T0329978

ADAM SMITH AND ECONOMIC SCIENCE

To Veronica and Nikie

Adam Smith and Economic Science

A Methodological Reinterpretation

Jan Peil

Assistent Professor in Economics,
University of Nijmegen, The Netherlands

Edward Elgar
Cheltenham, UK – Northhampton, MA, USA

Published by
Edward Elgar Publishing Limited
Glensanda House
Montpellier Parade
Cheltenham
Glos GL50 1UA
UK

Edward Elgar Publishing, Inc.
136 West Street
Suite 202
Northampton
Massachusetts 01060
USA

A catalogue record for this book
is available from the British Library

Library of Congress Cataloguing in Publication Data
Peil, Jan.
   [Adam Smith en de economische wetenschap. English]
   Adam Smith and economic science : a methodological
reinterpretation / Jan Peil.
   Rev. ed. in English of the Dutch-language book : Adam Smith en de
economische wetenschap : een methodologische herinterpretatie.
   Includes bibliographical references and index.
   1. Smith, Adam, 1723–1790. 2. Economists–Great Britain.
3. Smith, Adam 1723–1790. Inquiry into the nature and causes
of the wealth of nations. I. Title
HB103.S6P4413 1999
330.15'3—dc21   99–15588
                              CIP

ISBN 978 1 85898 919 8
Printed and bound by CPI Group (UK) Ltd, Croydon, CR0 4YY

Contents

Preface

My interest in Adam Smith was first aroused in the 1980s when I was conducting research in the field of economics and ethics as an assistant of Prof.dr. M.A.D. Plattel at Tilburg University. After a pilot study of Smith's economic thought – published in Berns, E. (ed.), *Adam Smith. Ethiek, politiek, economie* – I decided to reread Smith's oeuvre from the perspective of present-day disputes about the principles of economics. Some earlier results of this rereading have been published in Blaug, M. (ed.), 'Adam Smith (1723–1790)', *Pioneers in Economics* and elsewhere.

The present study of the relevance of Smith to current economic debate continues the work of these earlier publications. It is, to be more precise, a revised edition in English of the Dutch-language book: *Adam Smith en de economische wetenschap: een methodologische herinterpretatie*. Although the text has been altered in part, the subject remains the same: 'How can Smith help us rethink economics in order to get a better understanding of the idea of the (free) market economy as it exists today?'

Since the publication of the Dutch-language version of this study in 1995, scholarship in the area has been enriched by the publication of a number of works including Jeffrey T. Young's *Economics as a Moral Science*. Despite these recent additions to the literature, the references in this edition remain largely unchanged. This is not to be taken as a reflection on the quality of recent studies, but reflects my belief that my original references remain the most useful for the particular topics discussed in this volume.

In presenting this book, I would like to thank all the people who have helped and encouraged me to continue the research on Smith and the principles of economics. Firstly, I would like to offer my sincere gratitude to Prof.dr. M.A.D. Plattel for his inspiration and continued interest in my research. Through the years he has always been willing to read and to give his learned comment on texts. As a social and moral philosopher with a special interest in economics, he has given me valuable advice in following the difficult and at times slippery path of inter-disciplinary research. There are, of course, many people who have been very helpful in one way or another in preparing the text for publication. I would like to thank in particular Drs. G. Clever and Prof.dr. H. Garretsen for their comments on earlier drafts, Drs. A.M. Iken and Mr. N. Martin for their assistance in editing the manuscript and Mrs. L. Roelen for formatting the manuscript into a camera ready copy. It has also been a pleasure to work with Ms. D. Evans, Mrs J. Leppard, Ms. F. O'Sullivan and Mrs V. Polding of Edward Elgar Publishing Ltd.

Introduction

The wealth of scholarship devoted to Adam Smith which has been published since the 1970's clearly indicates a growing awareness of his relevance to contemporary debate on the principles of economics. Smith has attracted the interest of economists from various schools and in their publications we observe both a shift in the direction of research and, more strikingly, a change in the mode of interpretation.

As early as 1978 Horst C. Recktenwald noted a growing interest in Smith's work as a coherent whole along with such new topics as his evolutionary historical approach to economics and interest in the institutional framework of market economies.[1] However, alongside that shift in research interests the flood of new publications also showed a major change in the interpretative model being brought to the study of Smith. Whereas earlier scholars had been primarily concerned with reproducing an *original* meaning supposedly immanent within Smith's text, a new generation of students were approaching that text in the spirit of dialogue. The same spirit of dialogue informs this study which is concerned with the question, 'How can Smith's text help us to better understand the idea of the free market today?'

Until quite recently the various schools of economic thought could be divided into supporters and opponents of the free market economy. Today, hardly any school disputes the relevance of competition and free exchange in stimulating efficiency or, more generally speaking, in producing and distributing wealth. At the same time it is important to note that this new unanimity has been accompanied by a growing unease with economics' traditional frame of reference in which the individual and society, the market and the state, positive and normative economics, general theory and historical understanding are interpreted as opposed binary pairs. Through a contextual reading of Smith we show that this oppositional interpretation of key concepts had no place in Smith's own frame of reference and consequently we suggest that rereading Smith may be of help in reframing contemporary economic discourse.

Employing an essentially hermeneutical model in our approach to Smith's text we demonstrate that his theory of the market economy is significantly distorted when interpreted in the framework of modern economics as exemplified by Joseph A. Schumpeter in his *History of Economic Analysis*.[2] This interpretation, according to which Smith's contribution to economic analysis is understood as a Walrasian general equilibrium theory *in nucleo,* is still generally accepted in mainstream economics.

In broad outline, our rereading of Smith in the context of the current debate on the principles of economics can be divided into three parts. The first part (Chapter I) focuses on the relevance of rereading Smith in general and the methodological considerations involved in reinterpreting his texts. The second part (Chapters II,

III and IV) discusses Smith's economic thought as one part of his all-encompassing *sympathy*-based moral philosophy. The third part (Chapter V) summarizes the lessons to be drawn from our rereading as they bear on current attempts to rethink the principles of economic science.

In more detail, Chapter I discusses the Adam Smith renaissance in relation to today's crisis in economics. In a discussion of the new trends in Adam Smith research we show that the reinterpretation and revaluation of Smith's oeuvre has been accompanied by the emergence of a new interpretative model.

In the new wave of Smith studies, the positivistic pursuit of the text's true meaning is giving way to a hermeneutical approach which acknowledges the presence of both the *horizon of the interpreter* and the *horizon of the author* in the act of interpretation. According to the hermeneutical model, textual interpretation is understood as producing meaning through the fusion of the horizon of the interpreter with the horizon of the author. The hermeneutical model implies a shift from the passive reading of a text in pursuit of its intrinsic and original meaning, to a more productive engagement with that text in which meaning is oriented toward the horizon of the reader's own interests and concerns.

Accordingly, in our discussion of the Smith renaissance we will be concerned both with the explication and elucidation of Smith's vision of the free market economy in relation to its historical circumstances, and with interpreting its relevance for our own time. Our rereading of Smith is thus conceived as a dialogue which contributes to a better understanding of the current debate on the principles of economic thought.

In Chapter II, through a contextual reading of Smith's work, we demonstrate that the conventional general equilibrium interpretation of *The Wealth of Nations* is riddled with anachronisms leading to a significantly distorted understanding of Smith's thought. The economistic-functionalistic approach, which is so typical of nineteenth and twentieth-century economic science, in fact finds no support in Smith's text. For Smith, we argue, economics was still an integral part of moral philosophy and his discussion of the market economy is related to the wider attempt to give sense and meaning to the processes of liberalization and commercialization experienced by Western societies since the sixteenth century.

Comparing Smith with other contributors to the new discourse on man and society such as Grotius, Pufendorf, Locke and Hutcheson, it becomes clear that Smith has a particularly distinctive view of the emerging commercial society. It appears that he supports arguments in favour of further liberalization and commercialization of society from the angle of a substantially new interpretation of the autonomy of the individual in giving shape and substance to his life and world. By reinterpreting phenomena of (mutual) sympathy, he produced an analysis which cannot be assimilated to the trend towards antipodal pairings such as the individual versus society, typical of nineteenth and twentieth century economic modernism.

Chapter III focuses on Smith's *sympathy*-based view of man and society. Our reading of Smith's discussion of *sympathy*, clarifies his criticism of the old doctrine that free, self-interested economic exchange was dangerous to the *bonum commune*, and explains why he would have opposed later attempts to explain the production and distribution of wealth by deduction from the behaviour of rationalistic atomistic individuals.

Smith's discussion and examples of the phenomenon of *(mutual) sympathy* are read as a dialogue between Smith and his readers which is intended to demonstrate that we give shape and substance to our lives and world through our longing for praise(worthiness) in a context of dialogically shared values and beliefs. Customs, fashion, law, utility and the production and distribution of wealth are all understood with reference to the communication, competition and concurrence immanent to the principle of *(mutual) sympathy*.

The principle of *(mutual) sympathy* also explains why the so-called *commercial* age is understood as the final stage in the evolution of man and society. In the commercial society people are supposed to act freely according to their personal (self-interested) interpretation of the social value patterns to which they feel themselves committed.

In Chapter IV we turn to the discussion of Smith's economics. Reinterpreting the theory of the market economy through the lens of Smith's *sympathy*-view and references to his view of philosophy and science, we show that considering Smith as an exponent of the mechanics of self-interest results in a serious misinterpretation of his theory of the market economy.

We argue further that Smith's reference to the *invisible hand* and *market prices gravitating towards natural prices* does not imply some universal causal laws which are waiting to be discovered by economists. When Smith uses these expressions he speaks metaphorically in order to suggest that free commerce is well-ordered because of the social value patterns to which the actors are committed. As participants in market economics, people are so familiar with the rules of this process that their freedom of action itself reflects these rules, giving them the appearance of causal laws. Hence real market prices continuously move up and down *as if* they are gravitating towards some *average* which the actors recognize as the normal or natural value.

In Chapter V we relate our new interpretation of Smith to the growing dissatisfaction with the framework of modern economics constructed around such antipodal pairs as the individual versus society, the market versus the state, positive versus normative economics, general theory versus historical understanding of experiences and phenomena. Referring to the new process approach to society and its economy, we show that Smith can be of help in the quest for a new, relational, understanding of the traditional antipodal pairs.

We illustrate this point through an examination of Smith's discussion of Newton's astronomy, in particular his interpretation of the principle of gravitation. Against the traditional interpretation of Smith which views the relation between the general theoretical and the evolutionary historical approaches in *The Wealth of Nations* as dichotomous, we argue that, for Smith, historical understanding and system analysis are both part of one and the same process of attributing meaning to human existence. *The Wealth of Nations* was Smith's contribution to the search for a new understanding of the production and distribution of wealth in societies undergoing the process of commercialization.

Smith's advocacy of the free market economy was entirely consistent with his *system of sympathy*. He proposed a transformation of the economy towards a free market economy because he believed that such a system was best suited to securing the basics of a truly human life, i.e, to living a free life in society in accordance with our longing for praise(worthiness).

Notes

1. Recktenwald, H.C., 'An Adam Smith Renaissance *anno* 1976? The Bicentenary Output – A Reappraisal of His Scholarship', *Journal of Economic Literature*, vol. 16, 1978, pp. 56–57.
2. For instance, Schumpeter, J.A., *History of Economic Analysis*, New York, 1954/1959, p. 189.

I An Adam Smith Renaissance Anno 1976

*Niemand sollte eigentlich über wirtschaftliche und politische Grundzusammen-
hänge mit Sachverstand urteilen oder die ökonomische Wissenschaft studieren, in
ihr forschen oder gar darüber lehren wollen, ohne den ›Wohlstand der Nationen‹
zu kennen.*

(H.C. Recktenwald, *Adam Smith. Der Wohlstand der Nationen*, München, 1988)

Introduction

In 1978, the *Journal of Economic Literature* published a survey of articles, books
and conference proceedings commemorating the bicentenary of *The Wealth of
Nations*. Written by Horst C. Recktenwald, the review's title raised a question
about the current state of Smith scholarship: *An Adam Smith Renaissance* anno
1976?[1] Since Recktenwald first posed that question a continuous stream of
publications on Smith has enabled us to answer it in the affirmative. Some twenty
years after the bicentennial it has become clear that 1976 did indeed mark the
beginning of a veritable Adam Smith renaissance. It is equally apparent that the
revival of interest in Smith mirrors wider changes within economics that have
taken place since the 1970s.

In this chapter we will examine the reasons for that renaissance in order to
understand why rereading Smith is of such importance to today's economist. The
chapter comprises five sections.

Sections 1 and 2 describe the current Adam Smith renaissance from an
historical perspective. Section 1 'samples' Smith's critical reception at fifty year
intervals from the publication of *The Wealth of Nations*, while section 2 describes
his current reception through an account of the main trends in recent research.

In sections 3 and 4, Smith's changing critical reception is considered from a
theoretical perspective. In section 3 we show that in the earlier phases of Smith
scholarship the interpretation of a text was understood primarily as the reproduction of the author's intention in writing the text. Because, in this model, meaning
is regarded as an immanent property of the text which simply awaits reproduction
by the reader, we shall describe the interpretive model employed in earlier
readings of Smith as *positivistic*.

In section 4 we show that in contemporary readings of Smith, interpretation is
no longer concerned with the reproduction, but with the production, of meaning
through a dialogue with the text. Because of its dialogical approach we designate
this the *new hermeneutical model* of interpretation.

Finally, section 5 outlines the substance of the dialogue with Smith to be found in the following four chapters. A brief sketch of the current debate on the market mechanism, the economic system, and the nature of self-interested economic behaviour indicates that our own dialogue with Smith will focus on the familiar topic of the production and distribution of wealth in commercial society. Referring to recent research on both Smith and the principles of economics it is argued that a contextual rereading of Smith can be of help in rethinking the very basics of modern economics – particularly in helping us to resolve the problems arising from the oppositional interpretation of dual concepts such as the individual and society, explaining and understanding (*Verstehen*), and positive and normative economics.

1 The Adam Smith Reception Before the 1970s

Smith's best-known work is, of course, *The Wealth of Nations*. However, for a fuller understanding of the reception of Smith's economic thought it is important to remember that he also published a book called *The Theory of Moral Sentiments* which, as the subtitle of the last authorized edition of 1790 indicates, concerns,

> the Principles by which Men naturally judge concerning the Conduct and Character, first of their Neighbours, and afterwards of themselves.[2]

The Theory of Moral Sentiments was well received and brought Smith international acclaim in the field of moral philosophy.[3]

The Wealth of Nations, Smith's second book, was published 17 years later in 1776.[4] According to the *Advertisement* of the last authorised edition of *The Theory of Moral Sentiments*, this book deals with,

> the general principles of law and government, and of the different revolutions which they had undergone in the different ages and periods of society ... in what concerns police, revenue, and arms.[5]

Like its predecessor, *The Wealth of Nations* was also enthusiastically received – this time contrary to the expectations of William Strahan, the publisher, and David Hume, the well-known heterodox thinker and close friend of Smith, both of whom felt that it would place too great a demand on the attention and intellect of the ordinary reader.[6]

A third work remained unfinished on Smith's death on July 17, 1790. The origins of this work lay in a promise made in 1759 in the concluding paragraph of *The Theory of Moral Sentiments* and reiterated in the afore-mentioned *Advertisement* of the sixth edition of *The Theory of Moral Sentiments*:

> In the last paragraph of the first Edition of the present work, I said, that I should in another discourse endeavour to give an account of the general principles of law and government, and of the different revolutions which they had undergone in the

different ages and periods of society; not only in what concerns justice, but in what concerns police, revenue, and arms, and whatever else is the object of law. In the *Enquiry concerning the Nature and Causes of the Wealth of Nations*, I have partly executed this promise; at least so far as concerns police, revenue, and arms. What remains, the theory of jurisprudence, which I have long projected, I have hitherto been hindered from executing, by the same occupations which had till now prevented me from revising the present work. Though my very advanced age leaves me, I acknowledge, very little expectation of ever being able to execute this great work to my own satisfaction; yet, as I have not altogether abandoned the design, and as I wish still to continue under the obligation of doing what I can, I have allowed the paragraph to remain as it was published more than thirty years ago, when I entertained no doubt of being able to execute every thing which it announced.[7]

While we know that the subject of the third book was *jurisprudence*, we can only guess at its precise contents for a week before his death Smith gave instructions that the manuscript, together with other texts, be destroyed.[8] Consequently, student notes made in classes in 1762–1763 and 1766 are our only remaining source of information on Smith's thoughts on jurisprudence.[9]

Smith had always considered *The Theory of Moral Sentiments* and *The Wealth of Nations* as related parts of a comprehensive project on man and society. However, prior to the 1970s it was common practice in studies of political economy, and thereafter of economics, to deal almost exclusively with *The Wealth of Nations*. The subject matter of *The Theory of Moral Sentiments* was generally regarded as lying outside the proper concerns of political economy or economics.

This section describes Smith's reception in the discourse of political economy and, later, of economics at fifty year intervals after the publication of *The Wealth of Nations*. The Adam Smith renaissance anno 1976 is discussed in the following section.

1.1 The Adam Smith Reception Anno 1826

The fiftieth anniversary of the publication of *The Wealth of Nations* was not marked by any conferences or symposia commemorating Smith's contribution to economic thought.[10] In 1826, *The Wealth of Nations* was still regarded as the main text on economic thought, and the literature on Smith consisted mainly of elaborations on, or supplements and corrections to his work.[11] Pioneers in this respect were David Ricardo (whose influence was mainly restricted to England) and Jean-Baptiste Say. Both Ricardo and Say shared a desire for the further systematization of economic analysis; for the rest, however, their interpretations of Smith differed significantly. Where Ricardo opted for a deductive method in economic analysis and based the theory of value more firmly on the so-called value of labour, Say chose the greater realism of an inductive method, while emphasizing utility and scarcity in his elaborations on value.[12]

While the Ricardian interpretation of Smith's economic thought set the tone in England, its reception was not entirely uncritical. Samuel Bailey, for example, argued that Smith not only championed a more realistic approach in his analysis, but also had a keener appreciation of the relative nature of value.[13]

Differences in the interpretation of Smith's economic policy were less radical. Smith's belief that we should aspire to a free market economy, even though this may never be completely realized, was widely shared. Further it was generally agreed that existing customs and conventions needed careful handling as did the de facto power relations in society. Nor was the possibility of direct government interference with the economy completely excluded.

1.2 The Adam Smith Reception Anno 1876

By 1876 the situation in England had changed dramatically in comparison with 1826. The Ricardian school had lost its dominant position and with the marginal revolution the era of so-called neoclassical economics was born bringing English economic thought into line with mainstream thought in Continental Europe and America once again. So too, the tendency towards greater professionalization was associated with the separation of normative and applied economics from positive economics which became synonymous with economic science.[14]

The position of *The Wealth of Nations* within English economic thought in the latter half of the nineteenth century is usefully illustrated by the assessments of T.E. Cliffe Leslie and Walter Bagehot.[15] Bagehot can be considered representative of the emerging school of neoclassical economics, while Leslie represents the heterodox historical school.

Both authors considered the Ricardian doctrine an aberration and both acknowledged Smith as the founder of the theory of the market economy. In their more detailed interpretations of Smith's contribution to economic analysis, however, significant differences are apparent.

Trying to relate *The Wealth of Nations* to *The Theory of Moral Sentiments*, Leslie was critical of Smith's natural law-based approach and praised his use of history and institutional observations. Further, he drew attention to Smith's sympathy-based approach in *The Theory of Moral Sentiments* and contrasted it with the self-interest approach of economic analysis. In general, Leslie found Smith's economic theories outdated because of their reference to the early stages of industrialization.[16]

Representing the emerging neoclassical approach to economics, Bagehot confined himself to *The Wealth of Nations* and especially to Smith's discourse on value and the price mechanism. According to Bagehot, Smith deserved our respect for placing the idea of the market mechanism at the centre of economic thought. About the theory itself, however, Bagehot was less positive. While he subscribed to the proposition that the value of a commodity had to be related to its costs of production, he rejected Smith's development of the concept. This, he suggested, would lead economic analysis down the false trail of the Ricardian labour theory of value.[17]

From the reports of the memorial meeting of the *Political Economy Club* on 31st May 1876, it is clear that politicians and statesmen saw *The Wealth of Nations* in a different light than economists. Robert Lowe, for instance, praised Smith unconditionally for his laissez-faire approach even going so far as to dismiss Smith's own reservations about his analysis. According to Lowe's commemorative speech, Smith had shown too little faith in his own doctrine, which by now could be considered beyond criticism.[18]

As the assessments of Leslie and Bagehot, show, the economists did not share this sanguine view of Smith as the ne plus ultra of their science. Far from being a discipline which had been all but perfected, they believed that economics needed to undergo a radical change. Accordingly, the comments of the economists on Smith at the time of the centennial of *The Wealth of Nations* should to a certain extent be read as commentary on that change.[19]

1.3 The Adam Smith Reception Anno 1926

On the evidence of the sesquicentennial publications it appears that *The Wealth of Nations* was increasingly regarded as a document whose importance belonged primarily to the history of economics. Its publication was now commemorated mainly by economists. Politicians and statesmen it seemed were no longer so eager to pay homage to the champion of the free market economy while the self-regulatory effects of the price mechanism were still not readily apparent.

Neoclassical economists such as Edwin G. Cannan, Paul H. Douglas and Jacob Viner are well represented in the commemorative literature.[20] Economists from heterodox schools such as the American institutionalists are nearly all absent. Apparently they were no longer interested in Smith, who was at that time canonized as the founding father of the theory of the self-regulating market economy. With hindsight this is remarkable, given that articles with new heterodox interpretations of Smith were already appearing in the 1920s.

The evaluations of Cannan and Douglas echo those of Bagehot in the 1870s. Cannan and Douglas read Smith against the background of the neoclassical theory of rational maximizing behaviour in a self-regulating system of interrelated markets. According to Cannan and Douglas, Smith's principles were sound but his analysis had become confused in his elaborations on the theory of value. Again, because of his labour theory of value, he was considered partly responsible for the mistakes of the English classical school. While Cannan and Douglas did in fact point out that Smith devoted more attention to the influence of supply and demand conditions on the market price of commodities than the English classical economists had after him, ultimately, they considered Smith's contribution to price theory to be outdated – as had Bagehot some fifty years earlier.[21]

Viner's reading of Smith can also be classified as neoclassical although it is broader in scope than those of Cannan and Douglas.[22] While the latter two, according to the prevailing methodological ideas, limited themselves to the so-called analytical parts of *The Wealth of Nations*, Viner dealt with the work as a whole. His reading even extended to *The Theory of Moral Sentiments*. Viner's assessment of Smith's contribution to economic analysis was more positive than those of Cannan and Douglas, he even praised Smith for being the first to succeed in representing a market economy as a coherent system. Furthermore he contradicted Cannan's view that Smith, because of his concept of the natural harmonious order, had been a supporter of unconditional laissez-faire politics.[23] According to Viner, Smith advanced the idea of a natural harmonious order in *The Theory of Moral Sentiments*, but not in *The Wealth of Nations*.[24]

In reading both *The Wealth of Nations* and *The Theory of Moral Sentiments*,

Viner might at first seem to be a precursor of the economists who in the 1970s rejected the accepted, selective, reading of Smith to plead for an integrated, contextual approach to the Smith oeuvre. Anticipating the discussion of contemporary readings of Smith later in this chapter, it should be noted that this impression is mistaken. Viner did indeed include both *The Wealth of Nations* and *The Theory of Moral Sentiments* in his reading, but the reading itself followed the lines laid out in traditional accounts of Smith. He considered *The Theory of Moral Sentiments* as an ethico-psychological text with an altruistic view of man, and *The Wealth of Nations* as an economic text advancing a selfish view of man.[25]

Further similarities with present-day integral and contextual readings of Smith may be found in the philosophically and historically oriented assessments of Smith's contribution to economic thought by scholars such as Jacob H. Hollander, John M. Clark and Glenn R. Morrow.[26] Morrow deserves a special mention in this respect because he had already indicated that the relation between *The Theory of Moral Sentiments* and *The Wealth of Nations* should be sought in Smith's special understanding of man's feelings of sympathy for his fellow men.[27] However, it was not until the 1970s that these new interpretations of Smith began to reach an audience outside the narrow circle of historians of economic thought. The views of Bagehot, Cannan, Douglas and Viner continued to dominate, being reproduced in texts such as Joseph A. Schumpeter's *History of Economic Analysis* and Mark Blaug's *Economic Theory in Retrospect*. In the wake of Schumpeter's *History of Economic Analysis*, it was widely held that Smith had reframed the economic analysis of his time into a theory that in hindsight could be classified as a Walrasian general equilibrium theory *in nucleo*.[28]

2 The Adam Smith Reception Since the 1970s

Given the trend in Adam Smith readings prior to the 1970s it might have been expected that the bicentennial literature would consist mainly of discussions of Smith's anticipation of the Walrasian equilibrium analysis. The avalanche of publications which has appeared since the 1970s, however, presents a quite different picture. By 1976 Smith's economic analysis was no longer considered outmoded or mistaken. Prominent specialists in various areas were once again finding a source of inspiration in Smith's work.[29] Many of Smith's ideas had taken on a new meaning in contexts such as international and welfare economics.[30] Schumpeter's argument that Smith's economic analysis was not truly original – and even inconsistent at numerous points – was widely contested.[31]

The selective reading of Smith's oeuvre by economists which concentrated exclusively on the 'scientific' sections of *The Wealth of Nations,* was also challenged.[32] *The Wealth of Nations* and *The Theory of Moral Sentiments* have increasingly been interpreted, in accordance with Smith's wishes, as two parts of one inclusive discourse on man and society. There is, in short, every reason to consider 1976 as marking a true renaissance in Adam Smith studies. Of course the history of Smith studies shows a number of new beginnings, reinterpretations and re-evaluations. Nevertheless, we will argue that the mid-1970s marks the beginning of a new phase in Smith scholarship which is qualitively different from earlier phases.[33]

Horst C. Recktenwald and Edwin G. West noted the change in the reception of Smith as early as 1978.[34] Reviewing the literature on Smith published since World War II, West concluded that Smith had once again become an important figure for economic analysis. Many of his ideas which had previously been criticized or simply forgotten, had taken on a new vitality.[35] Recktenwald too mentions the rehabilitation of Smith as an economist, but his survey also points to a shift in the focus of research beyond the traditional boundaries of economic science.[36] Besides a reappraisal of Smith's economic analysis, Recktenwald signalled three other trends in the new wave of Adam Smith research, namely:

- an emphasis on reading Smith's work comprehensively, as a coherent whole;
- a special interest in Smith's history of man and society as background for his economic theory, and
- a new concern with the role of the state and other socio-political institutions in Smith's market economy.[37]

The growing importance of these three trends in the last twenty years is reflected in the prevalence of titles such as, *Markt, Staat und Solidarität bei Adam Smith* (1981); *Wealth and Virtue: The Shaping of Political Economy in the Scottish Enlightenment* (1983); *'Free Trade' and Moral Philosophy: Rethinking the Sources of Adam Smith's* Wealth of Nations (1986); *Adam Smith and His Legacy for Modern Capitalism* (1991); *Adam Smith in his Time and Ours: Designing the Decent Society* (1993); and *Economics as a Moral Science: The Political Economy of Adam Smith* (1997).[38]

In this section the main trends in recent Smith research will be considered along the lines laid out by Recktenwald in his survey of the bicentennial literature. A more theoretical discussion will be given in sections 3 and 4, where it will be demonstrated that the new interpretation of Smith has been accompanied by a change in the model of interpretation.

2.1 The Emphasis on Viewing Smith's Work as a Coherent Whole

The conventional reading of Smith treats *The Theory of Moral Sentiments* and *The Wealth of Nations* as separate texts, each of which has its own narrowly defined area of competence. *The Wealth of Nations* is regarded as a statement of Smith's economic thought, but only the first two books are considered relevant to discussions about his contribution to economic analysis.[39] The other three books are regarded as discourses on economic history and normative or applied economics.[40] *The Theory of Moral Sentiments* is classified as a text on ethics and psychology. It is also considered to be of limited interest to economists on the grounds that its allegedly altruistic view of man contradicts the first principle of economics: that man acts rationally according to his self-interest.

In contrast to this traditional compartmentalization of his oeuvre, more recent readings of Smith have tended to *view his work comprehensively, as an integrated whole.*[41] On the assumption that Smith's writings refer to a single unifying theory of man and society, a considerable amount of research has been devoted to the reconstruction of that underlying theory. So too the conventional view that *The Theory of Moral Sentiments* refers to an altruistic view of man and *The Wealth of Nations* to a selfish view of man, has been challenged and dismissed as based on an erroneous reading of Smith's text.

Attempts are now being made to understand Smith's economic thought as an integral part of a more encompassing moral philosophy.[42] At the same time, greater emphasis is being placed on the need to understand Smith's economic thought in its original context. Smith cannot be read against the precepts of modern economics, it is argued; rather he needs to be understood within the context of the classical division of philosophy into logic, natural philosophy and moral philosophy. This means that not only *The Theory of Moral Sentiments* and *The Wealth of Nations* but also his unpublished manuscripts and the student lecture notes on what today we would call ethics, politics, law, and the philosophy of science, should be read as discourses on moral philosophy.[43]

2.2 The Rehabilitation of Smith as an Economist

During the first half of the twentieth century interest in Smith had become almost purely historiographical. In the 1940s and 1950s it was widely believed that *The Wealth of Nations* had little to offer contemporary economic analysis and policy.[44] Where Smith's achievement was respected, it was largely for his integration of the fragmented economic theory of his time into a coherent whole. However, it should be noted that the praise he received on this account was less for the creativity of this systematization than for the drudgery which must have been necessary in order to consolidate the ideas and theories which had until then been widely dispersed in the works of various authors.[45] Furthermore, many economists, including Pieter C. van Traa in the Netherlands, accepted the critical judgement of Schumpeter that the logical rigour of Smith's economic analysis left much to be desired.[46]

Looking at the current discussion of Smith's economic analysis it is immediately apparent that there has been a radical shift in the interests and the appreciation of economists. Evidence of the high regard in which many economists hold Smith's scientific achievements is to be found in numerous publications. Comparative studies for instance, have demonstrated that many 'new' ideas were already present in Smith's work in a more or less developed form.[47] Samuelson has even attempted to reconstruct Smith's economic theory in terms of current economic modelling. Together with Hollander, among others, he praises the consistency and the realism of Smith's analysis.[48]

2.3 A Special Interest in the Social Philosophy Behind Smith's Economic Analysis

Traditional readings of Adam Smith can be characterized as *economistic* interpretations. Typically, they assume that Smith's economic analysis and current mainstream economic theory share the same referential frame. More precisely, Smith is thought to employ an analytic model in which atomistic individuals efficiently strive after their own interest and contribute, by means of the price mechanism, to an efficient allocation of factor endowments in the economy as a whole.[49]

New readings based on *The Wealth of Nations* and *The Theory of Moral Sentiments* have contested this interpretation with the result that a different picture of Smith's economic thought has emerged to counter the abstract mechanistic theory of the market economy which economists were used to reading in *The Wealth of Nations*. Against the idea of atomistic individuals acting like calculating machines driven by price signals, more recent readings typically place an emphasis on understanding behaviour in relation to its concrete socio-historical context. This means that in the new reading of Smith's economic analysis, individuals are still considered as economic agents, but their agency is no longer interpreted as atomistic, mechanistic and rationalistic. Instead, recent scholarship on Smith pays far greater attention to the ways in which his individuals act according to prevailing social values and rules.

Examples of this reading strategy are to be found in the interpretations offered by Ludwig M. Lachmann, Gerald P. O'Driscoll Jr., Mario J. Rizzo, Ronald L. Meek and Andrew S. Skinner. In arguing for the importance of analysing the market economy as a process, Lachmann, O'Driscoll and Rizzo refer to Smith as the author who pointed out that order originates in, and evolves spontaneously with, concrete interaction.[50] Meek and Skinner present a different – institutionalist – interpretation in their reading of Smith's discussions on ethics, economics and law as parts of a comprehensive history of man and society.[51]

2.4 A New Institutional Interest in Smith's Market Economy

In the 1960s Smith was known as the author of the theory that the price mechanism creates general equilibrium by acting as an *invisible hand*. Little attention was paid to readings of Smith, such as Viner's, that opposed the conventional laissez-faire interpretation of that *invisible hand* metaphor. Opponents of laissez-faire ideology distanced themselves from Smith while adherents quoted him readily.

Studies by Franz-Xaver Kaufman, Hans G. Krüsselberg, Manfred Trapp, and Spencer Pack among others, demonstrate a growing desire to establish exactly what Smith really said about the price mechanism and government policy.[52] As such, it is clear that present-day interest in Smith is not primarily concerned with re-opening the question of his attitude to laissez-faire politics.

Instead, contemporary research suggests the possibility of using Smith as a lens through which to examine and question the relationship between the individual actor, society and government.[53]

Summarizing the main trends in contemporary Smith research, it is clear that Recktenwald was right to speak of an Adam Smith renaissance in 1978. Not only is the number of papers and books that have been published since the 1970s remarkable, there has also been a radical shift in the perception of Smith's work.

In the next two sections we will consider this change of perception from a more theoretical point of view. The Adam Smith renaissance will be explained as part of a more general shift in the understanding of the principles of modern economics. It will be shown that the shifting interpretation of Smith is parallelled by a shift in its frame of reference, or, more precisely, its model of interpretation.

3 The Traditional Model of Interpretation

To gain a clearer understanding of the contemporary Adam Smith renaissance an insight into the background of this renewed interest in Smith is required.

In the previous section we characterized the *new* reading of Smith through reference to four main trends: (1) reappraisal of Smith's economic analysis, (2) reading Smith's work comprehensively, as a coherent whole, (3) a special interest in the social philosophy behind Smith's economic theory, (4) a new concern with the role of the state and other socio-political institutions in Smith's market economy. Reviewing these trends, it is apparent that they relate to one central question: 'What is Smith's concept of the relationship between the individual, society and government?' This question is central to discussions of Smith's view of the relationship between the market and other institutions of social organization and coordination, and more generally between economics, ethics and politics. Questions concerning the conceptual relation of the individual, society and government are also at the centre of present-day debates on the principles of economic analysis and economic policy. Consequently it is apparent that the Adam Smith renaissance is not simply scholarly in origin but has its roots in the debate surrounding the changing interpretations of the basic concepts of modern economic thought.

In outlining the frame of reference that informs the contemporary reading of Smith, the studies of West and Recktenwald provide an obvious point of departure. Both authors recognize the radical change in the orientation of Smith studies and their surveys might be expected to shed some light on the changing frame of reference which has accompanied that reorientation. However, a closer reading of West and Recktenwald proves disappointing in this respect.

While recognizing that there have been major changes in the reception of Smith, West sees no particular significance in this phenomenon, rather he considers it self-evident that every generation will have its own interpretation of Smith and that this interpretation will reflect that generation's own specific interests and ideas, or horizon. In his view, time always colours the relationship between the interpreter and the text. In West's view, the recurring debate on Smith's contribution to economic analysis is simply further proof that the observer's frame of reference always influences the process of observation. Further, West points to the renewal of that debate as evidence that *The Wealth of Nations* is one of economics' classic texts. Thus West regards the current renaissance in Smith studies simply as proof of his lasting contribution to economic science.[54]

In general West's understanding of the idea that time qualifies any interpretation seems to lack any positive connotation: at its most extreme it tends towards a meaningless relativism which implies that every reader and every period will have their own interpretation. He is, however, equivocal in this respect. In his account of *The Wealth of Nations*, West clings to the idea of a fixed meaning and thus does not exclude the possibility that the meaning of the author is accessible to the interpreter on all occasions.

Nor, unexpectedly, does Recktenwald's survey contribute much to a deeper insight into the renewed interest in Smith. Given his comprehensive discussion and the fact that he devotes a special section to explain and evaluate the Adam Smith renaissance, this is surprising. However, the title of Recktenwald's section on the Smith renaissance, *The 1976 Revival and the Lasting Radiation*, indicates that we may have to look further to find the actual explanation of the revival of interest in Smith. Recktenwald's review of the reappraisal of Smith's scholarship lacks a sound discussion of its background. He describes the revival in Smith scholarship as a genuine Adam Smith renaissance, but he does little to elaborate on the specific reasons for this renewed interest in Smith.

For the most part Recktenwald shares West's view of the changes in Adam Smith interpretation. Like West he believes that each generation's interpretation of Smith is inevitably coloured by the spirit of the age. Consequently he believes that contemporary interest in economic growth and development has played a large part in generating the increased attention to Smith.[55] Recktenwald's relativism differs from West's only in that it is more positive. In Recktenwald's account, the spirit of the age may colour the reception of Smith's texts, but it also helps reveal new and important facets of his work.[56] It is because each generation rewrites the history of ideas for itself that Smith's text retains its intellectual vitality.[57]

Recktenwald traces the present-day Smith renaissance back to the lasting radiation of Smith's ideas.[58] The renaissance literature is considered both as a confirmation of the importance of those ideas and as a contribution to a better understanding of that lasting radiation by removing misinterpretations of Smith's oeuvre.[59]

In their assessment of the Smith renaissance of the 1970s as just another phase in a continual process of revision, Recktenwald and West neglect one of the most distinguishing features of the current Smith revival, namely that it employs an interpretative model which is radically different from that used in earlier readings of Smith. Their blindness to this difference may be due in part to the fact that their own work is still informed by the spirit of the traditional interpretative model.

Like earlier readers of Smith, West and Recktenwald apply an interpretative model which leans heavily on the positivistic tradition in the philosophy of science. This tradition has always appealed to economists aspiring to make economic analysis conform to the example of the natural sciences. The close relationship between the traditional interpretative model and the positivist tradition in the philosophy of sciences is particularly clear in its determination to define the immanent meaning of a text. Traditional readings assume that a text has an intrinsic meaning which can be discovered by using appropriate methods. Thus Recktenwald's approach implies that Smith's work has an immanent message that will be gradually uncovered through the on-going process of reading and rereading his texts.

The traditional model of interpretation assumes that a text possesses a unitary and original truth which corresponds to the author's original intention to express a particular view of the world. Interpreting a text according to this traditional model, involves nothing more than reproducing what has always been there, i.e. the never changing (semper idem) meaning of the text.

The fact that the traditional interpretative model is inspired by a positivistic concept of science derived from the natural sciences does not of course imply that historical texts are likened to natural scientific facts. Thus Recktenwald and West clearly recognize that in Smith's case we are dealing with texts which should be understood in their historical context. They also recognise that the contemporary hermeneutical context of the investigator will influence the interpretation of the text. It is, however, characteristic of scholars employing the traditional interpretative model to proceed as though the double hermeneutics of the historical and the contemporary horizons, can be separated.

The traditional interpretative model is distinguished by its failure to consider the possibility of the inextricable interlacing of both horizons. Instead, it typically reduces the double hermeneutics to two single hermeneutics in which the original meaning remains a single, unitary, object. Thus, despite his recognition that the contemporary horizon encourages the discovery of the historical riches of the text, Recktenwald holds fast to the idea of the text's unchanging meaning, pointing out that different readings enliven the intrinsic meaning of the original text.

The assumptions implicit in Recktenwald's approach can be clarified by an example taken from Eric D. Hirsch's *Validity in Interpretation*.[60] According to Hirsch a text has an objective and invariant *meaning*, which corresponds to the intention of the author. Interpretation aims at reproducing that *meaning*. In addition to the *meaning* of the text, Hirsch distinguishes what he terms the text's *significances*. These are the perceptions of the unchanging *meaning* which themselves change through time. *Significances* are, as it were, reproductions of the original *meaning* in contemporary colours. Hirsch clarifies the difference between *meaning* and *significances* with the example of *a red object* which,

> 'will appear to have different colour qualities when viewed against differently coloured backgrounds. The same is true of textual meaning. But the meaning of the text *(its sinn)* does not change any more than the hue and saturation of the red object changes when seen against different backgrounds'.[61]

In Hirsch's view, the *meaning* of a text remains unchanged just like the colour of an object when it is placed against different backgrounds. Recktenwald echoes this cognitive model when he speaks of the lasting radiation of Smith's work. In his explanation of the Smith renaissance, the *meaning* of a text remains an object independent of the reader, thanks to, or in spite of, its contemporary colouring.

This interpretative model not only informs Recktenwald's and West's assessments of the present-day Adam Smith renaissance, it has also provided the interpretative frame for past Smith revivals. In these revivals Smith's economics was typically used to demonstrate the validity of the interpreter's own approach to economics over and against other rival approaches. Here too we see an attempt to uncouple the double hermeneutics into two single hermeneutics in order to grasp Smith's 'genuine' economic analysis.

Despite having their own theories of economic analysis and policy, earlier Smith readers did not engage in dialogue with Smith in order to gain a better understanding of their economic world. In their reading of Smith they aimed at the reproduction of the master's economic analysis in order to support or criticize contemporary economic theories. Although it was assumed that the real meaning of Smith's texts could be determined, readers actually used Smith's texts as a sort of lucky dip from which they could quote various, even mutually contradictory, ideas according to the needs of the situation.

Today's readings of Smith are based on a radically different interpretative model in which interpretation is no longer viewed as the passive reproduction of an already given meaning, but as an activity which itself helps generate the text's meaning. Recent Smith scholarship is characterized by a trend to engage in a dialogue which it is hoped will help us rethink some of the fundamental principles of economics and consequently lead to a better understanding of today's economic problems.

In order to better understand this new hermeneutic model, however, it is useful to consider the ways in which the old model has actually been employed in the various phases of Smith scholarship.

Today the history of modern economic analysis is usually divided into four periods. By virtue of their dominant style of analysis, the first three are called respectively the classic, the neoclassic and the Keynesian periods. There is a clear correspondence between this periodization and the different phases in the history of Adam Smith reception.

The beginning of the classical period saw intense debate about the direction in which Smith's theory of the free market economy should be further developed. In line with the different options, there were various interpretations of *The Wealth of Nations*. In Britain, Ricardo's theory of production and distribution of wealth eventually gained the upper hand and Smith came to be viewed as the founder of a theory of political economy which saw the economy as a system tending to stasis through the operation of the price mechanism. The economy was analysed as a system of class relations, i.e. as a system of exchange between labour, capital and land. Value was explained by means of a labour theory of value.

The transition to the second, neoclassical, period took place in the second half of the nineteenth century. Once again the object and method of economic analysis was the subject of keen debate among British (political) economists. In the struggle to seize the high ground from the declining classical school, economists of various schools quoted Smith indiscriminately in order to bolster their position. When the neoclassical school eventually gained the upper hand, the neoclassical interpretation of *The Wealth of Nations* became canonical. After the break with the so-called distortions of Ricardian economics, Smith was reinvented as a precursor of the neoclassical approach.

By representing Ricardian economics as misconceived, and their own style of economic analysis as the rightful heir of Smith's epoch-making theory of the self-regulating market economy, the neoclassicals successfully created the impression that with their approach the process of accumulating sound scientific knowledge in the field of economics had been restored. Selectively referring to the parts of Smith's discussion of the market economy of which they approved, the neoclassicals succeeded in bringing about a fundamental change in economic analysis. They abandoned the classical perspective in which the market mechanism acted as the *causa efficiens* of social economic processes, and introduced an analysis in which the economy was reduced to market relations between atomistic, rationalistic individuals. In this way, the Ricardian dynamic and social point of view was replaced by a static and individualistic perspective. Explaining individual economic behaviour and social economic phenomena became synonymous with reconstructing them as effects of the principles of rational choice. Price adjustments in and between markets were supposed to stabilize the economy, producing a state of general equilibrium.

The third period began in the 1920s when, with mounting evidence of persistent inequilibrium in the economy, a new controversy of the schools flared up. In particular the idea that the price mechanism automatically clears all markets, including the labour market, was criticized. In the 1940s, however, the quarrels faded away and a new research programme incorporating revolutionary Keynesian ideas on macro-economic demand management was formulated.

The impact of this development was also registered in the history of Smith's reception. With his contribution to economic analysis widely regarded as outdated Smith fell into oblivion. In the *History of Economic Analysis*, still a standard work on the history of economic thought, Schumpeter described *The Wealth of Nations* as the majestic culmination of the first classical phase in economic analysis.[62] In accordance with the contemporary shift from a Marshallian to a Walrasian approach to price theory, Schumpeter read Smith against the background of Walras's general equilibrium analysis, the so-called *Magna Charta of economic theory*.[63] He concluded that Smith points toward Say and, through the latter's work to Walras, and further noted that Smith's thought is not strikingly original and is, moreover, lacking in logical consistency.[64]

The manner in which Smith was quoted in earlier discussions of principles, shows that at the time a more positivistic interpretative model was used than West and Recktenwald recognize in their surveys of recent literature. Frequently the reader completely ignored his own horizon in interpreting Smith. Reading was considered a form of direct observation whose aim was the reproduction of Smith's original thought. Donald Winch has commented unfavourably on these interpretations from an historiographic perspective.[65]

The extent to which a particular reader follows the positivistic tradition is, however, less important than the fact that in any positivistic model of interpretation it is erroneously assumed that the double hermeneutics of the contemporary and the historical horizon can be separated into two distinct hermeneutics. Without pre-empting our discussion of the new interpretative model, we note that ascribing *meaning* to a text implies a relationship between the reader and the text. Reading is no more a reproduction of the genuine ideas of the author than an observation is a reprint of an independent reality. Just as an observer *creates* his object in observing it, so a reader *produces* meaning in reading the text. To read a text is thus akin to entering into a discussion with the text's author. In short, the double hermeneutics operative in reading a text allows distinction but not separation.

From this hermeneutic perspective it will be clear that Recktenwald and many other economists actually ask the wrong question in reading Smith. In the terms suggested by Hirsch's analogy they ask: 'What *is* that red object?' while the question should be: 'What does that red object *mean*?' When applied to reading Smith, the question is not: 'What *is* the content of the text?' but, 'What does the content of this text *mean*?' Interpreting Smith is not aimed at reproducing the content of his texts but at producing meaning in dialogue with Smith. This new hermeneutical approach is found in contemporary Smith research in which economists enter into a discourse with Smith on the principles of economics. In that discourse the researchers are both the recipients and providers of meaning. This new attitude towards Smith, which underlies the Adam Smith renaissance anno 1976, will be more extensively discussed in the next section.

4 The New Interpretative Model of Smith's Work

As in previous revivals, the current resurgence of interest in Smith takes place against the backdrop of present-day discussions of the principles of economics. The Adam Smith renaissance of 1976 is closely linked to the process of reorientation in which economics has found itself since the 1960s. The new economics of the 1940s, influenced by Keynes' *General Theory of Employment, Interest and Money*, could not satisfy changing expectations. Keynesianism failed to provide a long term synthesis which could satisfy both adherents and opponents of the neoclassical doctrine.

As will be more fully discussed in the following section, the course of current debates on principles can be broken down into two distinct stages. The first stage is closely related to earlier debates. Economists who favour a break with the doctrine of *homo economicus* and the price mechanism, are opposed to economists who plead for closer scrutiny and stricter application of these principles. It is not surprising that in this debate Smith's *invisible hand* metaphor of the price mechanism has been revived.

Again, the controversy has proved insoluble because both parties continue to address the question from totally different theoretical perspectives.[66] Consequently, discussions are dominated by pseudo-contradictions, such as positive versus normative economics, the rational behaviour of individual agents versus socio-historical evolution, and the market mechanism versus state control.

The second stage, which increasingly defines the present context, differs essentially from the first in that the afore-mentioned contrasts are losing their grip on the way economic life is understood. Instead of a clash between opposing frames of reference, as in the first stage, the debate on principles has now moved towards designing and testing new interpretations of the free market economy. The question of whether we should oppose or support the free market economy is becoming increasingly irrelevant. Instead, current debate focuses on the nature of the free market economy.

Accordingly, current debate is less concerned with the choice between a number of well-known positions within the traditional frame of ideas, such as laissez-faire versus state control, than with the frame itself and the concepts implied by it, such as the free market and state intervention. Many concepts which were, until recently, taken for granted in economics, have been re-examined in this second stage of the principles debate.

As might be expected, the second stage of debate over the principles of economics has seen a revival of interest in Smith. Rethinking the free market economy makes a discourse with Smith almost inevitable given his reputation as the founder of free market economics. Moreover, because *The Wealth of Nations* has been widely considered the work in which economics first became a science distinct from *moral philosophy*, the rereading of Smith has taken on additional importance for both the history of economic thought and the debate on the principles of economic science. Consequently the new wave of Adam Smith research concentrates on: (1) the integral reading of Smith's work; (2) the reconstruction of Smith's economic analysis; (3) the attempt to clarify the history of man and society that informs Smith's thought, and (4) a reappraisal of Smith's views on economic policy and law. These issues correspond to the main questions of the current debate between the various schools of economic thought.

The selective reading of Smith characteristic of the first phase of renewed interest in Smith is often carried over into the second stage, despite the desire for an integral reading of his oeuvre. This, in combination with the interference of two different interpretative models, means that the results of the new wave of Adam Smith research are often hard to compare or appear to be contradictory. Two examples help illustrate this confusion.

The first example concerns the resemblance between Smith's economic analysis and the Walrasian general equilibrium theory. On the one hand readings by Maurice Brown, Peter L. Danner and Jeffrey T. Young, can be described as *second stage* readings in that they help us understand Smith's various discourses as parts of a comprehensive moral philosophy.[67] At the very least these readings raise serious doubts about the validity of interpreting Smith's economic analysis according to the precepts of Walrasian general equilibrium theory in that they indicate that Smith's view of man was not compatible with the rationalism and atomism presupposed in the general equilibrium theory.

On the other hand there are readings such as those by Samuel Hollander and Paul A. Samuelson which are based on *first stage* assumptions. These authors suggest that Smith anticipated the Walrasian general equilibrium theory and that criticism of Smith's analytical skills by scholars such as Schumpeter and Van Traa are ill-founded. These readings praise Smith for his analytical skills thus confirming the traditional view of Smith the economist which other *second stage* authors seek to correct.[68]

The second example of this confusion concerns the relationship between economics and other social sciences. Here we encounter *second stage* readers looking to Smith for inspiration in the attempt to resolve problems in the field of economics and law, or economics and politics, because in his work the separation of economics, politics and jurisprudence has not yet taken place.[69] There are also integral readings which attempt to reconstruct either the moral philosophy informing Smith's economics, or his history of man and society in order to reassess the separation of economics and other social sciences.[70]

On the other hand there are readers who, clinging to the *first stage* of the Smith appraisal, discuss his economics in accordance with the traditional division of the social sciences. Hollander, for example, asserts that the economic analysis of books I and II of *The Wealth of Nations* can be read separately from the historical discourse of book III.[71] It is also a distinctive feature of this group of readers that they reassess Smith's economic analysis with reference to theories current at the time.[72]

The influence of *first stage* readings can still be felt in the *second stage* of more recent Smith research, but the integral reading of Smith is increasingly gaining ground and the methodological gulf separating current from traditional readings is growing ever wider. Present-day Smith research is organized like an economic discourse with Smith's views on economics being considered as viewpoints in an ongoing discussion. The relationship of the researcher to Smith's texts is increasingly dialogic and is directed at deepening our insight into the principles of economics.

Particularly in its *second stage*, the new wave of Smith scholarship has shown that it is not simply another battle between hostile camps keen to demonstrate their competence in the art of quoting to defend established points of view. The implicit question in Viner's discussion of Smith – whether quoting Smith has any value for economic analysis, given that everyone can find something to support a given viewpoint in Smith's work – is not applicable to the many thorough studies published in the past 20 years.[73] These publications show that the way in which Smith's texts are now being read differs fundamentally from earlier approaches. They are based on an interpretative model which differs profoundly from the traditional model at various points.

1 Present-day readings of Smith grant far more autonomy to the text and are far less concerned with the author's original intention. In earlier readings which appealed to the authority of Smith in order to bolster the reader's own economic theories, questions of intention were of course far more prominent.

Today's readers approach Smith's texts with a shared interest in the idea and the concrete reality of the free market economy. Accordingly it is not Smith's authority, but the subject matter which provides the principal focus of interpretation. Contemporary readers do not try to enter the inner thoughts of the text's author, but seek instead for a better understanding of the subject which the other, in casu Smith, has discussed. Within the new interpretative model, the text's subject matter can be regarded as the *locus*, i.e. the place, where author and interpreter meet.

2   Another typical feature of the new hermeneutical model is that interpretation is regarded as discursive, i.e. as a discussion about a matter raised in the text. While the discussion originates in a shared interest in the subject of the text, author and reader do not directly share the same view of that subject. Without difference no discourse could exist.

Readings are undertaken in the expectation of a deeper insight into a particular topic. They do not seek to impose a particular set of preconceived ideas on the text. To gain a better insight into the subject matter, the reader will, according to the new interpretative model, engage in an exchange between his own viewpoint and the written one of the other, i.e. of the author.

3   The contemporary interpretation of Smith's texts is, so to speak, a discussion by economists and other scientists responding to ideas originating in these texts. This form of discursive engagement corresponds with the approach to the problem of textual hermeneutics adopted by such contemporary philosophers as Hans-Georg Gadamer, Jacques Derrida, Paul Ricoeur and others. Even though their ideas on textual interpretation differ, their views on the activity of interpretation have much in common. Obviously a thorough discussion of the theory of hermeneutics and linguistics is beyond the scope of the present work. However, it is important to recognize that the current reception of Smith's texts reflects recent developments in the theory of hermeneutics.

The idea that a text possesses an objective meaning which exists independently of the interpreter has become virtually obsolete. Instead, as Gadamer asserts, interpretation is increasingly seen as a process of fusing horizons: a process in which understanding and meaning are relational terms that connect the text and the reader, the past and the present. The interpreter approaches a text from his own, contemporary, perspective, i.e. he inhabits a frame of thought, or *univers de discourse*, which differs markedly from the historical patterns of thought encoded in the text. Thus, the hermeneutic circle can never be closed: that is to say, when the interpreter immerses himself in the historical text in order to reconstruct its original meaning he is always accompanied by his own horizon.[74]

A text cannot be understood without relating it in some way to one's own situation. An historical text cannot be likened to an objectively fixed guiding principle. To some degree, a pure reconstruction of an historical text always entails a fusion of the historical context with the interpreter's own context.

This fusion of temporal horizons, however, should not be seen simply as a barrier which makes it impossible for us to understand the original contents of the text: the fusion of temporal horizons also has its positive side. Our contemporary horizon enables us to bring a new perspective to the historical horizon, as a result of which the historical meaning of the text is, so to say, given a new life.

4   A fourth characteristic of much current Smith research is closely related to the hermeneutic concept of the independence or decontextualization of the written,

as opposed to the spoken, text. Contemporary hermeneutics places considerable emphasis on the contextual dependence of spoken language. Spoken language, it is pointed out, *indicates* the surrounding reality, or rather the pragmatic context of the speech act. Beside communicating a specific message, it also gestures towards the speaker and the person to whom the message is addressed. Written language, however, has gained independence; it has freed itself from the situational context and in so doing has lost this pragmatic base.

This *decontextualization* is the most essential characteristic of the written text. Ricoeur asserts: 'By virtue of being written the text becomes autonomous with regard to the intention of the author. What the text means is no longer identical to what the author meant'. The author effectively disappears into the background.[75]

The autonomy of the text is described in terms of *distantiation*: the fact of writing distances the text from its authorial source. As Ricoeur says, the text has in its most literal sense been *emancipated* from the author, i.e. it is no longer under the author's control.[76]

The pronounced interlacing with the concrete situational context of the speaker and the listener, which is so characteristic of spoken language, disappears in the written text. This *decontextualization* now offers the possibility of new contextualizations. Texts float in the air, until the reader has placed them in a new context or has reintegrated them. The value of the written text lies in the possibility of its *recontextualization*. Therefore, in the words of Ricoeur, 'The text's career escapes the finite horizon lived by its author. What the text means now matters more than what the author meant when he wrote it'.[77] Of course *recontextualization* cannot take place at random, the freedom of interpretation is bound by the text as composed by the author.

Contemporary readings of Smith are frequently informed by the spirit of this new hermeneutics. The principle that 'What the text means now, is more important than what the author meant' can be seen as the motto of current approaches to Smith's oeuvre. Why this should be so becomes clearer when we consider the fifth characteristic of today's readings.

5 Presentday economists seek a more productive dialogue with Smith's texts than the simple attempt to reconstruct their historical meaning. Through the reading of Smith's manuscripts, economists are attempting to understand how the vision of the free market was worked out in the late-eighteenth century. Through this reconstruction they hope to learn how this vision should be translated to the present. Such a reading is in effect an *interpretation of an interpretation:* the interpretation of Smith's manuscripts is discussed in order to understand its relevance to the present.

6 In the application of this model of *interpretation of an interpretation* to Smith's work a clear line may be discerned. Smith's writings are mainly studied in connection with the debate on the free market economy. Economists are becoming more and more conscious that the free market is not constituted by a uniform system of causal laws. The idea of the market refers to a pattern of rules which is in various ways realized in historical situations. Thus, the market

knows no regularity in the traditional scientific sense of universal causal laws, which should by definition be uniformly implemented. Market behaviour is not *law-governed* but *rule-governed.*

It is characteristic of the *market mechanism* that the system or pattern of rules and its strategic implementation in behaviour presuppose each other. On the one hand the system or the pattern of a free market economy is given shape *in* and *through* strategic behaviour, but on the other hand, historically contingent behaviour always happens within the framework of that self-same free market system or pattern. The ordering pattern of rules we call *the free market* therefore exists only in a *virtual* sense. The pattern presents itself to the economic subject as a *previously* given set of rules in that it continually takes shape in the economic processes *retrospectively.*

It is this insight which guides contemporary economic commentary on Smith's texts. Economists attempt to comment on and to interpret, for our own times, the vision of the free market which Smith's manuscripts describe with reference to the historical circumstances of his day. The focus of contemporary research lies on the ways in which Smith's texts can illuminate the virtual pattern of the free market in our own era.

5 Adam Smith and the New Debate on the Principles of Economics

In the following chapters Smith will be reinterpreted from the perspective of the current debate on the principles of economics. Two questions are central to our rereading of Smith: (1) What do we mean by the free market economy? and (2) Which type of economic thought best fits this idea?

We put these two questions to Smith because *The Wealth of Nations* is still considered the classic text on the free market economy. Since it is customary to refer to *The Wealth of Nations* in debates on the market economy, a reconsideration of various theories of the market economy cannot be undertaken without a rereading of this primary text.

A second reason to address our questions regarding the principles of economics to Smith is that he discussed the market economy within the broader frame of *moral philosophy.* That is, his discussion of the evolving market economy was motivated by a need to understand the world as a meaningful whole. This approach is especially interesting at this time when the debate on principles shows more and more clearly that modern conceptual dichotomies such as the individual versus society, the analysis of the economic system versus understanding economic processes in its historical context, and positive versus normative economics, obstruct an adequate conception of the market economy.

When in the following chapters we consider how Smith can help in the reinterpretation of basic economic concepts we do so in the belief that a proper understanding of Smith's moral philosophical perspective on the market economy may be of help in interpreting and evaluating the latest developments in the debate on the principles of economics. Compared to the discussions of the 1960s and 1970s, the debate has changed from a rivalry between different approaches rooted in the oppositional interpretation of basic concepts, into a rivalry between different relational reinterpretations of these same concepts.

Adapting Robert L. Heilbroner's and William Milberg's observation that *there is a crisis of vision in modern economics*, we would say that in the 1980s and the 1990s the crisis of vision has changed into a crisis of modern economics itself.[78] Reinterpretation of basic concepts such as the *free market economy* and the *price mechanism* is an integral part of today's debate on the principles of economics.

Present-day discussions no longer focus on traditional controversies such as the market versus the state. Post Keynesians, neo-institutionalists, neo-Austrians, New Classicals and non-Walrasian equilibrium theorists now agree that the market should occupy centre stage in the economy. They all understand the market economy as a process and are searching for a deeper insight into what free-market adherents and opponents formerly presupposed: the so-called price mechanism. In the (neo)classical economy the intrinsic coordination properties of interrelated markets were part of the assumptions and not of the explanation. Critics also paid little attention to coordination by market exchange because in the traditional frame of modern economics it was synonymous with the criticised (neo)classical mechanistic understanding of the price mechanism.

If we look at the discussions of the 1980s and 1990s and compare, for example, Jan E. Kregel's Post Keynesian economics with Robert E. Lucas' New Classical economics, we find that in both approaches, albeit in different ways, the old frame of reference with its oppositional interpretation of twin-concepts such as the individual and society is challenged.

With reference to the notion of fundamental uncertainty, Kregel still emphasizes the importance of an adequate social and institutional framework to guide the individual in his economic activities. The collectivistic view according to which individual behaviour is thought to be determined by macro-economic structures, however, is absent from Kregel's Post Keynesian writings. The individual is now interpreted as a real subject whose subjectivity is considered to be freedom of action in relation to its context, as Kregel's discussion on the creativity of the entrepreneur in the anniversary volume for George L.S. Shackle shows.[79]

The New Classical economist Robert E. Lucas, on the other hand, still retains the old device of methodological individualism. His analysis of the market economy based on general equilibrium *cum* rational expectations, however, no longer explains social phenomena by reducing them to the behaviour of strictly atomistic individuals. In *Understanding Business Cycles*, for example, Lucas' analysis supposes that individuals act with reference to a common outlook on the economy.[80]

In addition to Kregel and Lucas, many other authors can be cited to illustrate that the growing dissatisfaction is not limited to the traditional oppositional interpretation of the individual and society, but also extends to other basic twin concepts, such as the market versus the state and positive versus normative economics. It suffices to mention authors such as Karl Brunner, Paul Davidson,

Frank H. Hahn, Ludwig M. Lachmann, Axel Leijonhufvud, Takashi Negishi, Arjo Klamer, Don Lavoie, Douglas C. North and Warren J. Samuels.[81] However, our aim is not to investigate the various ways in which economists are currently experimenting with new relational interpretations of the aforementioned basic concepts of economics. Nor are we concerned with investigating in what measure these experiments run parallel to Smith's economic theories.[82]

Unlike traditional Smith readings, which look for parallels and differences between the genuine ideas of the founding father and contemporaneous theory, this study aims to discover in what ways a dialogue with Smith can illuminate the problems associated with the aforementioned twin concepts. Through our dialogic reading of Smith's texts we hope to contribute to the new relational interpretation of these concepts.

By advancing an hermeneutical rereading of Smith we want to show that there really is a promised land beyond the prison house of binary oppositions in which economics had been incarcerated until recently. As indicated above, Smith's texts are pre-eminently suited to a dialogue aimed at rethinking the principles of economics. Taking seriously Smith's statements about his planned trilogy – i.e. *The Theory of Moral Sentiments, The Wealth of Nations* and the unpublished *Theory of Jurisprudence* – means that there can be no adequate reading of Smith which does not rethink economics by taking it beyond the framework constituted by such binary antitheses as the following:

– *either* the economy has to be explained by deduction from the universal characteristics of its atoms, i.e. the individual subjects *or* economic behaviour is predetermined by the economy's social structure;
– *either* economics has to be modelled like mechanics, i.e. economics is the mechanics of self-interest *or* we should stop with analysing the economy as a system because interpreting the economy as a system of causal laws is a naturalistic fallacy produced by the modern scientistic mind;
– *either* a market economy without any interference by government mirrors the economic order implied by the autonomy of the individual economic subject *or* the economy has to be controlled by the government because of the inevitable coordination failures arising from a market economy;
– *either* science focuses exclusively on what is, so economic science – positive economics – is value-free in contrast to normative and applied economics *or* there are only subjective opinions because the objective, pre-given real world of positive economics is an illusion that masks the normativity of its theories, its explanations and predictions.

In the following chapters we will interpret Smith's discussion of the market economy as part of a more encompassing project – understanding the evolving commercial society as a meaningful whole. With regard to traditional Smith-interpretations it will be our hypothesis that the supposed dichotomies and other inconsistencies in Smith's work reflect a clash between two frames of reference: while Smith himself was still thinking in the tradition of *moral philosophy* when he dealt with the analysis and explanation of economic phenomena as part of understanding the world as a meaningful whole, later readers have approached his texts as if they were written from a modernist perspective, characterized by oppositions such as the individual versus society, the market versus the state, general theory versus historic understanding, and science versus metaphysics. We will reinterpret Smith's idea of the free market economy as part of a dialogue with Smith in order to contribute to new relational interpretations of the aforementioned basic concepts of economic thought.

Notes

1. Recktenwald, H.C., 'An Adam Smith Renaissance *anno* 1976? The Bicentenary Output – A Reappraisal of His Scholarship', *Journal of Economic Literature*, vol. 16, 1978, March, pp. 56–83.
2. Cf. Recktenwald, H.C., *Adam Smith, sein Leben und sein Werk*, München, 1976, 70.
3. See for instance Raphael, D.D and A.L. Macfie (eds.), *The Theory of Moral Sentiments*, Oxford, 1976, pp. 25–34.
4. The full title is *An Inquiry into the Nature and Causes of the Wealth of Nations*.
5. TMS, Advertisement:
    'In the last paragraph of the first Edition of the present work, I said, that I should in another discourse endeavour to give an account of the general principles of law and government, and of the different revolutions which they had undergone in the different ages and periods of society; not only in what concerns justice, but in what concerns police, revenue, and arms, and whatever else is the object of law. In the Enquiry concerning the Nature and Causes of the Wealth of Nations, I have partly executed this promise; at least so far as concerns police, revenue, and arms.'
6. 'the sale was from the first better than the publishers expected, for on the 12th of April, when it had only been a month out, Strahan takes notice of a remark of David Hume that Smith's book required too much thought to be as popular as Gibbon's, and states, "What you say of Mr. Gibbon's and Dr. Smith's book is exactly just. The former is the most popular work; but the sale of the latter, though not near so rapid, has been more than I could have expected from a work that requires much thought and reflection (qualities that do not abound among modern readers) to peruse to any purpose."'
    (Rae, J., *Life of Adam Smith*, London, 1885; reprint: Bristol, 1990, pp. 285–286)

    'reading of it necessarily requires so much attention, and the public is disposed to give so little'
    (Mossner, E.C. and I.S. Ross, 'From David Hume', *The Correspondence of Adam Smith*, Oxford, 1987, p. 186)
    See also Recktenwald, H.C., *Adam Smith, sein Leben und sein Werk*, München, 1976, p. 18.
7. TMS, Advertisement. See also the final sentences of *The Theory of Moral Sentiments*:
    'I shall in another discourse endeavour to give an account of the general principles of law and government, and of the different revolutions they have undergone in the different ages and periods of society, not only in what concerns justice, but in what concerns police, and arms, and whatever else is the object of law.'
    (TMS VII.iv.37)
8. 'a week before his death, he expressly sent for them *[Black and Hutton]*, and asked them then and there to burn sixteen volumes of manuscript to which he directed them. This they did without knowing or asking what they contained.'
    (Rae, J., *Life of Adam Smith*, London, 1895; reprint: Bristol, 1990, p. 434)

9. LJ(B): 'Report dated 1766': notes, discovered by E.G. Cannan in 1895 and published in 1896 under the title: *Lectures on Justice, Police, Revenue, and Arms, delivered in the University of Glasgow by Adam Smith.* LJ(A): 'Report of 1762–1763': discovered by J. Lothian in 1958 and first published in *The Glasgow Edition of the Works and Correspondence of Adam Smith.* See also the *Introduction* in Meek, R.L., Raphael, D.D. and P.G. Stein (eds.), *Lectures on Jurisprudence*, Oxford, 1978/1987, pp. 5–13.

10. Cf. Black, R.D.C., 'Smith's Contribution in Historical Perspective' in Wilson, T. and A.S. Skinner (eds.), *The Market and The State. Essays in Honour of Adam Smith,* Oxford, 1976, p. 44.

11. See for instance Ricardo in the *Preface* of the *Principles of Political Economy and Taxation*, third edition, 1821:

    'The writer, in combating received opinions, has found it necessary to advert more particularly to those passages in the writings of Adam Smith from which he sees reason to differ; but he hopes it will not, on that account, be suspected that he does not, in common with all those who acknowledge the importance of the science of Political Economy, participate in the admiration which the profound work of this celebrated author so justly excites.'

    (Pelican edition by R.M. Hartwell, Harmondsworth, 1971, p. 50).

12. Cf. Backhouse, R.E., *A History of Modern Economic Analysis*, Oxford, 1985, pp. 26, 32–33, 34–35 and 43–44; Black, R.D.C., 'Smith's Contribution in Historical Perspective' in Wilson, T. and A.S. Skinner (eds.), *The Market and the State. Essays in Honour of Adam Smith*, Oxford, 1976, pp. 44–47; Hutchison, T.W., *On Revolutions and Progress in Economic Knowledge*, Cambridge, 1978, pp. 26–57 and 84–85; Sowell, T., *Classical Economics Reconsidered*, Princeton, 1974, pp. 112–148.

13. Another important critic of the Ricardian economics was Richard Jones, who is generally considered to be the forerunner of the English historical school. Jones' *Essay on the Distribution of Wealth and the Sources of Taxation* from 1833 is critical of Ricardo's method of discussing economic processes in a framework of universal causal laws. Cf. Backhouse, R.E., *A History of Modern Economic Analysis*, Oxford, 1985, pp. 36–37 and 212–213; Black, R.D.C., 'Smith's Contribution in Historical Perspective' in Wilson, T. and A.S. Skinner (eds.), *The Market and the State. Essays in Honour of Adam Smith*, Oxford, 1976, pp. 44–47; Hutchison, T.W., *A Review of Economic Doctrines. 1870–1929*, Oxford, 1966, p. 7, and Hutchison, T.W., *On Revolutions and Progress in Economic Knowledge*, Cambridge, 1978, pp. 77 and 223.

14. With regard to the division of economics in positive, normative and applied economics, see among others Hutchison, T.W., *'Positive' Economics and Policy Objectives*, London, 1964 and Plattel, M. and J. Peil, 'An Ethico-Political and Theoretical Reconstruction of Economic Thought' *Research Memorandum 149*, Department of Economics, Tilburg University, 1984.

15. Leslie, T.E.C., 'The Political Economy of Adam Smith', *Fortnightly Review*, November 1870, reprinted in Leslie, T.E.C., *Essays in Political and Moral Philosophy*, London, 1879, pp. 148–166; Bagehot, W., 'The Centenary of *The Wealth of Nations, The Economist*, 1876, reprinted in St John-Stevas, N. (ed.), *The Collected Works of Walter Bagehot*, London, 1968, part 3, pp. 84–112; Bagehot, W., 'Adam Smith and Our Modern Economy', *Economic Studies*, 1880, reprinted in St John-Stevas, N. (ed.), *The Collected Works of Walter Bagehot*, London, 1968, part 11, pp. 298–328.

16. Black, R.D.C., 'Smith's Contribution in Historical Perspective' in Wilson, T. and A.S. Skinner (eds.), *The Market and the State. Essays in Honour of Adam Smith*, Oxford, 1976, pp. 52–54. With regard to Leslie, see also Backhouse, R.E., *A History of Modern Economic Analysis*, Oxford, 1985, pp. 213–214; Hutchison, T.W., *A Review of Economic Doctrines.*

1870–1929, Oxford, 1966, pp. 1, 19–21, and Hutchison, T.W., *On Revolutions and Progress in Economic Knowledge*, Cambridge, 1978, pp. 63 and 203–205.

17. Black, R.D.C., 'Smith's Contribution in Historical Perspective' in Wilson, T. and A. Skinner (eds.), *The Market and The State, Essays in Honour of Adam Smith*, Oxford, 1976, pp. 55–56; Backhouse, R.E., *A History of Modern Economic Analysis*, Oxford, 1985, pp. 214–215; Hutchison, T.W., *A Review of Economic Doctrines. 1870–1929*, Oxford, 1966, pp. 1, 6–7, 15 and 75; and Hutchison, T.W., *On Revolutions and Progress in Economic Knowledge*, Cambridge, 1978, pp. 63 and 203–205.

Though we have mentioned Bagehot as a representative of the neoclassical view of Smith, it is important to realize that the neoclassicals were not unanimous in their assessment of Smith's economics. Jevons, for instance, valued *The Wealth of Nations* positively because he understood this book as a mathematical theory, combined with concrete applications and historical examples. He especially appreciated Smith's treatise on the division of labour and he emphasized that Smith used the notion of *utility* in his analysis. However, he rejected Smith's distinction between productive and unproductive labour, because from the utility viewpoint this distinction was pointless. Cf. Black, R.D.C., 'Smith's Contribution in Historical Perspective' in Wilson, T. and A.S. Skinner (eds.), *The Market and The State, Essays in Honour of Adam Smith*, Oxford, 1976, pp. 54–55.

It is also worth mentioning Jevons' comment in which Ricardian economics is rejected in favour of the so-called French school:

'The most obvious conclusion which I always reach is that the only way of attaining a true system of political economy is to reject, once and for all, the muddled and ludicrous hypotheses of the Ricardian school. The truth lies in the French school' *[and here he recognises the importance of Say's influence]* 'and the sooner we realise this, the better it will be.'

(in Reynaud, P.-L., 'Jean-Baptiste Say', in Recktenwald, H.C. (ed.), *Political Economy. A Historical Perspective*, London, 1973, p. 115).

18. Lowe, R., 'What are the more important results which have followed from the publications of the *Wealth of Nations* ... and in what principal directions do the doctrines of that book still remain to be applied' in *Political Economy Club, Revised Report of the Proceedings at dinner of May 1876, held in celebration of the Hundredth Year of Publication of the* Wealth of Nations, London, 1876, pp. 11, 19 and 21, cited in Black, R.D.C., 'Smith's Contribution in Historical Perspective' in Wilson, T. and A.S. Skinner (eds.), *The Market and The State. Essays in Honour of Adam Smith*, Oxford, 1976, pp. 49–50. Cf. Hutchison, T.W., *A Review of Economic Doctrines. 1870–1929*, Oxford, 1966, pp. 1–5.

19. See, for instance, Hutchison, T.W., *A Review of Economic Doctrines. 1870–1929*, Oxford, 1966, pp. 1–31 and *On Revolutions and Progress in Economic Knowledge*, Cambridge, 1978, pp. 58–93 about the degeneration of (English) classical economics.

20. For a survey of the lectures held at the London School of Economics and at the University of Chicago, see: Black, R.D.C., 'Smith's Contribution in Historical Perspective' in Wilson, T. and A.S. Skinner (ed.), *The Market and The State. Essays in Honour of Adam Smith*, Oxford, 1976, p. 56, note 51. The lectures given at the University of Chicago have been published in Clark, J.M. (ed.), *Adam Smith 1776–1926*, Chicago, 1928.

21. Cannan praised Smith for the following three important innovations in economic thinking:

'The first thing was the definite substitution of income – "produce" as he called it – for the older idea of a capital aggregation of "treasure" or something akin to "treasure". ... The second great change which Adam Smith made in general theory was to substitute wealth per head for wealth in the aggregate, whatever that may be. ... Thirdly, Adam Smith may fairly claim to be the father, not of economics generally – that would be absurd – but of what in modern times has been called, with opprobrious intention, "bourgeois economics," that is the economics of those economists who look with favour on working and trading and investing for personal gain.'

Cannan's criticism was the following:

'Very little of Adam Smith's scheme of economics has been left standing by subsequent inquirers. No one now holds his theory of value, his account of capital is seen to be hopelessly confused, and his theory of distribution is explained as an ill-assorted union between his own theory of prices and the physiocrats' fanciful Economic Table. His classification of incomes is found to involve a misguided attempt to alter the ordinary useful and well-recognised meaning of words, and a mixing up of classification according to source with classification according to method or manner of receipt. His opinions about taxation and its incidence are extremely crude, and his history is based on insufficient information and disfigured by bias.'

(Cannan, E.G.,'Adam Smith as an Economist' in Wood, J.C. (ed.), *Adam Smith. Critical Assessments*, part II, London, 1983, pp. 20, 22 and 24).

Douglas shared Cannan's views, albeit that he formulated various points somewhat less sharply and sometimes with more nuances than Cannan did:

'The contributions of Adam Smith to the theory of value and distribution were not great, and in commemorating the publication of the *Wealth of Nations* it might seem to be the path of wisdom to pass these topics by in discreet silence and to reserve discussion instead for those subjects, such as the division of labour, where his realistic talents enabled him to appear at a better advantage. Yet the errors of an able thinker are, if properly interpreted, only slightly less illuminating than his substantive contributions, and deserve analysis in the history of economic thought. There is, however, another reason why Smith's doctrines on value and distribution merit examination. This is because Smith's formulation of the problems of exchange value and of the distribution of the national product among the factors of production was such as almost inevitable gave rise to the doctrines of the post-Ricardian socialists and to the labour theory of value and the exploitation theory of Karl Marx.'

(Douglas, P.H. 'Smith's Theory of Value and Distribution' in Clark, J.M. (ed.), *Adam Smith, 1776–1928*, Chicago, 1928, New York, 1966, p. 77).

22. Viner, J., 'Adam Smith and Laissez-Faire' in Clark, J.M. (ed.), *Adam Smith, 1776–1926*, Chicago, 1928, New York, 1966.

23. See Cannan, E.G., 'Adam Smith as an Economist' in Wood, J.C. (ed.), *Adam Smith. Critical Assessments*, part II, London, 1983, pp. 26–28.

24. Viner, J., 'Adam Smith and Laissez-Faire' in Clark, J.M. (ed.), *Adam Smith, 1776–1926*, Chicago, 1928, New York, 1966:

'There is much weight of authority and of evidence, ..., that Smith's major claim to originality, in English economic thought at least, was his detailed and elaborate application to the wilderness of economic phenomena of the unifying concept of a co-ordinated and mutually interdependent system of cause and effect relationships which philosophers and theologians had already applied to the world in general. Smith's doctrine that economic phenomena were manifestations of an underlying order in nature, governed by natural forces, gave to English economics for the first time a definite trend toward logically consistent synthesis of economic relationships, toward "system-building." Smith's further doctrine that this underlying natural order required, for its most beneficent operation, a system of natural liberty, and that in the main public regulation and monopoly were corruptions of that order, at once gave to economics a bond of union with the prevailing philosophy and theology, and to economists and statement a program of practical reform.'

(pp. 116–117)

'In his *Theory of Moral Sentiments*, Smith develops his system of ethics on the basis of a doctrine of a harmonious order in nature guided by God, and in an incidental manner applies his general doctrine with strict consistency to the economic order. In his later work, the *Wealth of Nations*, Smith devotes himself to a specialized inquiry into the nature of the economic order. It is a commonplace among the authorities on Adam Smith that it is impossible fully to understand the *Wealth of Nations* without recourse to the *Theory of Moral Sentiments*. The vast bulk of economists, however, who have read the *Wealth of Nations* without reading the *Theory of Moral Sentiments*, have not regarded Smith's masterpiece as an obscure book, as one especially hard to understand. On the other hand, the very authorities who are most emphatic in asserting the need of reference to the *Theory of Moral Sentiments* to understand the *Wealth of Nations*, once they embark upon their self-imposed task of interpreting the latter in the light of the former, become immersed in difficult problems of interpretation for which scarcely any two writers offer the same solution. The system of individual liberty is much in evidence among the interpreters of Smith, but that natural harmony which should also result is strikingly lacking. The Germans, who, it seems, in their methodological manner commonly read both the *Theory of Moral Sentiments* and the *Wealth of Nations*, have coined a pretty term, *Das Adam Smith Problem*, to denote the failure to understand either which results from the attempt to use the one in the interpretation of the other. I will endeavour to show that the difficulties of the authorities result mainly from their determination to find a basis for complete concordance of the two books, and that there are divergences between them which are impossible of reconciliation ... . I will further endeavour to show that the *Wealth of Nations* was a better book because of its partial breach with the *Theory of Moral Sentiments*, and that it could not have remained, as it has, a living book were it not that in its methods of analysis, its basic assumption, and its conclusions it abandoned the absolutism, the rigidity, the romanticism which characterise the earlier book.'
(pp. 119–120)

'There would be little ground for insistence upon reconciliation between the *Theory of Moral Sentiments* and the *Wealth of Nations* if it were simply a case of comparing one book written in 1757 with another written in 1776. It may not be as common as it should be for a man in his full maturity to advance beyond the level of his first book; but it surely is not a rare phenomenon requiring to be explained out of existence. In every respect which is of concern to the economist as such, with the possible exception of his treatment of benevolence, the apparent discrepancies between the *Theory of Moral Sentiments* and the *Wealth of Nations* mark distinct advances of the latter over the former in realism and in application of the saving grace of common sense. But in the last year of his life Smith made extensive revisions and additions to the *Theory of Moral Sentiments*, without diminishing in any particular the points of conflict between the two books. This would make it seem that in Smith's mind, at least, there was to the last no consciousness of any difference in the doctrines expounded in the two books. Though we grant this, however, are we obliged to accept his judgement and to strain interpretations in order to find consistency prevailing where inconsistency appeareth to reign supreme? I think not. There persisted within the *Wealth of Nations*, through five successive editions, many, and to later eyes obvious, inconsistencies. When Smith revised his *Theory of Moral Sentiments* he was elderly and unwell. It is not altogether unreasonable to suppose that he had lost the capacity to make drastic changes in his philosophy, but had retained his capacity to overlook the absence of complete coordination and unity in that philosophy.'
(pp. 137–138)

25. Idem.
26. Hollander, J.H., 'The Dawn of a Science' and 'The Founder of a School', Clark, J.M., 'Adam Smith and the Currents of History', Morrow, G.R., 'Adam Smith: Moralist and Philosopher' in Clark, J.M. (ed.), *Adam Smith, 1776–1926*, Chicago, 1928, New York, 1966.
27. See also Peil, J., 'Adam Smith. A Reconstruction of His Economic Thought', *Research Memorandum 8802*, Institute of Economics, University of Nijmegen, 1988.
    Towards the end of the nineteenth century, especially German authors like Hasbach, Oncken and Zeiss, had occupied themselves with the relationship between *The Theory of Moral Sentiments* and *The Wealth of Nations*. Ever since, the question of the relation between Smith's two works is known as *Das Adam Smith Problem*. A recent, interesting discussion of the *Adam Smith Problem* is provided by Dupuy, J.-P., 'A Reconsideration of *Das Adam Smith Problem*', *Stanford French Review*, vol. 17, 1993, pp. 45–57. In chapter III it will be shown that Dupuy's argument that Smith's *sympathy*-theory ultimately undermines itself, cuts no ice.
28. Schumpeter, J., *History of Economic Analysis*, London, 1954/1972, pp. 188–189:
    'The rudimentary equilibrium theory of chapter 7, by far the best piece of economic theory turned out by Adam Smith, in fact points towards Say, and through the latter's work to Walras.'
29. See for instance Buchanan, J., 'Public Goods and Natural Liberty' in Wilson, T. and A.S. Skinner (eds.), *The Market and the State. Essays in Honour of Adam Smith*, Oxford, 1976, pp. 271–286, and Musgrave, R.A., 'Adam Smith on Public Finance and Distribution' in Wilson, T. and A.S. Skinner (eds.), *The Market and the State. Essays in Honour of Adam Smith*, Oxford, 1976, pp. 296–319.
30. For instance Richardson, G.B., 'Adam Smith on Competition and Increasing Returns' in Wilson, T. and A.S. Skinner (eds.), *The Market and The State. Essays in Honour of Adam Smith,* Oxford, 1976, pp. 350–360; Bloomfield, A.I., 'Adam Smith on the Theory of International Trade' in Skinner, A.S. and T. Wilson (eds.), *Essays on Adam Smith,* Oxford, 1975, pp. 445–481, and Hla Myint, U., 'Adam Smith's Theory on International Trade in the Perspective of Economic Development', *Economica*, vol. 44, 1977, pp. 231–248.
31. Samuelson, P.A., 'A Modern Theorist's Vindication of Adam Smith', *The American Economic Review*, vol. 67, 1977, pp. 42–49.
32. See Campbell, R.H., Skinner, A.S. and W.B. Todd (eds.), 'General Introduction' to *An Inquiry into the Nature and Causes of the Wealth of Nations,* Oxford, 1976, pp. 1–60, as well as Winch, D., *Adam Smith's Politics: An Essay in Historiographic Revision,* Cambridge, 1978.
33. Early signs of the change in the Smith reception may be found in the numerous essays and books on Smith by Alec L. Macfie and Andrew S. Skinner, for example:
    Macfie: 'The Scottish Tradition in Economic Thought', *Scottish Journal of Political Economy*, vol. 2, 1955, pp. 81–103; 'Adam Smith's Moral Sentiments as Foundation for his Wealth of nations', *Oxford Economic Papers*, vol. 11, 1959, pp. 209–228; 'Adam Smith's Theory of Moral Sentiments', *Scottish Journal of Political Economy*, vol. 8, 1961, pp. 12–27; 'The Moral Justification of Free Enterprise. A Lay Sermon on a Adam Smith Text', *Scottish Journal of Political Economy*, vol. 14, 1967, pp. 1–11, and *The Individual in Society*, London, 1967.
    Skinner: 'Economics and History', *Scottish Journal of Political Economy*, vol. 12, 1965, pp. 1–22; 'Natural History in the Age of Adam Smith', *Political Studies*, vol. 15, 1967, pp. 32–48; 'Introduction' to *The Wealth of Nations*, Aldershot, 1970, pp. 11–97; 'Adam Smith: Philosophy and Science', *Scottish Journal of Political Economy*, vol. 19, 1972, pp. 307–319; *Adam Smith and the Role of the State*, Glasgow, 1974; 'Adam Smith: Science and the Role of the Imagination' in Todd, W.B. (ed.), *Hume and the Enlightenment:*

Essays Presented to Ernest Mossner, Austin, 1974, pp. 164–188; *A System of Social Science*, Oxford, 1979; 'Adam Smith: An Aspect of Modern Economics, *Scottish Journal of Political Economy*, vol. 26, 1979, pp. 109–125; 'A Scottish Contribution to Marxist Sociology?' in Bradley, I. and M. Howard (eds.), *Classical and Marxian Political Economy: Essays in honour of Ronald L. Meek,* New York, 1982, pp. 79–114; 'Adam Smith' in Eatwell, J., Milgate, M. and P. Newman (eds.), *The Invisible Hand – The New Palgrave*, London, 1987/1989, pp. 1–42, and 'The Shaping of Political Economy in the Enlightenment' in Mizuta, H. and C. Sugiyama (eds.), *Adam Smith: International Perspectives*, London, 1993, pp. 113–139.

34. Cf. Recktenwald, H.C., 'An Adam Smith Renaissance *anno* 1976? The Bicentenary Output – A Reappraisal of His Scholarship', *Journal of Economic Literature*, vol. 16, 1978, pp. 56–83, and West, E.G., 'Scotland's Resurgent Economist: A Survey of the New Literature on Adam Smith', *Southern Economic Journal*, vol. 45, 1978, pp. 343–369.

35. West divides his survey into six parts of which the latter four are devoted to the *new literature*. He describes the themes of these parts as follows:

'Part I will review recent discussion on economic methodology as it concerns the work of Adam Smith. Part II will examine the post-war interpretations of Adam Smith's theory of value and growth. Part III will analyse new comparisons of Smith's theory of competition with neo-classical theory. Also in the light of recent literature Part IV will compare Smith's classical assessment of monopoly with the modern or neo-classical. A recent "vindication" of Smith's international trade theory is examined in Part V. Part VI will conclude the paper by "parading" the new literature on Smith's analysis of institutions, politics, and the role of the state.'
(p. 344)

In 1988, West published a new updated survey: 'Developments in the Literature on Adam Smith: An Evaluative Survey' in: Thweatt, W. (ed.), *Classical Political Economy. A Survey of Recent Literature*, Boston, 1988, pp. 13–44. West's *Adam Smith and Modern Economics* (1990) can be seen as a new, more detailed version of the above-mentioned surveys, in which the period under consideration has been extended to 1990: the year of the 'bicentenary of the death of that great economist' (p. 1). We limit ourselves to the first survey in which West's perspective on Smith is most explicitly worded.

36. Recktenwald formulates the purpose of his article as follows:

'To organise my reflections after reading a vast literature, I shall concentrate very restrictively on seven topics: The new Glasgow edition of Smith's complete works as well as the four central issues mentioned above *[i.e., the four main themes in present-day Smith inquiry]*. I begin this essay with the lasting appeal of Smith's ideas, and I shall close with my reappraisal of his scholarship.'
(p. 57)

In 1980 and 1985 Recktenwald published a German-language version of the above-mentioned survey: 'Eine Adam Smith Renaissance anno 1976? Eine Neubeurteilung seiner Orginalität und Gelehrsamkeit' in Grüske, K. (ed.), *Markt und Staat. Fundamente einer freiheitlichen Ordnung in Wirtschaft und Politik. Ausgewählte Beitrage,* Göttingen, 1980, pp. 39–69 and in *Ethik, Wirtschaft und Staat. Adam Smiths Politische Ökonomie Heute*, Darmstadt, 1985, pp. 345–390.

37. Recktenwald, H.C., 'An Adam Smith Renaissance *anno* 1976? The Bicentenary Output – A Reappraisal of His Scholarship', *Journal of Economic Literature*, vol. 16, 1978, pp. 56–57.

38. Kaufmann, F.-X. and H.G. Krüsselberg (eds.), *Markt, Staat und Solidarität bei Adam Smith*, Frankfurt am Main, 1981/1984; Haakonssen, K., *The Science of a Legislator: The Natural Jurisprudence of David Hume and Adam Smith*, New York, 1981; Hont, I. and

M. Ignatieff (eds.), *Wealth and Virtue. The Shaping of Political Economy in the Scottish Enlightenment*, Cambridge, 1983; Teichgraeber III, R.F., *'Free Trade' and Moral Philosophy. Rethinking the Sources of Adam Smith's* Wealth of Nations, Durham, 1986; Berns, E. (ed.), *Adam Smith. Ethiek, politiek, economie*, Tilburg, 1986; Brown, M., *Adam Smith's Economics: Its Place in the Development of Economic Thought*, London, 1988; Lange, D., *Zur sozial-philosophischen Gestalt der Marktwirtschaftstheorie bei Adam Smith*, München, 1983; Werhane, P.H., *Adam Smith and His Legacy for Modern Capitalism*, New York, 1991; Muller, J.Z., *Adam Smith in his Time and Ours: Designing the Decent Society*, New York, 1993; and Young, J.T., *Economics as a Moral Science: The Political Economy of Adam Smith*, Cheltenham, 1997.

39. See for instance Tobin, J., 'Theoretical Issues in Macroeconomics' in Feiwel, G.R. (ed.), *Issues in Contemporary Macroeconomics and Distribution*, London, 1985, pp. 104–106.

40. See for example Hollander, S., 'The Historical Dimension of the Wealth of Nations', *Transactions of the Royal Society of Canada*, Series IV, 14, 1978, pp. 227–292.

41. Recktenwald, H.C., 'An Adam Smith Renaissance *anno* 1976? The Bicentenary Output – A Reappraisal of His Scholarship', *Journal of Economic Literature*, Volume 16, 1978, March, p. 56.

42. See among others Billet, L., 'The Just Economy: The Moral Basis of the Wealth of Nations', *Review of Social Economy*, volume 34, 1976, pp. 295–315; Danner, P.L., 'Sympathy and Exchangeable Value: Keys to Adam Smith's Social Philosophy', *Review of Social Economy*, vol. 34, 1976, pp. 317–331; Young, J.T., 'Natural Price and the Impartial Spectator: A New Perspective on Adam Smith as a Social Economist', *International Journal of Social Economics*, vol. 12, 1985, pp. 118–133, and Young, J.T., 'The Impartial Spectator and Natural Jurisprudence: An Interpretation of Adam Smith's Theory of the Natural Price', *History of Political Economy*, vol. 18, 1986, pp. 365–382.

43. See among others the survey by Recktenwald, H.C., 'An Adam Smith Renaissance *anno* 1976? The Bicentenary Output – A Reappraisal of His Scholarship', *Journal of Economic Literature*, vol. 16, 1978, pp. 56–57, and Campbell, R.H., Skinner, A.S. and W.B. Todd (eds.), 'General Introduction' to *An Inquiry into the Nature and Causes of the Wealth of Nations*, Oxford, 1976, pp. 1–60.

44. For example Moos, S., 'Is Smith out of Date?', *Oxford Economic Papers*, vol. 3, 1951, June, pp. 187–201:

    'At a time when the more advanced countries are run by a vast body of local and central administrators, when national economies are protected by elaborate systems of tariffs, quotas, subsidies, and exchange controls, the student of economics knowingly smiles at the very mention of the name of Adam Smith. It means those concepts of unproductive labour, of free trade, and of labour as measure of value considered typical of eighteenth-century thought. Today we know better.'

45. Cf. Schumpeter, J.A., *History of Economic Analysis*, New York, 1954:

    'We know already that the skeleton of Smith's analysis hails from the scholastic and the natural-law Philosophers: besides lying ready at hand in the works of Grotius and Pufendorf, it was taught to him by his teacher Hutcheson.'
    (pp. 182–183)

    'the fact is that the Wealth of Nations does not contain a single analytic idea, principle, or method that was entirely new in 1776.'
    (p. 184)

    'the Wealth of Nations contained no really novel ideas ... it cannot rank with Newton's *Principia* or Darwin's *Origin* as an intellectual achievement.'
    (p. 185)

'His very limitations made for success. Had he been more brilliant, he would not have been taken so seriously. Had he dug more deeply, had he unearthed more recondite truth, had he used difficult and ingenious methods, he would not have been understood.'
(p. 185)

46. In fact Van Traa even tended towards a negative judgement of Smith when he argued that Smith's fame was due largely to the omission of sources and to the favourable political economic climate. According to Van Traa, success was practically unavoidable because, in his *Wealth of Nations,* Smith served the wishes of the powerful lobby for political and economic liberalization by a clear and concise plea for a politics of *laissez-faire.* See Van Traa, P.C., *Geschiedenis van de Economie,* Amsterdam, 1969, pp. 47–49.

47. For example West, E.G., 'Scotland's Resurgent Economist: A Survey of the New Literature on Adam Smith', *Southern Economic Journal,* vol. 45, 1978, pp. 343–369; West, E.G., 'Developments in the Literature on Adam Smith: An Evaluative Survey' in Thweatt, W.O. (ed.), *Classical Political Economy. A Survey of Recent Literature,* Boston, 1980, pp. 13–44; West, E.G., *Adam Smith and Modern Economics. From Market Behaviour to Public Choice,* Aldershot, 1990.

48. Samuelson, P.A., 'A Modern Theorist's Vindication of Adam Smith', *The American Economic Review,* vol. 67, 1977, pp. 42–49.

49. For instance, Blaug, M., *Economic Theory in Retrospect,* Cambridge, 1985, pp. 57 and 60–61, and Tobin, J., 'Theoretical Issues in Macroeconomics' in Feiwel, G.R. (ed.), *Issues in Contemporary Macroeconomics and Distribution,* London, 1985, p. 105.

50. O'Driscoll Jr., G.P. and M.J. Rizzo, *The Economics of Time & Ignorance,* Oxford, 1985, pp. 107, 111–112, 147, 153 and 192.

51. Meek, R.L., 'Smith, Turgot, and the "Four Stages" Theory', *History of Political Economy,* vol. 3, 1971, pp. 9–27; Meek, R.L., *Smith, Marx and after: Ten Essays in the Development of Economic Thought,* New York, 1977, and Skinner, A.S., 'A Scottish Contribution to Marxist Sociology?' in Bradley, I. and M. Howard (eds.), *Classical and Marxian Political Economy: Essays in Honour of Ronald L. Meek,* New York, 1982, pp. 79–114.

52. Kaufmann, F.-X. and H.G. Krüsselberg (eds.), *Markt, Staat und Solidarität bei Adam Smith,* Frankfurt, 1981; Trapp, M., *Adam Smith, politische Philosophie und politische Ökonomie,* Göttingen, 1987, Pack, S.J., *Capitalism as a Moral System: Adam Smith's Critique of the Free Market Economy,* Aldershot, 1991.

53. In addition to the literature mentioned in notes 37 and 52, see also Manenschijn, G., *Moraal en eigenbelang in Thomas Hobbes en Adam Smith,* Amsterdam, 1979; Fellmeth, R. *Staatsaufgaben im Spiegel politischer Ökonomie. Zum Verhältnis von Wirtschaft und Staatstätigkeiten in Werken von Adam Smith und Adolph Wagner,* München, 1981; Myers, M.L., *The Soul of Modern Economic Man. Ideas of Self-Interest. Thomas Hobbes to Adam Smith,* Chicago, 1983; Berns, E., *Adam Smith. Ethiek, politiek, economie,* Tilburg, 1986; and Muller, J.Z., *Adam Smith in his Time and Ours: Designing the Decent Society,* New York, 1993.

54. West, E.G., 'Scotland's Resurgent Economist: A Survey of the New Literature on Adam Smith', *Southern Economic Journal,* vol. 45, 1978, p. 343:
'Smith still has enemies as well as champions. But perennial controversies over *The Wealth of Nations* are signs that endorse it as a classic. Of course, interpreters come and interpreters go, and each reflects the preoccupations of his generation ... The present paper is probably no exception. But that is a risk that must be faced.'
Just like Recktenwald, West typifies the interest in Smith during the bicentenary as exceptional:

'Hundreds of essays were written on him in the bicentenary year 1976, although many of these no doubt were prompted more from the spirit of veneration than anything else. Much of the writings nevertheless has, I believe, been seminal. This is so either in the sense of a new appreciation of Smith's insight and a fresh exploration of paths he opens for us in the 20th century, or in the sense of presenting Smith in a new perspective in the light of a deeper understanding of the historical circumstances of his time.' (p. 343)

55. Recktenwald, H.C., 'An Adam Smith Renaissance *anno* 1976? The Bicentenary Output – A Reappraisal of His Scholarship', *Journal of Economic Literature*, vol. 16, 1978, March, p. 57:

'Surely the change in perspective to greater focus on growth and development is an important cause for extending interest, as R. D. C. Black emphasizes in his stimulating and scholarly survey.'

It should also be noted that Recktenwald's reference to Black is incomplete and therefore does not accurately represent the latter author's view on the Adam Smith renaissance. See Black, R.D.C., 'Smith's Contribution in Historical Perspective' in Wilson, T. and A.S. Skinner (eds.), *The Market and The State. Essays in Honour of Adam Smith,* Oxford, 1976, pp. 42–63.

56. Recktenwald, H.C., 'An Adam Smith Renaissance *anno* 1976? The Bicentenary Output – A Reappraisal of His Scholarship', *Journal of Economic Literature*, vol. 16, 1978, p. 73:

'Each epoch in its own way has tended to view and evaluate anew Smith's scientific performance and, of course, relevance.'

57. Recktenwald expresses similar sentiments about new research regarding other classical authors such as Schumpeter and Say in the introduction to Recktenwald, H.C., Scherer, F. and W. Stolper, *Schumpeters monumentales Werk – Wegweiser für eine dynamische Analyse*, Düsseldorf, 1988:

'Die Autoren folgen meinem Konzept, das der Klassiker-Edition zugrunde liegt: Sie prüfen kritisch, was in Schumpeters Werk bahnbrechend war und was heute noch klassisch ist, wenn wir die Elle *unserer* Einsicht, Methode und Erfahrung als Mass anlegen, wobei auch das Urteil der Nachfolger einbezogen wird.' (p. 5)

58. According to Recktenwald, the more fundamental reasons for the lasting appeal and interest in Smith are:

'(1) The very catholicity of Smith's work inspires. ...
(2) His subject matter is timeless, even biblical; ...
(3) The self-interest and not selfishness is the very foundation of his edifice of thought; ...
(4) Smith's goal seems to be congruent with the perennial tasks of economics, ...
(5) ... Smith's realism; ...
(6) His great capacity for model-building ...
(7) ... his personal integrity and his fresh yet disciplined style ...'

(Recktenwald, H.C., 'An Adam Smith Renaissance *anno* 1976? The Bicentenary Output – A Reappraisal of His Scholarship', *Journal of Economic Literature*, vol. 16, 1978, pp. 57–58)

59. In this connection, see Recktenwald:

'Let me round off my reflections on this topic. As far as I see, many errors and enigmas said to flaw Smith's work come under five headings: (1) a failure to see his works as a unitary whole, (2) an unfortunate mixing of parts of his models in his different works and, as a corollary, a deliberate and unjustified shifting from one subsystem to another, (3) a lacuna associated with the unfinished "theory and history of law and government," (4) an excessive stress by his critics on historical illustrations and ingenious or curious value judgments (commonly unimportant for his argument or overstated by isolating), and (5) the anachronistic habit of interpreting his words and ideas in the light of later insights, and experience, or of methods Smith would not have accepted.

Furthermore, many caricatures and *clichés*, alleged errors, or silly criticisms (Smith as the prototype of Manchester liberalism or as an advocate of "bourgeois economics" and of selfish materialism, who deals inadequately with ethical values) are all popular in literature and textbooks (for two centuries the object of moralists' mockery). They stem from careless thinking, impatient reading, prejudice, or oversimplification.'
(Recktenwald, H.C., 'An Adam Smith Renaissance *anno* 1976? The Bicentenary Output – A Reappraisal of His Scholarship', *Journal of Economic Literature*, vol. 16, 1978, pp. 65–66)

See also Recktenwald, H.R., 'Einführung des Herausgebers' in Baumol, W.J., *Jean-Baptiste Say und der »Traité«*, Düsseldorf, 1986, pp. 7–8:

'Schliesslich erstaunt es auch, wie viele Verdrehungen, Irrtümer und grobe Missdeutungen die *kritischen* Analysen der ersten sechs klassischen Werke in dieser Faksimile-Edition bereits aufgedeckt haben. Man hat diese Fehler sogar über mehrere Generationen unkritisch tradiert. Dabei liegen die Gründe für solche Karikaturen einzelner Theorien nicht nur in unscharfem Denken, unzureichender Analytik oder oberflächlicher Lektüre der Interpreten und Kritiker. Sie beruhen, nicht selten, ganz einfach auf Vor-Urteilen, wie ich sie vor allem gegenüber Smiths *Gesammtwerk* im einzelnen offengelegt habe.'

60. Hirsch, E.D., *Validity in Interpretation*, London, 1967, p. 216. Cf. Buuren, M.B. van, *Filosofie van de algemene literatuurwetenschap*, Leiden, 1988, pp. 106 ff.
61. Ibidem.
62. Schumpeter, J., *History of Economic Analysis*, New York, 1954, pp. 51–52 and 143. Schumpeter identified three such periods: the first culminated in Smith's *Wealth of Nations*, the second centred around the work of John Stuart Mill and the third around the work of William S. Jevons, Carl Menger, Léon Walras and Alfred Marshall. Ibid., pp. 380 and 953. See also chapter II, section 1.
63. Schumpeter, J. *History of Economic Analysis*, New York, 1954, pp. 242 and 827.
64. Ibidem, p. 189. See also note 45 and chapter II, section 1.
65. Winch, D., 'Commentary' on West, E.G., 'Developments in the Literature on Adam Smith: An Evaluative Survey' in Thweatt, W.O. (ed.), *Classical Political Economy. A Survey of Recent Literature*, Boston, 1988, pp. 45–46:

'Professor West rightly anticipated that the main difference between his and my perspective on recent developments in Smith scholarship turns on a historiographic question: How much can now be learned about Smith by treating him from a Whig-historical perspective within which the main issue is one of deciding in what respects he anticipated or foreshadowed, or failed by a large or small margin to foreshadow, what later generations of economists regard as significant? While this perspective continues to dominate the history of economics, and has sometimes served to clarify modern economic debate, it has often, in my opinion, obscured understanding of the historical subject; and while historiographic fiat can be laid down respecting the questions which it is legitimate to ask of the past, I still find something distinctly odd about an examination of classic works which largely results in interpretations that amount to little more than mirror-images of our latest concerns.

Although West recognizes the dangers of anachronistic readings, he believes that they are more acute in the case of Smith's philosophy and politics than his economics. This may be due to the reassuring sense of continuity between past and present which economists are able to enjoy by confining their attention to *The Wealth of Nations*, and more especially to those aspects of it which appear to be amenable to the latest form of economic analysis. In view of the economic focus of this book, West's concentration on literature produced within the economists' guild is understandable, though it is perhaps less justifiable in relation to Smith than the other classical authors considered in this book. I can only record my opinion at the outset that much of the work which has significantly modified and enlivened traditional perspectives on Smith in recent years has been done by those who are outside this guild.'

66. See also Plattel, M.A.D., 'Het vraagstuk van positieve en normatieve economie' in De Gaay Fortman, B. (ed.), *Economie en waarde*, Alphen aan de Rijn, 1982, pp. 48–67; Plattel, M.A.D. and J.J.M. Peil, 'An ethico-political and theoretical reconstruction of economic thought', *Research Memorandum 149*, Department of Economics, Tilburg University, 1984, Tilburg; M.A.D. Plattel, 'Economische wetenschap en ethiek', *Tijdschrift voor Theologie*, vol. 25, 1985, pp. 4–19.

67. Brown, M., *Adam Smith's Economics. Its Place in the Development of Economic Thought*, London, 1988; Danner, P.L., 'Sympathy and Exchangeable Value: Keys to Adam Smith's Social Philosophy', *Review of Social Economy*, vol. 34, 1976, pp. 317–331; Young, J.T., 'Natural Price and the Impartial Spectator: A New Perspective on Adam Smith as a Social Economist', *International Journal of Social Economics*, vol. 12, 1985, pp. 118–133 and Young, J.T., 'The Impartial Spectator and Natural Jurisprudence. An Interpretation of Adam Smith's Theory of Natural Price', *History of Political Economy*, vol. 18, 1986, pp. 365–382.

68. Hollander, S., *The Economics of Adam Smith*, Toronto, 1973, and 'The Historical Dimensions of the Wealth of Nations', *Transaction of the Royal Society of Canada*, Series IV, vol. 14, 1976, pp. 227–292; Hollander, S., 'On Professor Samuelson's Canonical Classical Model of Political Economy', *Journal of Economic Literature*, vol. 18, 1980, pp. 559–578; Samuelson, P.A., 'A Modern Theorist's Vindication of Adam Smith', *The American Economic Review*, vol. 67, 1977, pp. 42–49, and Samuelson, P.A., 'The Canonical Classical Model of Political Economy', *Journal of Economic Literature*, 1978, vol. 16, pp. 1415–1434. See also Recktenwald, H.C. in Trapp, M., *Adam Smith, politische Philosophie, und politische Ökonomie*, Göttingen, 1987.

69. For instance, Kaufmann, F.-X. and H.G. Krüsselberg (eds.), *Markt, Staat und Solidarität bei Adam Smith*, Frankfurt am Main, 1981; Skinner, A.S. and T. Wilson (eds.), *The Market and the State. Essays in Honour of Adam Smith*, Oxford, 1976, and Trapp, M., *Adam Smith, politische Philosophie und politische Ökonomie*, Göttingen, 1987.

70. In addition to titles mentioned in notes 38, 42, 53 and 68, see also Meek, R.L., 'Smith, Turgot, and the "Four Stages" Theory', *History of Political Economy*, vol. 3, 1971, pp. 9–27; Skinner, A.S., *A System of Social Science* and 'A Scottish Contribution to Marxist Sociology?' in Bradley, L. and M. Howard (eds.), *Classical and Marxian Political Economy: Essays in Honour of Ronald L. Meek*, New York, 1982, pp. 79–114.

71. Hollander, S., 'The Historical Dimension of the Wealth of Nations', *Transactions of the Royal Society of Canada*, Series IV, vol. 14, 1976, pp. 227–292.

72. See the survey by West, E.G., 'Scotland's Resurgent Economist: A Survey of the New Literature on Adam Smith', *Southern Economic Journal*, vol. 45, 1978, pp. 343–369 and West, E.G., 'Developments in the Literature on Adam Smith: An Evaluative Survey' in Thweatt, W.O. (ed.), *Classical Political Economy. A Survey of Recent Literature*, Boston, 1988, pp. 13–44.

73. Viner, J., 'Adam Smith and Laissez-Faire', *Journal of Political Economy*, vol. 35, 1927, pp. 198–232.

74. Gadamer, H.-G., *Wahrheit und Methode*, Tübingen, 1960, cited in Buuren, M.L. van, *Filosofie van de algemene literatuurwetenschap*, Leiden, 1988, p. 112.

75. Ricoeur, P., *Du texte à l'action*, Paris, 1986, p. 111, cited in Buuren, M. van, *Filosofie van de algemene literatuurwetenschap*, Leiden, 1988, p. 125.

76. Ibidem.

77. Ricoeur, P., *Interpretation Theory: Discourse and the Surplus of Meaning*, Fort Worth, 1976, p. 30, cited in Buuren, M. van, *Filosofie van de algemene literatuurwetenschap*, Leiden, 1988, p. 125.
78. Heilbroner, R.L. and W. Milberg, *The Crisis of Vision in Modern Economic Thought*, Cambridge, 1995.
79. See Kregel, J.A., 'Imagination, Exchange and Business Enterprise in Smith and Shackle' in Frowen, S.F. (ed.), *Unknowledge and Choice in Economics: Proceedings of a Conference in Honour of G.L.S. Shackle*, London, 1990, pp. 81–95.
80. Lucas, R.E., 'Understanding Business Cycles', in Brunner, K. and A.H. Meltzer (eds.), *Stabilization of the Domestic and International Economy*, Carnegie-Rochester Conference Series on Public Policy, vol. 5, Amsterdam, pp. 7–29, in Hoover, K.D., *The New Classical Macroeconomics*, part III, Aldershot, 1992, pp. 245–267. Cf. Pesaran, M.H., *The Limits to Rational Expectations*, Oxford, 1987.

The New Classicals, in their theories inspired by Muth, assume that the basis of the economic processes is an objective structure, which is known to the individual economic subjects, or will become known (to them) by means of a learning process.

'The ... version of the rational expectations hypothesis (REH), due to Muth, ... states that subjective expectations held by economic agents will be the same as the conditional mathematical expectations based on the "true" probability model of the economy, or more generally, that the agents' subjective probability distribution coincides with the "objective" probability distribution of events.'

(Pesaran, M.H., *The Limits to Rational Expectations*, Oxford, 1987)

With regard to the objective basic structure, the New Classicals presuppose that, when the individual economic subjects are well informed and also apply that information rationally, all markets are cleared by means of price adaptation.

By adopting the rational expectations hypothesis, the New Classicals assume that the frame of behaviour and action of the economic subject reflects the causal laws which are the basis of the economy. This implies that with regard to the principles of economics, they hold fast to the old functionalistic, cause and effect approach which is directly opposed to the hermeneutic approach currently being developed among Post Keynesians, neo-institutionalists and neo-Austrians. With reference to this new hermeneutical approach, it may even be contended that while the New Classicals recognize the importance of the process view to economic analysis, they actually reproduce, by substituting the rational expectations assumption for the auctioneer assumption, the Walrasian model of explanation in which economic processes are reduced to the economic behaviour and actions of atomistic rationalistic individuals directed by pre-given laws.

In the new hermeneutical approach the insight that the action of individual subjects is embedded in a social context, is not translated in the presupposition that causal laws are at the basis of the economy, of which the actors perhaps have no complete knowledge but certainly sufficient knowledge. In the hermeneutic approach, the economy as a whole is understood as being constituted by a number of processes which take place according to intersubjectively produced norms and values, sedimented in institutions.

81. See among others Brunner, K., 'Mensbeeld en "Maatschappij"-opvatting', *Rotterdamse Monetaire Studies*, 26, 1987; Davidson, P., *Controversies in Post Keynesian Economics*, Aldershot, 1991; Hahn, F.H., 'Reflections on the Invisible Hand', *Lloyds Bank Review*, April 1982, pp. 1–21; Lachmann, L.M., *The Market as an Economic Process*, Oxford, 1986; Leijonhufvud, A., *Information and Co-ordination*, New York, 1981; Negishi, T., *Economic Theories in a Non-Walrasian Tradition*, Cambridge, 1986; Klamer, A., 'Towards the Native's Point of View. The Difficulty of Changing the Conversation', in Lavoie, D. (ed.) *Economics and Hermeneutics*, London, 1990, pp. 19-33; Lavoie, D., 'Introduction, in Lavoie, D. (ed.), *Economics and Hermeneutics*, London, 1990, pp. 1-15;

North, D.C., *Institutions, Institutional Change and Economic Performance*, Cambridge, 1990, and Samuels, W.J. (ed.), *Economics as Discourse. An Analysis of the Language of Economics*, London, 1990.

82. In order to avoid misunderstanding, it is useful to reiterate the point that our Smith inquiry differs fundamentally from that of authors such as West. As we have explained above, scholars such as West typically approach Smith's texts as the site of a meaning which they believe to be unequivocal and objectively determinable. Their purpose is to establish whether in Smith's work, in accordance with this view of interpretation, one can find initiatives for present-day scientific theories on, for instance, the division of labour, money and banking, international trade, moral hazard, principal agent and public choice.

II A Contextual Approach to *The Wealth of Nations*

it will be necessary to show just how much our view of Smith has come to depend on certain perspectives of a general nineteenth-century provenance, and to question a powerful stereotype that has grown up around the subject.

(D. Winch, *Adam Smith's Politics. An Essay in Historiographic Revision*, Cambridge, 1978, p. 2)

Introduction

For most economists Adam Smith is primarily associated with the related ideas of the self-interested individual and of the price mechanism which coordinates the actions of these individuals in accordance with public interest. Because of this idea of the self-coordinating market economy, Smith's economic theory has come to be regarded as a Walrasian general equilibrium theory *in nucleo* since the breakthrough of the Walrasian general equilibrium approach in modern economics in the 1930s and 1940s.

Clearly the market economy is central to *The Wealth of Nations* and it is equally apparent that Smith believed that if people are free to act according to their self-interest in the context of a commercial society, the market economy best serves the prosperity of all. However, it is highly debatable whether Smith's understanding of the market economy corresponds with economistic models such as the Walrasian general equilibrium theory.

In rethinking Smith's idea of the market economy we are not simply concerned with questioning the interpretation advanced by (neo)classical economics, but with examining the positivistic interpretative model underlying the economist's traditional reading of Smith. Instead of selecting and interpreting Smith's texts from the perspective of an ahistorical, causal-law-oriented economic science, we propose employing a Gadamerian hermeneutics of listening in order to hear what Smith himself wanted to tell us about economics in the context of an evolving commercial society.

In this chapter we begin the process of reinterpreting Smith by considering his economics as an integral part of the eighteenth-century debate on the nature of commerce. The chapter comprises four sections. The first two sections aim to provide a preliminary general impression of Smith's place in eighteenth-century economic thought.

Section 1 places Smith's oeuvre against the background of the dramatic social changes which occurred in sixteenth-, seventeenth- and eighteenth-century Europe. In the context of these changes it becomes clear that *The Wealth of Nations* should be read as an extension of Smith's other texts on man and society. That is to say, that Smith's economics should be interpreted as an integral part of the moral philosophy through which Smith attempted to understand, comment on, and influence the changes that had overtaken his world.

Section 2 focuses on Smith's particular position within the discourse of modern economics. It will be argued that Smith's theory of the market economy was the result of reinterpreting and integrating new commercial ideas originating with merchants, civil servants and administrators on the one hand, and new political philosophies of individual liberty and private property on the other hand, through the use of a model of human social relations based on the concept of *sympathy*.

A discussion of this concept will be presented in sections 3 and 4. Section 3 reconstructs Smith's view of man and society through a consideration of its contemporary intellectual context. It will be shown that Smith's reinterpretation of *sympathy* marked a radical departure from the vision of authors such as Hugo Grotius, Samuel Pufendorf, Thomas Hobbes, John Locke and Francis Hutcheson. We will show that, by reinterpreting man's longing for *mutual sympathy*, Smith presented a view of social relations that avoided the opposition between man and society characteristic of the new, modern philosophy of his own day. If man's longing for *mutual sympathy* is understood as involving a never-ending process of competition for, and concurrence in, mutual appreciation, it becomes clear that, according to Smith, the evolving market economy was part of an historical evolution towards societies which would become increasingly, and ever more directly, coordinated by *mutual sympathy*.

Section 4 presents some preliminary conclusions concerning Smith's economics which will be dealt with more extensively in Chapters III and IV.

1 *The Wealth of Nations*: An Integral Part of Smith's Moral Philosophy

By contemporary standards Smith was a writer of considerable versatility.[1] He not only discussed subjects which are now seen as belonging to different disciplines – such as economics, ethics, literature, law, psychology and sociology – his writings on economics, our primary area of interest, are also a mix of what, since John Neville Keynes, have been called positive, normative and applied economics. So much so, that if we were to apply the disciplinary guidelines followed by economists since the late nineteenth century, then we could limit our reading of Smith to the first two books of *The Wealth of Nations*.[2]

As we have noted, however, this selective reading distorts Smith's own frame of reference. Smith's work belongs to what Peter Gay calls the *prehistory* of the modern inquiry into man and society, and predates its now familiar disciplinary divisions.[3] The differentiation of the discourse on man and society into separate branches of knowledge, and more specifically, the division of the discourse on the nature and causes of wealth into positive, normative and applied economics, took place only in the nineteenth century.[4]

Smith himself indicates at several points in his text that he considers *The Theory of Moral Sentiments* and *The Wealth of Nations* to be integral parts of a general and historical discourse on the principles and institutions which guide human thought and behaviour. As we have noted, Smith's most significant remarks on this subject are to be found in *The Theory of Moral Sentiments*. The first remark dates from 1759 and the second from the year of Smith's death, 1790. These remarks deserve our close attention for two reasons. Firstly, in combination with the reinterpretation of *sympathy* developed in *The Theory of Moral Sentiments*, they briefly describe the purpose and plan of Smith's discourse on man and society, and, secondly, taken together, they indicate that Smith remained convinced of the relevance of his research project until the time of his death and that he never doubted the internal and external coherence of the three elements that made up that project.

In the first edition of *The Theory of Moral Sentiments* of 1759, Smith concludes his discussion of the *sympathetic* view of man and society with the promise that he will provide a more extensive discussion of *law* and *government* at a later date:

'I shall in another discourse endeavour to give an account of the general principles of law and government, and of the different revolutions they have undergone in the different ages and periods of society, not only in what concerns justice, but in what concerns police, revenue, and arms, and whatever else is the object of law.'[5]

In the following five editions of *The Theory of Moral Sentiments*, Smith did not substantially alter his *sympathetic* account of man and society, nor did he withdraw his promise of a complementary discussion of *law* and *government*. The sixth edition – the last prepared personally by Smith – even contains an *Advertisement* which repeats the promise of a separate study of *law* and *government* and itemizes the subjects which were and were not discussed in his second publication, *The Wealth of Nations*:

'In the last paragraph of the first Edition of the present work, I said, that I should in another discourse endeavour to give an account of the general principles of law and government, and of the different revolutions which they had undergone in the different ages and periods of society; not only in what concerns justice, but in what concerns police, revenue and arms, and whatever else is the object of law. In the *Enquiry concerning the Nature and Causes of the Wealth of Nations*, I have partly executed this promise; at least so far as concerns police, revenue, and arms. What remains, the theory of jurisprudence, which I have long projected, I have hitherto been hindered from executing, by the same occupations which had till now prevented me from revising the present work. Though my very advanced age leaves me, I acknowledge, very little expectation of ever being able to execute this great work to my own satisfaction; yet, as I have not altogether abandoned the design, and as I wish still to continue under the obligation of doing what I can, I have allowed the paragraph to remain as it was published more than thirty years ago, when I entertained no doubt of being able to execute every thing which it announced.'[6]

Scholars sensitive to Smith's own vision of *The Wealth of Nations* and *The Theory of Moral Sentiments* as integral parts of one, all-encompassing, project often characterize that project as *a general social theory, a cultural history* or *a system of social sciences*.[7] While these descriptions usefully suggest Smith's concern with presenting a general and historical analysis of the principles and institutions guiding human thought and behaviour, in the present study we consider Smith's project as his contribution to the debate about man and society in an age of liberalization and commercialization which was central to the moral philosophy of the eighteenth century. Accordingly we retain the idea of *moral philosophy* that Smith himself used, because this refers to a type of theorizing about man and society that is fundamentally different from those that were to emerge in the social sciences of the nineteenth and twentieth centuries. In contrast to the specialized and functionalistic approach of these later social sciences, Smith's work was *moral philosophy* according to the traditional understanding of the subject. Living in an age of emergent modernity, Smith continued to discuss the new social forces in holistic terms inherited from an earlier period and, consequently, his approach differs fundamentally from that of a modern science such as economics, even where it deals with economic problems from a broad perspective.

For a better understanding of Smith's *moral philosophy* we will briefly consider the social and intellectual context of *The Theory of Moral Sentiments* and *The Wealth of Nations*.

In the broadest of terms, Smith wrote at a time when people were confronted with the disintegration of the organic, feudal society and the emergence of a society characterized by specialization and structural differentiation. Smith's work is a product of both worlds: quite plainly it is representative of the increasingly powerful forces of modernity yet in its endeavour to understand the evolving new world according to the holistic perspective of moral philosophy it remains, in important respects, a text rooted in the pre-modern.

While the tensions between the modern and the pre-modern structure the social context of Smith's discourse, its intellectual context is provided, again in the broadest sense, by the Enlightenment. Smith's work shares the characteristic preoccupations of an intellectual movement distinguished by its constructive opposition to feudal society: a desire for liberation from the authoritarian power of the sovereign and the Church, and most importantly its faith in the power of human reason to change the world.[8]

As Emile Durkheim notes, this modernization and secularization of the worldview introduced specialization and structural differentiation.[9] As society began to be differentiated into separate sections, a further specialization of the various branches of knowledge took place. What we now consider to be independent parts of society with respect to their content, spatial situation and internal coherence – for example, the political and economic spheres – took shape during the sixteenth, seventeenth, and particularly, the eighteenth centuries.[10]

The process of social differentiation brought about increasing individual independence which further encouraged freedom of thought and action. Freedom of thought extended to questioning the Christian worldview which had hitherto provided Western society with its spiritual shelter and moral orientation. Hobbes, Pufendorf, Locke and many others, who tried to find an explanation and justification for contemporary social processes, no longer accepted the idea of an eternal, all-pervasive, divine order established by divine revelation and grounded in faith. Henceforth they took man and society as their direct object of enquiry as they searched for laws and patterns of order in society and human behaviour. Instead of assuming the existence of a God-given order, they set out to determine the order of nature for themselves through the use of the human faculties of sense and reason.[11]

This new approach to the understanding of man and society initiated a process that could be called the *rationalization of the worldview*.[12] In fact we can distinguish between two distinct kinds of rationality which are attendant on this changing perspective. Firstly, we see a growing preoccupation with what we might call, after Max Weber, *value rationality,* i.e. rationality embodied in values and norms, or, more generally, in the meaning people give to, and derive from, their world.[13] This is accompanied by an increasing interest in *formal* or *functional rationality*, i.e. an interest in representing social processes and individual behaviour and actions in terms of cause and effect, or, ends and means relations.

The modernization of the worldview is thus identified with the emergence of two processes of rationalization. Although these processes were ultimately to become oppositional, they were initially closely interwoven. The differentiation of the various spheres of life involved an increase in, and a greater emphasis on, functional rationality. Simultaneously these drastic social changes made new demands on ethical orientation which were beyond the scope of medieval philosophy and theology. As the need for the rationalization of the content and validity of values and norms arose, so the interest in rationality in content flourished and spread. Thinkers such as Hobbes and Locke offered their interpretations of the individual's desire to rationalize values and order. However, the general interest in value rationality was short lived. The explication of functional rationality, which was inherent to specialization, soon came to be practiced at the expense of rationality in substance or content. Modern society became rationalistic in the sense that rationalism came to be exclusively understood in terms of functional rationality.

Smith's work belongs to the first stage of the rationalization process and should be considered as part of the general reorientation stemming from the social changes of the sixteenth, seventeenth and eighteenth centuries. It initiates an analysis of a bourgeois society which was to become more manifest as social life was increasingly differentiated into autonomous spheres, such as the economic, the political, the public and the private. On the one hand Smith focused on the functional rationality of various social spheres which were becoming increasingly differentiated from each other, while at the same time he set out to demonstrate, as an expression of value rationality, the coherence of these specialising spheres in relation to the evolution of modern society as a whole. Thus, whenever Smith deals with a certain aspect of society – e.g. the economy in *The Wealth of*

Nations – he does so without isolating the particular sphere with which he is concerned from its wider social context. He does not limit his investigation to the functional rationality of wealth production and distribution, but considers economic processes as an aspect of society as a whole. In other words, Smith consistently attempts to understand the economy in the light of human and social value patterns.

Nineteenth- and twentieth-century readings of *The Wealth of Nations* which ignore its specific context are flawed insofar as they fail to recognize that the structural differentiation which began in the seventeenth and eighteenth centuries developed to such a degree that, in the nineteenth and twentieth centuries, functional rationality came to dominate content rationality. The relation of the specialism to the whole then degenerated to a point where it became simply a part of a larger functionalistic system.

One example of the anachronistic approach to Smith's work is provided by Schumpeter's *History of Economic Analysis* which remains a standard work on the history of economics. Although Schumpeter sets out to describe and analyse the origins and development of economics in their socio-historical context, he attaches little importance to the influence of the socio-historical context on the development of economic discourse.[14] Thus, the numerous socio-historical background sketches in the *History of Economic Analysis*, some of which are quite extensive, ultimately function as nothing more than intermezzos detached from the central theme – the history of economic analysis. Throughout Schumpeter's account, the selection and discussion of authors and their texts is determined by an idea of what constitutes economic analysis that emerged only in the nineteenth century.

Specifically, Schumpeter's model of the history of economics develops according to the late nineteenth- and twentieth-century view that economic analysis can only be called a pure economic science when it has been separated from so-called normative and applied economics. Furthermore, Schumpeter considers the Walrasian general equilibrium analysis as a sort of *Magna Charta* of economics, and his history effectively traces the evolution of that prototype of economic theory from its earliest origins in ancient times.[15]

The *History of Economic Analysis* tells two stories about Smith. On the one hand there is an introductory story about Smith's life, time and works. Placed within its social, political and intellectual context, Smith's work is considered as part of the natural law tradition in philosophy, specifically that of Grotius and Pufendorf both of whom emphasize the urge for greater freedom of the individual.[16] In a discussion of Smith's work as an integrated whole, *The Theory of Moral Sentiments* – its ethical part, according to Schumpeter – is described as the text in which Smith discussed the principles of economic behaviour.

Alongside this first story runs a second narrative which deals with Smith's economic analysis. Here we are told that if we want to know something about Smith's contribution to economic analysis, the first two books of *The Wealth of Nations* are sufficient to our needs. The other books are dismissed as treatises on economic history and economic policy. The best Smith achieved in the field of economic analysis is to be found in Chapter VII of Book I where, Schumpeter claims, he outlines an equilibrium theory, which anticipates the Walrasian general equilibrium analysis:

> 'The rudimentary equilibrium theory of Chapter 7, by far the best piece of economic theory turned out by A. Smith, in fact points toward Say and, through the latter's work, to Walras. The purely theoretical developments of the nineteenth century consist to a considerable degree in improvements upon it.'[17]

Notwithstanding his remarks about Smith's mix of economic analysis and other discourses on, for example, policy proposals, Schumpeter suggests we look upon *The Wealth of Nations* as a fully-fledged product of economic science. Despite finding hardly any original ideas in *The Wealth of Nations* Schumpeter describes it as the *peak success* of the first *classical situation* in economic analysis – i.e. the period from 1750 to 1800.[18]

At first sight Schumpeter's discussion of Smith's work might seem acceptable: he first presents an overview of the author's life and work and then collates the pieces of *sound* economic analysis from the various texts. Problems of inconsistency or incoherence seem to be problems intrinsic to Smith's texts rather than Schumpeter's account. However, on further reflection this treatment of Smith seems less convincing and suggests a number of interpretative problems. For example, Schumpeter's reading of Smith's economic analysis is based on the modern assumption that economic analysis – positive economics – can and should be separated from other forms of economic discourse such as normative economics. Schumpeter fails to justify this approach, while his introductory remarks on Smith suggest that this selective reading of Smith's economic analysis is not in accordance with what he considers to be the text's own frame of reference, i.e. the tradition of natural law philosophy.

Another question arises from Schumpeter's description of *The Wealth of Nations* as the *peak success* of the first *classical situation* in economic analysis. Apart from the alleged similarity to Walras' equilibrium analysis, Schumpeter provides no further justification for assigning it this elevated status. Indeed, Schumpeter himself raises doubts about the importance of *The Wealth of Nations* in his denial of its analytic originality. *The Wealth of Nations* is, according to Schumpeter, a compilation of ideas already formulated by others.[19] Inevitably this raises the question why *The Wealth of Nations* should be regarded as the *peak success* of the first *classical situation*?

William Letwin provides one answer to this question which, however, raises further doubts about Schumpeter's interpretation. According to Letwin, *The Wealth of Nations* is the first text in which economic phenomena are explained with reference to the idea of a coherent economic system based on a small number of basic principles. Because of this, *The Wealth of Nations* is, in Letwin's opinion, the founding text of an independent economic science.[20]

For a fuller appreciation of Letwin's interpretation of Smith's economics, it is, however, important to note that he talks about economic science as an analysis of economic behaviour or processes as parts of an economic system rather than a specifically Walrasian general equilibrium analysis. It is also worth mentioning that Smith's economic theory is, in Letwin's interpretation, still related to other explanatory systems.[21] In this connection it is interesting to note that Letwin's comparison of Smith's contribution to economics with Newton's revolutionary contribution to physics had already been made by John Millar, a contemporary of Smith, who sought to express his admiration for Smith's ground-breaking work in the *History of Civil Society*.[22]

In short, there are serious reasons to doubt the conventional interpretation of Smith exemplified by Schumpeter's *History of Economic Analysis*. The historical context and the questions raised by Schumpeter's approach suggest the necessity of rereading Smith. In contrast to the conventional approach – reading Smith from the functionalist positivist view of (Walrasian) neoclassical theory – we opt for an interpretation which relates Smith's economics to his other discourses on moral philosophical problems.[23] The question of prosperity and wealth, we will suggest, was to Smith part and parcel of the moral philosophical debate, as he himself indicated:

'No society can surely be flourishing and happy, of which the far greater part of the members are poor and miserable.'[24]

2 Smith and Modern Economic Thought

In our discussion of Smith and economic science *The Wealth of Nations* will be read as a contribution to the debate, ongoing throughout the seventeenth and eighteenth centuries, on the nature of the evolving commercial society. It will be interpreted as the product of an age when liberalization and commercialization had rendered the old scholastic worldview obsolete and when new rival philosophies were being articulated which reflected man's desire to shape the world according to his own faculties.[25]

After the fall of the Roman Empire a feudal socio-economic structure had developed in Europe in which the production and distribution of wealth was determined by tradition, succession and military power. In this mode of production individual freedom of behaviour was restricted by a hierarchy of direct, personal relationships, while economic processes showed cyclical patterns.[26]

The contemporary Thomistic philosophy reflected this world by describing it as the expression of the order of God. According to Thomistic teachings, knowledge of that order was attained through Divine revelation or by reason. In the latter case, people spoke of *natural laws*, to distinguish them from man-made laws which were termed *positive laws*. Natural laws were the knowable side of the *lex aeterna*, i.e. the eternal, Divine light which radiated through God's creation.[27]

The roots of the Thomistic philosophy in a synthesis of the Christian doctrine of the Church fathers and Aristotelian philosophy are particularly clear in the field of economics where the distinction between the art of household management and the art of acquiring and accumulating pecuniary riches was derived from Aristotle's ideas about *oikonomikê* and *chrêmatistikê*. *Oikonomikê* encompassed natural economic activities, including the exchange of use values, i.e. the exchange necessary for providing natural wants. It was taught at the universities, unlike the art of acquiring and accumulating money by exchange for its own sake which was institutionally denounced and suppressed.[28]

For a clearer understanding of the problems new economic theories had to solve in the age of commercialization and liberalization – the sixteenth, seventeenth and eighteenth centuries – it is important to note that scholastic and modern views on barter and trade are radically opposed. Barter and trade were not forbidden by scholasticism, but they were subject to important restrictions. In line with Aristotle's idea of *oikonomikê*, barter and trade were considered natural and therefore permitted, provided they served to satisfy needs which could not be realized by one's own labour. It was even considered one of the duties of the head of the family, the *oikonomikos*, and of the statesman, the *politikos*, to engage in natural barter and trade, while ensuring that the prices were fair for both of the parties involved. However, barter and trade motivated by the urge for personal gain were considered unnatural and were discouraged. It was apparently taken for granted that barter and trade motivated by the idea of personal gain, always had a detrimental effect on the well-being of the individual and society, i.e. the *bonum commune*. As we all know, in modern economics this idea was to be turned upon its head.

We should, however, avoid creating the impression that European feudal society was harmonious and stable. This was certainly not the case in the fourteenth and fifteenth centuries. After a long period of growth and expansion a crisis occurred in the fourteenth century which finally ended in the disintegration of the feudal social structure and led to the rise of nation states with expanding market economies, such as France and Britain.

In that crisis, conflicts of interest between Church, nobility, king and merchants eroded the old feudal principles with the result that power and influence became ever more dependent on personal wealth. The urge to accumulate personal wealth clashed with the feudal idea that production and distribution of commodities should be aimed at satisfying the needs of all members of the community according to the preordained social hierarchy. The coordination of the production and distribution of commodities became increasingly the concern of free commerce. Production aimed at satisfying needs changed into the production of a tradeable surplus. Trade and exchange became the instruments through which the surplus, embodied in commodities, could be transformed into general personal riches, i.e. money.

In the sixteenth century the tendency towards the commercialization and liberalization of the economy was reinforced by significant population growth and a considerable expansion of world trade. Privatization of common land and the introduction of paid labour took place in the countryside. In the cities the opposition to the guild system increased and merchants forced the king to grant more trade concessions. The monarchies of Europe even used such concessions as a means of securing the financial support of the citizenry in their power struggle with the nobility. The monarchies' use of foreign trade to satisfy their need for money in turn led to resistance from those who were deprived of trade concessions.[29]

In the seventeenth and eighteenth centuries the commercialization and the liberalization of the economy proceeded at such a pace that in Britain, for example, the economy at large began to be coordinated by market-exchange. At this point debate began to focus on the question whether all markets, including the markets for subsistence goods and raw materials, should be allowed to operate freely.[30] Smith's *Wealth of Nations* may be understood as an expression of the emergence of a full-grown market economy.

In the economic literature of sixteenth-, seventeenth- and eighteenth-century Europe, criticism of traditional Scholastic-Aristotelian economic thought was initially limited to anonymous pamphlets by merchants and civil servants who denounced specific impediments to production and trade from a personal standpoint. In the course of the seventeenth and the eighteenth centuries, however, an international discourse of economics developed out of these fragments of heterodoxy which was eventually to establish itself as the new orthodoxy. *The Wealth of Nations* was the culmination of that process, transforming the fragments of new economic thinking into a coherent system based on a very limited number of principles, i.e. the theory of the market economy.[31] As such *The Wealth of Nations* marked the beginning of a new era in economic thought. In the words of Say (1767–1832):

> 'if one reads Smith as he deserves to be read one perceives that before him there was no political economy.'[32]

Prior to *The Wealth of Nations*, the debate about the commercialization and liberalization of the production and distribution of wealth had been fragmented, partly because of the diversity of the problems discussed, but more importantly, because a unifying frame of reference was lacking.[33] *The Wealth of Nations* provided that frame by reconstructing the various phenomena of economic commerce as parts of an all-encompassing self-regulating system – the market economy. Because of Smith's concept of the market economy, the commercialization and liberalization processes in different regions or countries could now be understood as parts of one movement, namely, the transformation of the feudal economy into the market economy.[34]

When nineteenth century (political) economists – believing themselves to be followers of Smith – also began to contemplate the production and distribution of wealth in Smith's 'abstract and philosophical light' they referred to the concept of the free market economy in *The Wealth of Nations* for a description of the economic 'machine whose regular and harmonious movements produce numberless agreeable things'.[35] It was in Smith's text too that they read about man's innate urge to continually improve his own situation:

'the desire of bettering our conditions, a desire which, though generally calm and dispassionate, comes with us from the womb, and never leaves us till we go into the grave. In the whole interval which separates those two movements, there is scarce perhaps a single instant in which any man is so perfectly and completely satisfied with his situation, as to be without any wish of alteration or improvement of any kind. Any augmentation of fortune is the means by which the greater part of men propose and wish to better their condition.'[36]

Elsewhere in *The Wealth of Nations* Smith also indicated that the urge to improve one's situation was a necessary and sufficient condition to fuel economic activity:

'It is not from the benevolence of the butcher, the brewer, or the baker, that we expect our dinner, but from their regard to their own interest. We address ourselves, not to their humanity but to their self-love, and never talk to them of our own necessities but of their advantages.'[37]

According to Smith, self-interest promotes the interest of society even more effectively than benevolence:

'every individual ... intends only his own gain, and he is in this, as in many other cases, led by an invisible hand to promote an end, which was no part of his intention. Nor is it always the worse for the society that it was no part of it. By pursuing his own interest he frequently promotes that of the society more effectually than when he really intends to promote it. I have never known much good done by those who affected to trade for the publick good.'[38]

Consequently, if we accept that Smith's interpretation of the so-called abstract and philosophical approach to the market economy was similar to the interpretation of (neo)classical economists and if Smith's view of man was in accordance with the (neo)classical idea of the *homo economicus*, then we would probably agree with Letwin when he writes that:

'It was Smith who taught Bastiat to speak of the "social mechanism", Cairnes to analyse Ricardo's work as an exercise in mechanistic explanation, and Jevons to describe the science of economics as the "mechanics of self-interest".'[39]

Even Schumpeter would seem at least partly correct in asserting that Smith's thought lacks originality, since self-interest had previously been identified as a motive for economic behaviour, and economic processes had even been explained as the consequence of some kind of economic mechanism.[40] There would also seem to be some truth in Schumpeter's assertion that Smith's analysis of the market economy constitutes an embryonic Walrasian general equilibrium analysis. Both Smith and Walras tried to demonstrate that the production and distribution of wealth was well-ordered when economic behaviour was motivated by self-interest framed in a system of interrelated markets.[41]

The conclusion that classical and neoclassical economists were good students of Smith, however, implicitly endorses the view that Smith's texts are inconsistent.

Illustrations of this view can be found not only in Schumpeter's *History of Economic Analysis* and earlier readings of Smith, but also in more recent discussions. Charles M.A. Clark, whose interpretation of Smith will be discussed more extensively in Chapter V, has, for example, perpetuated the assumption in his argument that (neo)classical economists stick to Smith's mechanistic approach and discard the alternative, socio-historical approach.[42] From the perspective of modern economics it might seem that Smith's texts are inconsistent, but it is important to ask whether these texts really presuppose the interpretation of notions such as *self-interest* and *an abstract and philosophical approach* familiar to modern economists? The conflict between Smith's opinion that his work constituted an integrated whole and the modern economists' view that his texts are inconsistent, is a serious reason to reconsider the traditional interpretation. Rethinking Smith's moral philosophical frame of reference in order to understand the meaning of concepts such as self-interest, will be an essential part of that process of reinterpretation. However, before we take a closer look at that frame of reference we will elaborate a little more upon Smith's part in the emergence of modern economics in the seventeenth and eighteenth centuries, and, particularly, upon the economists' apparent difficulty in interpreting that contribution as a consistent whole.

We have noted above that the commercialization and liberalization of Britain in the seventeenth and eighteenth centuries had progressed to such an extent that the production and distribution of wealth were mainly coordinated by the market. In the discussion of the question whether the distribution of raw materials and subsistence goods should also be abandoned to the forces of supply and demand, Smith adopted an exceptionally extreme position.[43] While other authors followed the precepts of traditional economics and held fast to the view that the government had to control the distribution of these goods to safeguard the poor's ability to earn a living, Smith believed that raw materials and subsistence goods should also be freely traded.[44]

Smith's plea for an unrestricted free market economy might be explained in terms of his conviction that free trade would ultimately prove a better weapon against poverty than government regulation. However, as Istvan Hont and Michael Ignatieff suggest, Smith's advocacy of free trade in all goods has deeper roots.[45] Smith supported the commercialization and liberalization of every branch of the economy, because he believed this would contribute to the realization of *the natural order of liberty and equity* in society, i.e. Smith's *utopia*.[46]

In order to be truly persuasive this utopian view of society required a theory of the free market economy which could successfully counter the traditional argument that free exchange in combination with inviolable private property rights was detrimental to the well-being of the poor and thus reprehensible. In formulating that theory, Smith brought together two different lines of modern economic thought: he integrated in his moral philosophical discussion of the emerging commercial society, the instrumental, policy-oriented approach of merchants, bankers and civil servants.

As Grotius, Pufendorf, Hobbes, Locke and Hutcheson demonstrate, moral philosophy was at that time breaking away from the precepts of the old scholastic philosophy. The commercialization and liberalization of society forced moral philosophers to alter the scope of their enquiries and to discuss ethico-political problems from a new economic point of view. Ideas such as individual rights and individual freedom and their compatibility with the idea of society were bolstered by accounts of solitary individuals succesfully making an independent living outside the traditional constraints of the feudal hierarchy.

The writings of Thomas Mun, William Petty, Josiah Child, Dudley North, Pierre de Boisguilbert and John Law show that at the same time merchants, bankers and civil servants felt a need for a public discussion about how to organize and stimulate commercial economic processes and relations.[47] In these texts hardly any attention was paid to the ethico-political aspects of these new economies. Ideas such as individual freedom and self-interest were axiomatic while the validity of argument was based on a model derived from the rationalist or empiricist tradition of modern science.[48]

That Smith developed his ideas against the views of commercial economics advanced by both moral philosophers and 'economists' has been noted by a number of scholars. However, these readers generally assumed that Smith did nothing but apply existing views. For the most part they fail to consider the possibility that he produced his own, different view which is integrally related to his discussions of the emerging commercial societies.

Interpreting Smith's idea of the well-ordered market economy, economists usually presuppose that the *father of economic science* adhered to a deistic natural law tradition. Bob Goudzwaard, for example, writes:

'Adam Smith was the father of economic science and at the same time a deist. That is no coincidence, as has occasionally been asserted. It was exactly in the climate of Deism, which looked upon man's social and economic life as a cosmos governed by natural laws fully accessible to man, that economic science could gradually develop. It would have to be a type of economic science based on a predominantly mechanistic world view. The clockwork of the clockmaker could now be opened by man, and the hidden mechanism carefully analysed.'[49]

Here Goudzwaard suggests that Smith's theory of the free market economy arose from a Newtonian belief that God created the cosmos as an independent self-regulating entity. Indeed, in the clockwork perspective on the cosmos the behaviour and actions of individual economic subjects can be seen as parts of an all-encompassing system organized by its immanent principle: the *price mechanism*. With reference to this Newtonian deism, it also becomes clear that the birth of mechanics and economics are understood as identical:

1 believing that God created the world as a clockwork mechanism, the founders of mechanics and economics modelled the physical and the economic on the same clockwork principle in their search for the hidden mechanism;

2 later scientists retained the idea of a world governed by natural laws but dropped the reference to God as its creator once secularization was accomplished.

At first sight the assumption that Smith adhered to some deistic belief may provide a plausible explanation for Smith's idea of modelling the various economic processes as parts of a self-regulating market economy. However, this raises the question whether there is any direct or indirect evidence in Smith's texts to show that he aimed at a mechanistic analysis framed in a deistic worldview. Goudzwaard fails to provide any evidence of this intention and nor does a look at Smith's use of the famous notion of the *invisible hand* take away doubts about Smith's alleged deism which suggests we think about the economy in terms of natural (causal) laws. In *The Wealth of Nations*, for example, Smith writes:

> 'and by directing that industry in such a manner as its produce may be of the greatest value, he intends only his own gain, and he is in this, as in many other cases, led by an invisible hand to promote an end which was no part of his intention. Nor is it always the worse for the society that it was no part of it. By pursuing his own interest he frequently promotes that of the society more effectually than when he really intends to promote it. I have never known much good done by those who affected to trade for the publick good. It is an affectation, indeed, not very common among merchants, and very few words need be employed in dissuading them from it.'[50]

Here Smith notices that when man intends his own gain he also tends to promote the public interest, and thus, to act according to one's own interest appears in its effects to be the same as acting as if guided by public interest. He does not argue that we may expect self-interested behaviour and actions to promote social welfare because it originates in some hidden, a priori, mechanism, or system of universal causal laws. But assuming that Smith adhered to a deistic natural law approach in his understanding of human behaviour, produces a contradiction between the analysis of the market economy as a system and understanding the commercial economy in its socio-historical context, as for example Charles M.A. Clark has demonstrated.

Further discussion of Smith's use of the *invisible hand* in Chapter IV will show that a different, metaphorical, understanding of the *invisible hand* and the *market mechanism* opens a new perspective on the idea of the market economy which accords with other so-called socio-historical and ethical parts of Smith's work.

Another striking example of interpretation problems which relate to the assumption that Smith adhered to pre-given frames of thought relates to differences about Smith's theory or theories of value.

Economists continue to debate whether Smith supported a subjectivist-utility theory of value or an objectivist labour theory of value. The Walrasian general equilibrium interpretation proposed by Schumpeter would lead us to believe that Smith rejected an objectivist approach to labour value. However, the alternative supposition that Smith advanced a subjectivist utility theory of value is also problematic given his distinction between *market* and *natural prices* and his use of the concepts *commanded* and *embodied labour*. These concepts suggest that Smith also subscribed to an objectivistic cost of production theory of value. Schumpeter attempts to explain the inconsistency away by blending the Walrasian general equilibrium interpretation with the Marshallian ideas of short-run and long-run prices.[51]

This equivocal mix of Walrasian and Marshallian notions, however, does not resolve the problems of interpretation. What, for example, are we to make of Emil Kauder's assertion that Smith's objective labour theory of value led English economists astray for decades? We cannot simply reply that it was not Smith, but Ricardo who had incorrectly read a labour theory of value in Smith's obscure discussion about commanded and embodied labour.[52]

Reinterpreting Smith's theory of value with reference to the supposed context of natural law philosophy does not solve these problems, as Terence W. Hutchison's *Before Adam Smith* shows.[53] In this study of the emergence of political economy in the seventeenth and eighteenth centuries, Hutchison devotes considerable attention to uncovering the roots of modern economics in moral philosophy. But ultimately his discussion of the moral philosophical context of Smith's economics produces little more than an extratextual statement that Pufendorf's natural law philosophy was dominant in Smith's day in Scotland. As such, Hutchison assumes that Smith shared Pufendorf's frame of reference in which the concepts of *utility* and *the individual* were understood against the background of the opposition between subjectivism and objectivism, between individualism and collectivism. In short, Hutchison concludes that Smith inherited the subjectivistic-individualistic approach from Pufendorf via his teacher Hutcheson, but diverged at some – even crucial – points towards an objectivistic-collectivistic approach.[54]

Hutchison's interpretation of Smith's economics is based on a supposed family relationship between the economics of Smith and Léon Walras. According to Hutchison, both Smith and Walras are linked by their debts to Pufendorf's natural law philosophy.[55] To substantiate his argument with respect to Walras, Hutchison refers us to the economist's own words and those of his father, Auguste Walras.[56] No such substantiation is supplied for Smith however – perhaps because none exists. Indeed in *The Theory of Moral Sentiments*, Smith explicitly distances himself from the atomistic and rationalistic interpretation of man presented by philosophers such as Pufendorf.[57]

Hutchison does acknowledge that Smith differed from Walras in that he did not consistently follow the principles of Pufendorf's doctrine. In *The Wealth of Nations*, Smith is assumed to have used an objective labour and cost-of-production theory of value beside a theory of value based on subjective utility and scarcity experience, current in his time. This however, does not appear to be a problem to Hutchison:

'it is not necessary here to take sides, very dogmatically, for or against a labour and cost-of-production explanation of value and price, as against theories based on utility and scarcity.'[58]

According to Hutchison the two explanations are not mutually exclusive, nevertheless he concludes that,

'It was *The Wealth of Nations* which opened up the divisions ... between theories of value based on scarcity and utility and those based on labour and cost of production.'[59]

Notwithstanding this conclusion, Hutchison rejects interpretations which opt for one theory to the exclusion of the other on the grounds that they inevitably lead to a misreading of Smith:

'What is to be criticised is the dogmatic, over-confident rejection, or exclusion of a vital and valuable line of thought, which has, in fact, subsequently become an essential component of the modern theory of value.'[60]

Hutchison seems to suggest that classical and neoclassical economists had a significantly different view of economics from Smith when they read the discussions of value in *The Wealth of Nations* from the perspective of opposing theories of value.

According to Hutchison, Smith combined a utility and scarcity approach with a labour and cost-of-production approach as is usual in modern theory of value. However, because Hutchison does not amplify this statement it is unclear what is meant by the reference to the so-called modern theory of value, let alone that it is not apparent how the modern approach connects to Smith's reflections on value.

In textbook economics we often find a mixture of a utility and scarcity approach for demand side analysis and a cost-of-production approach for supply side analysis. From the Walrasian perspective the validity of such a mixture is however questionable. Walrasian economics is entirely reliant on the utility and scarcity model of value, for every economic decision is, after all, reduced to utilitarian perception of labour and leisure, and of the individual actor's present and future consumption. In short, in Walrasian economics there is one, and only one, way of understanding value: value is the expression of the utility and scarcity experience of the atomistically perceived economic subject.

This conclusion is supported by the passages Hutchison quotes from Walras pere et fils on Pufendorf's relevance to economics. Auguste and Léon Walras pay tribute to Pufendorf because he understood value in terms of subjective utility and scarcity experiences.

The question thus becomes, how can this be reconciled with Smith's discussion of value, of which Hutchison asserts that it is not an extension of Pufendorf's theory of value, nor an aberration from it?[61] In the following chapters we will see that Hutchison is correct in claiming that Smith does not use different models of value but discusses value from different perspectives using a model which differs radically from the traditional oppositional utility and cost-of-production models. Our rereading of Smith will suggest that the problems of Hutchison's interpretation lie in his assumption of a family resemblance between Smith and Pufendorf. It will be shown that rather than sharing Pufendorf's atomistic and rationalistic view of man, Smith criticizes Pufendorf, not because he favours the opposing holistic or organicist view, but because he is opposed to the antipodal interpretation of twin concepts such as the *individual* and *society*, and *reason* and *sentiment*.

In contrast to interpretations of Smith such as Hutchison's, we do not assume from the outset that the various streams of seventeenth- and eighteenth-century economics share a common understanding of such terms as the *individual, society, sentiment,* and *utility.* In our rereading of Smith, his economics will be interpreted as part of his contribution to the debates about how to conceive the new world of evolving individual freedom and commerce.

In the next section we take a first step in the direction of this rereading by discussing briefly some of the main topics of the modern moral philosophy that emerged in the sixteenth, seventeenth and eighteenth centuries.

3 Adam Smith and the New Moral Philosophy

Modern moral philosophy distinguished itself from medieval scholasticism in its urge to understand man and his world by means of man's own faculties of sense and reason. Theories about man and society which referred to the idea of a Divine order which was supposed to be known thanks to revelation or to participating in God's reason, were questioned and increasingly rejected.

The new moral philosophy mirrored and stimulated the general desire in society for emancipation from Church and king, from tradition and authority. However, ideas about what the new world should look like and how to understand and explain its order showed considerable diversity. The break with the scholastic idea of a preordained cosmic order in which everything had its meaning and purpose gave rise to numerous problems regarding content and method to which widely divergent solutions were proposed.

In this section we investigate how Smith handled these questions and compare his approach to other contemporary theories of man and society. To this end we consider Smith's moral philosophy alongside the ideas of Grotius (1583–1645), Pufendorf (1632–1694), Locke (1632–1704) and Hutcheson (1694–1746) – all of whom played a major role in the moral philosophical debate in Scotland in the first half of the eighteenth century, the formative period for Smith's intellectual development.

In reconstructing the development of Smith's moral philosophy in relation to the ideas of these philosophers, we will concentrate on the themes of *human nature, natural law* and *natural order,* and *nature and sources of knowledge.*[62] Successively, an outline will be given of how these items are dealt with in:

1 The Aristotelian-Thomistic tradition in philosophy,
2 The modern philosophy of Grotius, Pufendorf, Locke and Hutcheson,
3 Smith's reinterpretation of the principles of modern philosophy.

3.1 The *lex aeterna*

The Aristotelian-Thomistic tradition was grounded in the idea of the *lex aeterna* which was conceived as a Divine light irradiating God's entire creation. Man's knowledge of the *lex aeterna* was ascribed to the principles of *inclinatio* and *participatio*. Through *inclinatio* – e.g. the urge to live, to have social intercourse and to be part of a community – man was thought to be unconsciously led to the realization of God's order; through *participatio* – the participation of man in God's reason – man was supposed to become conscious of that part of the order God wished to be knowable to mankind, i.e. the so-called *lex natura* (law of nature).

As a preeminently teleological philosophy, scholasticism understood man and his world through reference to the evolving cosmic plan, of which only God, the creator, was to know the final goal. Thus, human nature and the natural order of society were seen as the given and knowable elements in an unknowable process of nascency. This meant that the knowledge given to man through creation was no more than potential knowledge. Scholastic philosophers spoke, for example, of *spermatikoi* which would only come to full growth upon the realization of God's plan of creation.[63]

The growing urge for emancipation from Church and king in the sixteenth, seventeenth and eighteenth centuries was mirrored in moral philosophy by new theories of man and society which dissociated themselves from the idea of the *lex aeterna* and such conceptual corollaries as *inclinatio* and *participatio*. Henceforth ideas such as *human nature* and *natural order* were to acquire new meanings.

3.2 Grotius, Pufendorf, Locke and Hutcheson
Grotius
Of all the philosophers who influenced Smith's education, Grotius remained closest to scholastic philosophy. Although he relinquished the idea of the *lex aeterna*, Grotius' new theory of man and society still leaned heavily on scholastic ideas.[64]

In Grotius we see an attempt to formulate an independent general theory of man and society, whose validity could be established without reference to the unknowable evolving cosmic plan of God. While in scholastic philosophy, natural law was considered a reflection of the *lex aeterna*, in Grotius' philosophy it acquired the connotation of a general law which would hold true irrespective of the existence or nonexistence of God.[65]

Grotius conceived human nature as a set of general human faculties and propensities. For him the natural order comprised a universal system of law which represented the preconditions of man's freedom to live according to his natural predisposition. Although he no longer referred to the *lex aeterna*, his conception of human nature and the natural order remained tied to scholastic precepts.

Thus, in his notion of the *lex prescriptiva* Grotius still refers directly to God as lawgiver.[66] So too, his discussion of the *lex indicativa* – the law which was knowable to man by virtue of his reason and senses – still draws upon the traditional scholastic idea that God had implanted in man a number of fundamental principles of law at the time of his creation. On the one hand Grotius tells us that man's own faculties enable him to learn the natural law, on the other hand he also argues that man is a reasonable and social creature because God made him that way. Ultimately Grotius' natural law turns out to be based on a human reason which is supposed to possess an a priori familiarity with God's plan as it relates to the basic assumptions of that law.[67]

For a clearer understanding of Smith's contribution to the discourse of modern moral philosophy it is important to note that Grotius conceived man as an essentially social being, and that he interpreted this idea of social being in the abstract and rationalist perspective of the stoic-scholastic tradition.[68] His discussions of private help illustrate this particular outlook on man and society.

Reflecting the experience of commercialization and liberalization Grotius gave more weight to private property than was usual among scholastic philosophers. He even discussed it as a subject of perfect natural law. Nevertheless, he also upheld the traditional scholastic principle that everybody should have an unconditional right to another person's private property if he has no other access to the bare means of subsistence. In this, Grotius remained faithful to the scholastic idea that God had put the earth at the disposal of mankind conceived as a positive community.[69]

As will be argued below, Smith also conceived man as an essentially social being, however, his arguments for this conclusion owe nothing to Grotius' stoic-scholastic framework. Having broken more completely with the scholastic interpretation of natural law, Smith was closer to Pufendorf's and Locke's attempts to explain and understand the world without any reference to the pre-given order or ratio of God. However, in his view of man and society Smith also departed radically from the atomistic model of man advanced by Pufendorf and Locke.

Pufendorf
Unlike Grotius who still assumed that the natural order was permeated by God's ratio, Pufendorf conceived natural law and natural order as man's rationalization of the world in which he lived.[70] If Pufendorf was influenced by the scholastic tradition, it was because he believed that God had provided man with the faculty of reason which would enable him to discover what social order was best suited to his needs as a human being.[71] This meant that, unlike Grotius, Pufendorf no longer believed that some basic principles of law and order were fundamental to human nature. Instead, Pufendorf merely presupposed that God gave man the faculty of reason in order to discover for himself the advantages of living in an ordered society.

In tracing the roots of modern economics in moral philosophy it is important to note that in Pufendorf's interpretation, man's reasoning about the world became functionalistic. Pufendorf explained the existence of well-organized human societies with reference to man's urge to escape from *imbecillitas*, i.e. the state of absolute poverty in which man would live if isolated from other people and exclusively dependent on his own faculties.[72] This meant that in contrast to Grotius, Pufendorf discussed human society as an artefact which was produced by man in order to avoid the state of *imbecillitas*.[73]

Pufendorf's atomistic view of man enabled him to 'improve' on Grotius' discussion of private property as an inviolable natural right to exclusive property. As we have noted, Grotius believed that there existed a natural right to property, but unlike

Pufendorf he believed that that right could be violated in times of famine and cata-strophy. Pufendorf, however, rejected the scholastic conception of mankind as a positive community to which God had given the earth as common property. Accord-ing to his atomistic view of man, mankind was a negative community: God had put the earth at man's disposal insofar as everyone could partake of it according to his need.[74] Therefore the natural right to private property no longer presupposed, as Grotius believed, a social agreement in which the original common property was turned into private property. Accordingly, the plea for distributive justice imply-ing a breach of strictly private property, could no longer be justified by referring to the original gift of the earth by God to mankind as a positive community.

However, Pufendorf's argument for a perfect natural right to exclusively private property was not yet conclusive. In substituting an atomistic for a social view of man, the idea that in the beginning all property was common property had lost its meaning. However, in a world of atomistic individuals every right to property, i.e. both private and common, presupposed an agreement with respect to this right. This did not merely undermine the arguments of the critics of the perfect natural right to exclusively private property, it also weakened the thesis that this right is implied by the proposition that man is an atomistic individual by nature.

Locke

The same use of the atomistic individual as a support for the principle of the perfect natural right to exclusively private property was made by Locke. In *An Essay Concerning Human Understanding*, Locke presents a vision of human thought and behaviour as proceeding from the desire to avoid pain and the inclination to pursue pleasure. According to Locke, men differed from animals in this respect only insofar as they did not react purely instinctively to stimuli of pain and pleasure. Man was able to give his vital urge for happiness a personal interpretation because the faculty of reason made it possible to identify, compare and select goals and means.[75]

Locke's hedonistic-utilitarian subjectivism gave the concept of property a dimension which it had previously lacked in the thought of Grotius and Pufendorf. While each of these authors had in their own way understood private property as the result of an agreement, and therefore a social phenomenon, Locke grounded the concept of private property exclusively in the atomistically conceived nature of man. According to Locke, the right to property represented the inviolable right of every individual to devote, in freedom, his natural faculties – in particular his capacity for labour – to his natural urge for life and happiness. In this view the right to private property was considered to be a natural right because it was part of man's natural right to life, freedom and happiness. The right to private property concerned the individual's right to control the material products of his own labour as he pursues life and happiness.[76]

Comparing Grotius, Pufendorf and Locke, it is evident that Locke advances the most radical model of man and society with his insistence on the individual's autonomy of thought and action. While Grotius continues to assume that man is a social being and that natural law is innate, Locke's *Essay Concerning Human*

Understanding treats man as an atomistic individual who himself produces his thoughts and organizes his behaviour from experiences of pain and pleasure. So too, despite the fact that Pufendorf's theories about man and society also employ an atomistic concept of the individual, his interpretation of that concept differs significantly from Locke's *pain and pleasure*-approach. Pufendorf's theories of man and society are based on thought experiments in which man is modelled as an atomistic individual striving for his own self-interest. In Locke's *pain and pleasure*-approach the discourse about man and society takes on the flavour of an evolutionary-historical analysis. That is to say, in the *pain and pleasure*-approach both man's ideas and behaviour and social processes and relations seem to be endogeneous to human experience, i.e. the real experience of the atomistic individual avoiding feelings of pain and pursuing feelings of pleasure.

Considering Locke's theory of the *pain and pleasure*-mechanism in relation to Grotius and Pufendorf, it is clear that he advances a far more radically individualistic model of man and society. But does Locke succeed where Hobbes failed? Does Locke's pain and pleasure mechanism obviate the need for a *Leviathan* to guarantee social order? Is it a necessary and sufficient condition to explain the creation of societies by essentially atomistic individuals? As Walter Euchner and John Dunn show, Locke himself did not believe so. Locke acknowledged the inadequacy of the atomistic principle of avoiding discomfort and striving for happiness in his final work, *The Reasonableness of Christianity as delivered in the Scriptures*:

> 'In his last work, ... Locke returned firmly to revelation. He did so in part to proclaim, as its title declares, *The Reasonableness of Christianity as delivered in the Scriptures*. But he did so more urgently because it was only by means of the Christian revelation that he retained the confidence that men's moral duties were effectively "made to all mankind". Natural law in its full extent had never been demonstrated by anyone (R 89), and by 1694 Locke had abandoned hope of demonstrating it himself (LC IV 768, 786).'[77]

As we have noted, Locke rejected the traditional theory of innate ideas in *An Essay Concerning Human Understanding* and attempted to explain human understanding by referring to nothing beyond the human faculties of reason and sense. However, any discussion of the social values and rules which preserve the well-orderedness of a society lay beyond the scope of this approach. If man is conceived as an essentially atomistic individual, his experience, beliefs and knowledge must also be regarded as strictly subjective, raising the question, 'how can we be confident in the well-orderedness of an open society when this well-orderedness presupposes common values and rules?' As we have indicated Locke is far from confident on this point. He distrusted public opinion, fashion and other forms of social values and rules created spontaneously by men. Locke's ultimate return to the principle of revelation and the idea of a God-given law shows his recognition that the *pain and pleasure*-principle was in itself incapable of providing a full account of the well-ordered open society.

Hutcheson   ·

Francis Hutcheson, Smith's professor in moral philosophy at Glasgow, had greater confidence in man's free will and ability to know and obey the rules of society. While he believed that man's thought and behaviour was rooted in experience, in contrast to Locke, he tried to integrate this idea in a renewed interpretation of the traditional view that man was a social being by nature.

Hutcheson refused to accept that man was essentially selfish, arguing instead that man's behaviour was not motivated by self-interest alone, but also by benevolence. Because of this benevolence, he argued, man possessed a natural inclination to live in a society and to contribute freely to the common good. In this Hutcheson rejected the Hobbesian view that man was essentially a selfish individual who, notwithstanding the expected benefits of social life, would only accept the rules of society, if they were enforced by an absolute sovereign, the only dependable safeguard except oneself against injuries by others.

According to Hutcheson it was necessary but not sufficient to consider the motive of benevolence alongside self-interest in order to understand the various examples of man's solidarity with others and of man's general interest in the common good. For a better understanding of man's behaviour, Hutcheson suggested that we should also pay attention to the feelings attendant on praise and disapproval.[78] Man, he argued, possessed a special *moral sense* which was sensitive to this type of feeling.[79] It is this *moral sense* which is central to Hutcheson's account of man's adherence to the law and interest in the common good of society.[80]

Smith agreed with Hutcheson that it was not reason but immediate sense and feeling which was the ultimate foundation of the perception of right and wrong, of pleasure and pain, and of approbation and disapprobation.[81] However, he disagreed with his teacher's supposition that man also had a *moral sense* in addition to his *external senses*. In his own attempt to explain moral sentiments Smith introduced his reinterpreted concept of *sympathy*, transforming Hutcheson's ideas about the mechanism of approbation and disapprobation into a general theory of man and society.

In his new theory of moral sentiments Smith conceived man not as an atomistic individual inclined to benevolence besides self-interest, but as an *individual in society*. As such, in Smith's interpretation, man experiences himself as an individual in relation to society, while society itself is experienced as a whole comprised of social processes which – by means of social values and rules – give sense, meaning and guidance to the feelings, thoughts, and behaviour and actions of its individual members.

3.3 Smith

Anticipating the discussion in Chapters III and IV, we have already noted that at the core of Smith's moral philosophy lies a new interpretation of man's tendency to *sympathy*.

It is important to clarify the differences between Smith's and Hutcheson's understanding of this concept. Hutcheson followed the traditional interpretation when he discussed *sympathy* as a form of *benevolence*:

'Benevolence is a word fit enough in general, to denote the internal spring of virtue, as Bishop Cumberland always uses it. But to understand this more distinctly, it is highly necessary to observe, that under this name are included very different dispositions of the soul. Sometimes it denotes a calm, extensive affection, or good-will towards all beings capable of happiness or misery: sometimes, 2. A calm deliberate affection of the soul toward the happiness of certain smaller systems or individuals; such as patriotism, or love of a country, friendship, parental affection, as it is in persons of wisdom and self-government; or 3. the several kind particular passions of love, pity, sympathy, congratulation.'[82]

In the opening chapters of *The Theory of Moral Sentiments* Smith, however, makes it clear that he intends to use the word *sympathy* to denote a wider sense of fellow-feeling:

'Pity and compassion are words appropriated to signify our fellow-feeling with the sorrow of others. Sympathy, though its meaning was, perhaps, originally the same, may now, however, without much impropriety, be made use of to denote our fellow-feeling with any passion whatever.'[83]

In a footnote to this passage, D.D. Raphael and Alec L. Macfie, the editors of the Glasgow Edition of *The Theory of Moral Sentiments,* remark that Smith's use of *sympathy* is often wrongly equated with *benevolence*.

'Smith's unusually wide definition of "sympathy" needs to be noted because some scholars, more familiar with his economics than his moral philosophy, have mistakenly equated sympathy with benevolence and have inferred that TMS deals with the altruistic side of human conduct and WN with its egoistic side.'[84]

This warning about the interpretation of Smith's use of *sympathy* is not superfluous, as, to take one example, Ben B. Seligman's equation of *sympathy* with *benevolence* in *Philosophic Perspectives in Economic Thought* demonstrates.[85] The editors' phrase, *Smith's unusually wide definition of 'sympathy'* may even require an additional warning. Smith is equally misunderstood when the phrase is understood as an instruction to extend the meaning of *sympathy* to include other motives such as altruism.

Sympathy does not refer to specific motives of behaviour and action. The fellow-feeling expressed by the notion of *sympathy* is of a completely different order than altruism and egoism. Smith's concept of *sympathy* denotes man's general interest in the happiness of other people, and as such it constitutes the intersubjective grounds in which man's assessment of behaviour and action in terms of *benevolence, prudence, justice* or *self-control* is founded.

In Chapter III Smith's reinterpretation of *sympathy* will be discussed at length. Here we will limit ourselves to a very brief outline of that discussion and focus on the new approach Smith introduced to the debate amongst modern philosophers about how to interpret the contemporaneous emancipation of man towards the condition of autonomous individual subjectivity. In contrast to the tendency to understand the individual's autonomy in an absolute sense, Smith presented a relational approach when reinterpreting *sympathy* as man's tendency to general fellow-feeling, as this implied that man's beliefs, thoughts, behaviour and actions are intersubjectively based in an ongoing process of communication, competition and concurrence.

According to Smith, our general tendency to fellow-feeling expresses itself in the first place in our inclination to identify imaginatively with other people in the sense of being able to 'put ourselves in their shoes'. But Smith also believed that we have an interest in the well-being of our fellow-men, in the sense that we also feel an urge to experience concurrence between our fellow-men's behaviour, its motivation and impact on other people, and our own performance and motivation when imagining ourselves in their situation. We are at ease and are even inclined to praise when there is concurrence; we feel uneasiness and disapproval where there is conflict.

Thus Smith reinterpreted the concept of *sympathy* in such a way as to suggest that man's beliefs, thoughts, behaviour and actions are intersubjectively based. This becomes particularly clear when Smith argues that *sympathy* implies *mutual sympathy*. The basic idea of his argument is that in our urge for concurrence we do more than try to persuade our fellow-men through praise or disapproval to conform to our way of life. The experience of our fellow-men's interest in our well-being, drives us to match our own behaviour to the feelings which, we imagine, this behaviour will rouse within our fellow-men. The understanding of behaviour generated by this interpretation of *sympathy* clearly indicates that Smith's perspective on man and society differs substantially from, for instance, the *pain and pleasure* and *moral sense* perspectives of other modern philosophers, and also from the *homo economicus* doctrines of later (neo)classical economists.

As we have noted, there are also more recent readings of Smith which, in line with older interpretations such as Leslie's, suggest that Smith's work contains two different views of man and society. According to these readings, one part of Smith's work hinges on the older Lockean or Pufendorfian view and anticipates the view of (neo)classical economics while the other part is supposed to be based on a totally different approach, often described as evolutionary-historic. Although we discuss this interpretative strategy extensively in a later chapter it is useful to offer here a brief explanation of the problems involved in the revival of the Lesliean reading.

The main question arising from the consideration of the various interpretations of Smith concerns the philosophical context in which Smith uses such concepts as natural law, pain and pleasure and self-interest. Or, more specifically, what are the arguments supporting the common assumption that Smith's vision of man and society is similar to that of, for example, Grotius, Pufendorf, Locke and Hutcheson? In this section we have suggested that there exist important differences between Smith's moral philosophy and that of his predecessors. Further we have indicated that with his reinterpretation of *sympathy* Smith introduced a fundamentally new view of man and society. We can usefully highlight three aspects of Smith's use of the concept of *sympathy* to further illustrate the differences between Smith's approach to moral philosophy and that of his predecessors.[86]

1 Smith's use of the concept of *sympathy* allows him to present man as an autonomous individual without lapsing into atomism and ethical relativism. Consequently Smith is able to explain the stability of the social order without recourse to the idea of an a priori order made known to man by revelation, or by a special faculty such as a reason with innate ideas, or a moral sense. *Mutual sympathy* implies intersubjectively shared frames of reference which, like an invisible hand, coordinate man's behaviour and thoughts.

2 The idea of *sympathy* allows Smith to explain social order with reference to social values, fashions, positive laws and other institutions without any complementary appeal to a knowledge of God's natural law. The concept of *sympathy* means that these social phenomena become the sediments of an intersubjectively shared frame of reference, which will be renewed and replaced in accordance with the evolution of the imaginary *sympathy*-discourse between people concerning praise and praiseworthiness.

3 Smith's interpretation of *sympathy* implies that a theory of man and society based on the principle of *sympathy* has a normative, teleological dimension. Analysing man and society from the *sympathy*-perspective implies that man's behaviour and social relations or processes are to be understood as ultimately centred on man's urge to experience praise or praiseworthiness. We should also note that this contrasts with Hans Medick's view that *sympathy* is just a formal emotional disposition of man.

'"Sympathy" erscheint in der "Theory of Moral Sentiments" weder als ein eindeutig festgelegter emotionaler Impuls noch als ein moralisches Prinzip, sondern als eine formale psychische Disposition jedes Menschen, deren Wirkzamkeit sich erst im Prozess sozialer Interaktion erweist.'[87]

Of course, Medick is right to argue that *sympathy* does not denote an urge for specific praise or praiseworthiness. Nor is it a moral principle with a specific content in the sense of a specific set of principles or rules of behaviour. Nevertheless, interpreting and explaining behaviour, social processes, values, laws and other institutions from the perspective of man's tendency to *mutual sympathy* implies a normative focus on the society in which the urge to *sympathy* will help complete man's development and bring about the final realization of his true nature.

Emphasizing the role of man's tendency to *mutual sympathy* in reading Smith's economics leads us to conclude that society is to be understood as an *evolutionary process*. Various papers and books concerned with rethinking the principles of economics have referred to Smith in discussing the *evolutionary process* approach in economics. Charles M.A. Clark even titles one of his papers *Adam Smith and Society as an Evolutionary Process*.[88]

In this paper Clark follows Leslie's suggestion that Smith began as a proponent of natural law philosophy – like Grotius, Pufendorf and Locke – who later adopted an evolutionary-historic perspective on man and society. We will examine Clark's dichotomized interpretation more extensively in a later chapter but it is important to note some basic flaws in his argument as this line of interpretation sets up a spurious opposition between the roles of the *economic system* and the *evolutionary process* in Smith's thought.

According to Clark, Smith eventually abandoned his attempt to explain economic life through reference to the *economic system* – an idea based on the natural law philosophy of scholars such as Grotius and Pufendorf and later adopted by (neo)classical economists. Towards the end of his life, Clark argues, Smith rejected the natural law tradition and came to believe that economics should be understood in terms of an *evolutionary process*. The fact that Smith never completed the frequently announced *theory of jurisprudence* is, Clark believes, proof of this apostasy.[89]

Assuming that Clark is correct, and that Smith's failure to complete his discourse on *jurisprudence* was indeed due to a loss of faith in natural law philosophy, then the question arises, why did Smith continue to edit various editions of *The Theory of Moral Sentiments* and *The Wealth of Nations* until his death in 1790? Both these works combine a *society-as-system* approach with a *society-as-an-evolutionary-process* approach. The fact that Smith continued to edit *The Theory of Moral Sentiments* and *The Wealth of Nations* over and over again until shortly before his death suggests that:

1 Smith felt no overwhelming desire to distance himself from the *society-as-system* approach, and

2 Smith did not feel that the *society-as-system* approach was incompatible with the *society-as-an-evolutionary-process* approach.

Consequently, Clark's belief that the *society-as-system* approach is incompatible with the *society-as-an-evolutionary-process* approach suggests that his understanding of these two approaches differs markedly from that of Smith. This impression is confirmed when we read Smith's comments on Grotius and Pufendorf in *The Theory of Moral Sentiments*, *Lectures of Jurisprudence* and *The Wealth of Nations*. These comments show that it is a mistake to conclude that when Smith uses concepts such as *self-interest, pain and pleasure* or *natural law*, he refers to the supposed functional-rationalist model of man and society.

As we will see in Chapter III, Smith makes it clear in both *The Theory of Moral Sentiments* and *Lectures of Jurisprudence* that he disagrees with Pufendorf's approach to understanding man and society. In *The Theory of Moral Sentiments*, he expressly dismisses Pufendorf's functional-rationalist understanding of man's motives of behaviour and action. In the *Lectures of Jurisprudence* he distances himself from Pufendorf's functional-rationalist approach, criticizing his attempt to ground an explanation of law in an appeal to a fictive natural state.[90]

The positive assessment of Grotius' contribution to the theory of natural law in *The Theory of Moral Sentiments* and *The Wealth of Nations*, may seem at first sight to confirm Clark's argument that Smith adhered to the older philosophy in which natural law was conceived as a God-given order. A closer look, however, shows that Smith valued other qualities in his predecessor.

Smith praised Grotius' discourse on justice and law because it was probably the first discourse which presented,

'any thing like a system of those principles which ought to run through [*the world*], and be the foundation of the laws of all nations: and his treatise of the laws and peace, with all its imperfection, is perhaps at this day the most complete work that has yet been given upon this subject.'[91]

However, his praise for Grotius' search for general principles did not prevent Smith being critical of the principles themselves. Smith even criticized Grotius' formulation of these principles. In the *Lectures* of 1762–1763, for example, Smith expresses his disagreement with the utilitarianism of Grotius' discourse on criminal punishment. This example is of particular interest because it demonstrates the importance Smith continued to place on the concept of *sympathy* which had been extensively discussed in *The Theory of Moral Sentiments* of 1759 and was not substantially modified in later editions.[92]

As will be shown in the following chapter, Smith agreed with Grotius that positive law had to be founded in a system of natural law. However, Smith did not conceive natural law as a principle of law instilled in man by God. Rather, Smith discussed the notion of justice in relation to the feelings of justice and injustice experienced by man in his sympathetic imagination. Referring to these feelings, not only does he explicate the meaning of justice, but he also demonstrates that without justice every society would ultimately dissolve into atoms.[93]

This explains why Smith announced his discourse of *Jurisprudence* as a discourse on,

'the general principles of law and government, and of the different revolutions they have undergone in the different ages and periods of society, not only in what concerns justice, but in what concerns police, revenue, and arms, and whatever else is the object of law.'[94]

According to Smith's discussion of *sympathy* in *The Theory of Moral Sentiments*, our sympathetic imagination enables us to do more than simply understand the workings of justice in our dealings with others. Smith's theory of *sympathy* also shows that the strict maintenance of justice is necessary to safeguard the sympathy-exchange without which our societies would dissolve and we would cease to exist as human beings. Thus, in Smith's theory of *sympathy*, social justice is mirrored and sustained by a set of general principles of law and government, but its meaning – and also the content of the accompanying principles – changes with the *ages and periods of society*.

As such, the concept of *sympathy* lends Smith's moral philosophy its evolutionary-historic dimension while simultaneously preventing it lapsing into relativism. Smith's contextualized, *sympathy*-based approach to the understanding of man and society has a teleological overtone: the urge for *mutual sympathy* is thought to develop over time, resulting in ever more advanced stages of society. An illustration of this may be found in Smith's use of the *four stages theory* of social

development in order to understand the changes which justice, law and government in Western Europe have undergone since the fall of the Roman Empire.[95]

This should also be kept in mind when reading Smith's discussion of private
property, and the free market economy or, as he described it, the 'natural system
of perfect liberty and justice'.[96] In all these cases the discussion has a teleological
overtone. Smith's argument is informed by his belief in the *utopia* which was to
be born from his own society: a *commercial society* in which *mutual sympathy* is
fully developed.[97]

4 Smith's Moral Philosophical Scope of Economics

Summarizing the preceding sections on Smith's contribution to modern moral
philosophy, and economics in particular, we can usefully focus on three subjects:
(1) the meaning of rationality in economics, (2) the economy as a system, and (3)
the division of economic thought into the areas of positive, normative, and applied
economics.

1 Hutchison may be correct in asserting that Walras adhered to Pufendorf's
   natural law philosophy, however, as we will demonstrate in later chapters, this
   certainly does not entail that Smith was also a follower of Pufendorf.

   In *The Theory of Moral Sentiments* and *Lectures of Jurisprudence,* Smith
   spoke out explicitly against Pufendorf's rationalistic approach. According to
   Smith, human behaviour and action are founded in *sympathy* and not in an
   individual's rationalistic calculus of private advantage and disadvantage. For
   Smith, *sympathy* refers to our experience that not only our behaviour but also
   our self-awareness is ultimately based in the intersubjectivity of the mutually
   shared urge to be beloved, to be praised and praiseworthy.

   Smith shared with other modern moral philosophers the need to understand
   man as an autonomous individual who makes his own life by means of his own
   faculties. However, Smith did not perceive the autonomous individual as an
   atomistic individual who enters society because of some natural need for
   company, or an expected advantage.

   Smith understood man as an *individual in society* in the sense that the
   individual and society presuppose each other. In Smith's *sympathy* perspective,
   man experiences and understands himself as an individual person against the
   background of his exchange with other people and more generally with
   society.

   Smith's distinctive view of man and society also explains why Pufendorf's
   rationalistic explanation of justice and law was rejected in *Lectures of Jurisprudence.* Smith discussed justice and law as founded in intersubjectively shared
   feelings and ideas. Pufendorf, in contrast, had dealt with justice and law as
   universal principles deducible from thought experiments in which calculating
   individuals are confronted with so-called natural states such as the state of
   imbecillitas.[97]

2   Schumpeter's description of Walras' general equilibrium analysis as the *Magna Charta* of (modern) economics may be correct, but Schumpeter misinterprets Smith's analysis of the market economy when he discusses it as a Walrasian general equilibrium theory *in nucleo*. Smith did indeed analyse market behaviour from the perspective of the market economy conceptualized as a self-regulating system. However, Smith's self-regulating system differs radically from the economic system exemplified in the Walrasian models of general equilibrium.

Walrasian general equilibrium economics is based on a belief in an a priori economic order or, so-called, system of fundamental economic laws. People are considered as atomistic individuals who will continuously reproduce the situation of general equilibrium if rational choice is the motivating and organizing principle of both individual and social economic life. Smith would have criticized this rationalistic interpretation of the free market economy for the same reasons he criticized Pufendorf's rationalistic discourse of man and society.

Smith not only rejected the rationalistic view of man and society, he also presented an alternative vision which implied a different interpretation of the free market economy than the a priori, law-governed system of the rationalists. In Smith's sympathetic understanding of man and society, the notion of the *free market economy* refers to a situation in which the production and distribution of wealth is coordinated by rules founded in the intersubjectivity of the *mutual sympathy exchange*.

In Smith's *sympathy*-based approach, individual behaviour and social processes are ruled by meanings and values which are generated and observed by people themselves as a result of their longing for *mutual sympathy*. The rationalistic idea of behaviour governed by fundamental causal laws is incompatible with this understanding of man and society. Discussing the system of free market economy means, in Smith's interpretation, discussing the horizon against which institutional rearrangements have to be made in a commercial society in order to guarantee a sound *mutual sympathy* exchange in the production and distribution of wealth. It is a horizon designed to persuade people needing a well-ordered society, that wealth should be produced and distributed according to rules established in the intersubjectivity of direct exchange in the same way as in other spheres of commercial society. A more extensive discussion of Smith's interpretation of the system of the free market economy will be presented in the following chapters.

3   Walrasian general equilibrium theory suggests that the discourses of positive, normative and applied economics are to be separated from each other. If one believes in a knowable, a priori, economic order, it is clear that true knowledge of that order will only be contaminated by discussion of values or economic policies. The true concern of the economist should be with the scientific theories which can be interpreted and employed as representations of universal causal laws.

In the *sympathetic* approach, (scientific) theories are also thought of as representing the world as a well-ordered system. However, this system is not understood as a reprint of an a priori order. Rather, as we will see, economic theory is thought of as reflecting the need of people living in orderly and prosperous societies to understand and to value the world as well-ordered. People want to feel that they are part of, and act in accordance with a meaningful well-organized whole. So, an economic theory is meant to 're-present' in an abstract and philosophical way the economic order people implicitly produce in their *sympathy*-based behaviour.

If we view *The Wealth of Nations* from this perspective, it will be clear that the interrelatedness of its positive, normative and applied economics should not be regarded as a failure or weakness on Smith's part. Smith did not anticipate the positivism of nineteenth- and twentieth-century economics according to which science is defined by its concern with the discovery of general, or universal, causal laws. In *The Wealth of Nations* Smith tried to persuade his audience to understand the production and distribution of wealth in contemporaneous commercial societies as a system regulated by self-interest in a context of fair competition.

In the following chapters Smith's oeuvre will be read as an argument for understanding the evolving commercial societies as societies in which the institutional framework is best accommodated to the organizing principle immanent to the tendency of *mutual sympathy*. That is, organizing by means of the rules of free exchange of ideas and goods in a context of fairness, or, in other words, a context in which everyone can express their urge for *mutual sympathy*. Smith's theory of the free market economy is the expression of this view with respect to the production and distribution of wealth.

Notes

1. For a concise description of Smith's life and work, see among others Recktenwald, H.C., *Adam Smith. Sein Leben und sein Werk*, München, 1976, and Jones, J., *Morals, Motives & Markets. Adam Smith 1723–1790*, Edinburgh, 1990.
2. Compare the argumentation in A.S. Skinner's edition of *The Wealth of Nations*:
    'The problem of size dictated that the whole of Smith's *The Wealth of Nations* could not be printed in the present series. Accordingly, it was decided to print Books 1 and 2 of the original work entire, thus presenting a volume which is solely concerned with Smith's contribution to the principles of economics.'
    (Skinner, A.S. (ed.), *The Wealth of Nations*, Harmondsworth, 1981, p. 7)
    Otherwise, Skinner understands *The Wealth of Nations* as a part of a comprehensive work on man and society. See Skinner, A.S., 'Introduction' in Skinner, A.S. (ed.), *The Wealth of Nations*, Harmondsworth, 1981, esp. p. 13.
    Some citations may illustrate mainstream economists' interpretation of Smith's economic analysis:
    'Adam Smith elevated it *[i.e. economics]* to the status of a separate discipline in 1776.'
    (Clower, R.W., 'Reflections on the Keynesian Perplex', *Zeitschrift für Nationalökonomie*, vol. 35, 1975, p. 2)

'If we count the publication of *The Wealth of Nations* in 1776 as marking the "birth" of economics as a separate discipline'
(Blaug, M., *The Methodology of Economics*, Cambridge, 1980, pp. 55–56)

'When the claim is made – and the claim is as old as Adam Smith – that a myriad of self-seeking agents left to themselves will lead to a coherent and efficient disposition of economic resources, Arrow and Debreu show what the world would have to look like if the claim is to be true.'
(Hahn, F.H., *On the Notion of Equilibrium in Economics*, cited in O'Driscoll Jr., G.P. and M.J. Rizzo, *The Economics of Time & Ignorance*, Oxford, 1985, p. 111)

'His pluralistic supply-and-demand analysis in terms of all three components of wages, rents, and profits is a valid and valuable anticipation of general equilibrium modelling.'
(Samuelson, P.A., 'A Modern Theorist's Vindication of Adam Smith', *The American Economic Review*, vol. 67, 1977, p. 42)

'The modern equilibrium theory is nothing else than a mathematically exact formulation of Smith's invisible hand which harmonizes the interests of egoistic individuals in an optimal manner.'
(Kornai, J., *Anti-equilibrium: Economic Systems Theory and the Tasks of Research*, Amsterdam, 1971, p. 349, cited in O'Driscoll Jr., G.P. and M.J. Rizzo, *The Economics of Time & Ignorance*, 1985, p. 110).

3. Gay, P., *The Enlightenment: An Interpretation / The Science of Freedom*, New York, 1977, pp. 319–320.
4. For different interpretations of the division of economics in positive, normative and applied economics see, for instance, Friedman, M., *Essays in Positive Economics*, Chicago, 1953, Hutchison, T.W., *'Positive' Economics and Policy Objectives*, London, 1964, Plattel, M.A.D. and J.J.M. Peil, 'An ethico-political and theoretical reconstruction of economic thought', *Research Memorandum no.149*, Tilburg University Department of Economics, Tilburg, 1984; Plattel, M.A.D., 'Economische wetenschap en ethiek', *Tijdschrift voor Theologie*, vol. 25, 1985, pp. 4–19.
5. TMS VII.iv.37.
6. TMS, Advertisement.
7. Cf.:
   'Adam Smith undoubtedly started with the purpose of giving to the world a complete social philosophy.'
   (Bonar, J., *Philosophy and Political Economy*, London, 1922, p. 149, cited in Hutchison, T.W., *Before Adam Smith: The Emergence of Political Economy, 1662–1776*, p. 414)

   'This is an economic work? It is far more than that; it is a history and criticism of all European civilization ... a philosophical work.'
   (Morrow, G.R., 'Adam Smith: Moralist and Philosopher' in Clark, J.M. (ed.), *Adam Smith, 1776–1926*, Chicago, 1928, New York, 1966, p. 157)

   'They *[The Scottish school in general and Adam Smith in particular]* in the eighteenth century thought of economics only as one chapter (not the most important) in a general theory of society involving psychology and ethics, social and individual law, politics, and social philosophy as well. This at least avoided the disintegration in thought, the lack of communication in practice which we almost accept today, though some deplore it without being able to do much about it.'
   (Macfie, A.L., *The Individual in Society. Papers on Adam Smith*, London, 1967, p. 16)

> 'All who are familiar with Smith's life and writings recognize that he was a philosopher by profession and that all his writings were conceived and executed as works of philosophy.'
>
> (Lindgren, J.R., *The Social Philosophy of Adam Smith*, The Hague, 1973, p. ix)

> 'Smith hatte nichts Geringeres als eine umfassende Philosophie- oder Kulturgeschichte der Menschheit zu schreiben geplant.'
>
> (Recktenwald, H.C. (ed.), *Adam Smith. Der Wohlstand der Nationen*, München, 1988, p. xxxii)

8. While in the Renaissance the liberation from the medieval feudal social structure was mainly sought in the rediscovery and return to the ideals of the ancient classics, the striving for freedom in the Enlightenment was characterized much more by an independent designing and experimenting with new ordering concepts. Cf. Peperzak, A., 'Kan de verlichting ons verlichten', *Tijdschrift voor Filosofie*, vol. 24, 1962, pp. 243–278; Gay, P., *The Enlightenment: An Interpretation / The Rise of Modern Paganism*, New York, 1966/1977 and *The Science of Freedom*, New York, 1969/1977; Darnton, R., 'The Social History of Ideas' in Darnton, R., *The Kiss of Lamourette: Reflections in Cultural History*, London, 1990, pp. 219–252.

9. Cf. Zijderveld, A.B., *De culturele factor. Een cultuursociologische wegwijzer*, The Hague, 1983, p. 79.

10. Cf. Polanyi, K., *Ökonomie und Gesellschaft*, Frankfurt am Main, 1979, pp. 129–219.

11. See for instance Euchner, W., *Naturrecht und Politik bei John Locke*, Frankfurt am Main, 1969; Fink, H., *Social Philosophy*, London, 1981, pp. 6–54; Manenschijn, G., *Moraal en Eigenbelang bij Thomas Hobbes en Adam Smith*, Amsterdam, 1979; Medick, H., *Naturzustand und Naturgeschichte der bürgerlichen Gesellschaft. Die Ursprünge der bürgerlichen Sozialtheorie als Geschichtsphilosophie und Sozialwissenschaft bei Samuel Pufendorf, John Locke und Adam Smith*, Göttingen, 1973, pp. 40–171, and Myers, M.L., *The Soul of Modern Economic Man. Ideas of Self-Interest. Thomas Hobbes to Adam Smith*, Chicago, 1983.

12. Zijderveld, A.B., *De culturele factor. Een cultuursociologische wegwijzer*, The Hague, 1983, pp. 68–73.

13. Zijderveld, A.B., *De culturele factor. Een cultuursociologische wegwijzer*, The Hague, 1983, pp. 72–73.

14. Schumpeter, J.A., *History of Economic Analysis*, New York, 1954, for instance p. 8. See also Hollander, S., *The Economics of Adam Smith*, Toronto, 1973, p. 6.

15. Schumpeter considers Walras' general equilibrium analysis as marking the breakthrough of rigorous, scientific analysis concerning the general principles of human behaviour and their economic effects. Cf. Schumpeter, J.A., *History of Economic Analysis*, New York, 1954, pp. 16 and 968. See also pp. 242:

> 'the Cantillon-Quesnay *tableau* was the first method ever devised in order to convey an *explicit* conception of the nature of economic equilibrium. ... Smith ... and others all struggled and fumbled for it, every one of them in his own way. But the discovery was not fully made until Walras, whose system of equations, defining (static) equilibrium in a system of interdependent quantities, is the Magna Charta of economic theory',

and p. 827:

> 'so far as pure theory is concerned, Walras is in my opinion the greatest of all economists. His system of economic equilibrium, uniting, as it does, the quality of "revolutionary" creativeness with the quality of classical synthesis, is the only work by an economist that will stand comparison with the achievements of theoretical physics. ... It is the outstanding landmark on the road that economics travels toward the status of

a rigorous or exact science and, though outmoded by now, still stands at the back of much of the best theoretical work of our time.'

The main questions of the economic analysis are, according to Schumpeter:

'how people behave at any time and what the economic effects are they produce by so behaving'

(p. 21)

With regard to Schumpeter's view of the object and the method of the economic analysis see also pp. 12, 15–16 and 20–21.

16. According to Schumpeter it is even possible to find an *embryonic Wealth of Nations* in Pufendorf. Schumpeter, J.A., *History of Economic Analysis*, New York, 1954/1959, pp. 122. See also pp. 94, 141, 182 and 185.

17. Id., p. 189. See also p. 187, pp. 308–309, p. 557 footnote 8, p. 918, p. 952, p. 999 footnote 1, and p. 1000 footnote 4.

18. Id., pp. 51–52 and 143.

19. Id., pp. 184–185. See also note 15.

20. Letwin asserts that with regard to Smith, Schumpeter fails to adequately recognize that a discourse is scientific if it is refers to an explanatory system based on just a small number of principles. According to Letwin, Schumpeter seriously underestimated Smith's work. Combining fragmentary thoughts into a system is not the same as compiling ideas of earlier authors, as Schumpeter suggests. In Letwin's opinion Smith's work was very creative, comparable to Newton's achievements in physics. Cf. Letwin, W., *The Origins of Scientific Economics*, London, 1963, pp. viii–ix and 227–228.

21. For instance Letwin, W., *The Origins of Scientific Economics*, London, 1963, p. 225.

22. Millar, J., *An Historical View of the English Government*, part II, London, 1787/1803, p. 429–430n:

'I am happy to acknowledge the obligations I feel myself under to this illustrious philosopher, by having, at an early period of life, had the benefit of hearing his lectures on the History of Civil Society, and of enjoying his unreserved conversation on the same subject. The great Montesquieu pointed out the road. He was the Lord Bacon in this branch of philosophy. Dr. Smith is the Newton.'

(Ross, I.S. (ed.), 'Dugald Stewart's Account of Adam Smith', in Wightman, W.P.D., J.C. Bryce and I.S. Ross (eds.), *Adam Smtih. Essays on Philosophical Subjects*, Oxford, 1980, p. 275)

23. Cf. Hutchison, T.W., *'Positive' Economics and Policy Objectives*, London, 1964, p. 25:

'When Smith referred to political economy "as a branch of the science of a statesman or legislator," the emphasis was on the function of policy prescription, as it had been with almost all his predecessors, whether natural law philosophers or practical pamphleteers. The term "science" had for Smith little of its modern methodological significance.'

24. WN 1.viii.36. See also Hont, I. and M. Ignatieff, 'Needs and Justice in the *Wealth of Nations*: An Introductory Essay' in Hont, I. and M. Ignatieff (eds.), *Wealth and Virtue. The Shaping of Political Economy in the Scottish Enlightenment*, Cambridge, 1983, pp. 1–2.

25. See Winch, D., 'Science and the Legislator: Adam Smith and After', *The Economic Journal*, vol. 93, 1983, pp. 501–520.

26. Fink, H., *Social Philosophy*, London, 1981, pp. 6–15 and Stamm, V., *Ursprünge der Wirtschaftsgesellschaft*, Frankfurt am Main, 1982, pp. 15–28.

27. Euchner, W., *Naturrecht und Politik bei John Locke*, Frankfurt am Main, 1969/1979, pp. 14–42 and Fink, H., *Social Philosophy*, London, 1981, pp. 15–20.

28. Beer, M., *Early British Economics from the XIIIth to the Middle of the XVIIIth Century*, London, 1938, pp. 15–45, 229 and Meikle, S., *Aristotle's Economic Thought*, Oxford, 1995.

29. For a more extensive survey of the dissolution of the feudal society and its system of producing and distributing wealth, see: Fink, H., *Social Philosophy*, London, 1981, pp. 21–54; Kittsteiner, H.-D., *Naturabsicht und Unsichtbare Hand*, Frankfurt am Main, 1980, pp. 105–133, and Stamm, V., *Ursprünge der Wirtschaftsgesellschaft*, Frankfurt am Main, 1982.

30. See also Hutchison, T.W., *Before Adam Smith: The Emergence of Political Economy, 1662–1776*, Oxford, 1988, pp. 112–113, 265–269, 293–294, 303–304, 345–346, and Hont, I. and M. Ignatieff, 'Needs and Justice in the *Wealth of Nations*: An Introductory Essay' in Hont, I. and M. Ignatieff (eds.), *Wealth & Virtue. The Shaping of Political Economy in the Scottish Enlightenment*, Cambridge, 1983, pp. 1–44.

31. Letwin, W., *The Origins of Scientific Economics*, London, 1963, pp. 79–228 and Hutchison, T.W., *Before Adam Smith: The Emergence of Political Economy, 1662–1776*, Oxford, 1988, pp. 352–371.

32. Cited in Hutchison, T.W., *Before Adam Smith: The Emergence of Political Economy, 1662–1776*, Oxford, 1988, p. 384.

33. Id. pp. 4, 372 and 374.

34. Letwin, W., *The Origins of Scientific Economics*, London, 1963, pp. 79–228. See also Klant, J.J., *Het ontstaan van de staathuishoudkunde*, Leiden, 1988.

35.   'Human society, when we contemplate it in a certain abstract and philosophical light, it appears like an immense machine, whose regular and harmonious movements produce numberless agreeable things.'
        TMS VII.iii.I.2.

36. WN II.iii.28.

37. WN I.ii.2.

38. WN IV.ii.9. See also:
        'This frugality and good conduct, ..., is upon most occasions, it appears from experience, sufficient to compensate, not only the private prodigality and misconduct of individuals, but the publick extravagance of government. The uniform, constant, and uninterrupted effort of every man to better his condition, the principle from which publick and national, as well as private opulence is originally derived, is frequently powerful enough to maintain the natural progress of things toward improvement, in spite both of the extravagance of government, and of the greatest errors of administration. Like the unknown principle of animal life, it frequently restores health and vigour to the constitution, in spite, not only of the disease, but of the absurd prescriptions of the doctor.'
        (WN II.iii.31)

        'The natural effort of every individual to better his own condition, when suffered to exert itself with freedom and security, is so powerful a principle, that it is alone, and without any assistance, not only capable of carrying on the society to wealth and prosperity, but of surmounting a hundred impertinent obstructions with which the folly of human laws too often incumbers its operations; though the effect of these obstructions is always more or less either to encroach upon its freedom, or to diminish its security.'
        (WN IV.v.b.43)

39. Letwin, W., *The Origins of Scientific Economics*, London, 1963, p. 225.

40. About, for instance, Pierre Nicole (1625–1695), Josiah Child (1630–1699), John Locke (1632–1704), Samuel Pufendorf (1632–1694), Sir Dudley North (1641–1691), Pierre de Boisguilbert (1646–1714), Bernard de Mandeville (1671–1733), Etienne Bonnet, Abbé de Condillac (1715–1780), Sir James Steuart (1713–1780), Ferdinando Galiani (1728–1787), Cesare Beccaria (1735–1794), Pierro Verri (1728–1797) see among others Schumpeter,

J.A., *History of Economic Analysis*, New York, 1954, Letwin, W., *The Origins of Scientific Economics*, London, 1963 and Hutchison, T.W., *Before Adam Smith: The Emergence of Political Economy, 1662–1776*, Oxford, 1988.

41. As indicated before, a reference to Walras and his general equilibrium theory without any further specification is a reference to the common understanding of Walras and his contribution to economic analysis as exemplified in Schumpeter's *History of Economic Analysis*, New York, 1959, pp. 998–1026. Cf. Tobin, J., 'Theoretical Issues in Macroeconomics' in Feiwel, G.R. (ed.), *Issues in Contemporary Macroeconomics and Distribution*, London, 1985, particularly pp. 105–107.

42. Clark, Ch.M.A., 'Natural Law Influences on Adam Smith', *Quaderni di Storia dell' Economica Politica*, vol. 6, 1988, pp. 59–86 and 'Adam Smith and Society as an Evolutionary Process', *Journal of Economic Issues*, vol. 24, 1990, pp. 825–844. Both titles are republished in Clark, Ch.M.A., *Economic Theory and Natural Philosophy. The Search for the Natural Laws of the Economy*, Aldershot, 1992, pp. 35–72 and 73–88.

43. See also Hont, I. and M. Ignatieff, 'Needs and Justice in the *Wealth of Nations*: An Introductory Essay' in Hont, I. and M. Ignatieff (eds.), *Wealth & Virtue. The Shaping of Political Economy in the Scottish Enlightenment*, Cambridge, 1983, pp. 1–44.

44. For example: 'Digression concerning the Corn Trade and Corn Laws' (WN IV.v.b)

'I cannot conclude this chapter concerning bounties, without observing that the praises which have been bestowed upon the law which establishes the bounty upon the exportation of corn, and upon that system of regulations which is connected with it, are altogether unmerited. A particular examination of the nature of the corn trade, and of the principal British laws which relate to it, will sufficiently demonstrate the truth of this assertion. The great importance of this subject must justify the length of the digression.'
(WN IV.v.b.1)

'Whoever examines, with attention, the history of the dearths and famines which have afflicted any part of Europe, during either the course of the present or that of the two preceding centuries, of several of which we have pretty exact accounts, will find, I believe, ... that a famine has never arisen from any other cause but the violence of government attempting, by improper means, to remedy the inconveniences of a dearth.'
(WN IV.v.b.5)

'The unlimited, unrestrained freedom of the corn trade, as it is the only effectual preventative of the miseries of a famine, so it is the best palliative of the inconveniences of a dearth; for the inconveniences of a real scarcity cannot be remedied; they can only be palliated. No trade deserves more the full protection of the law, and no trade requires it so much; because no trade is so much exposed to popular odium.'
(WN IV.v.b.7)

'That system of laws, therefore, which is connected with the establishment of the bounty, seems to deserve no part of the praise which has been bestowed upon it. The improvement and prosperity of Great Britain, which has been so often ascribed to those laws, may very easily be accounted for by other causes. That security which the laws in Great Britain give to every man that he shall enjoy the fruits of his own labour, is alone sufficient to make any country flourish, notwithstanding these and twenty other absurd regulations of commerce; and this security was perfected by the revolution, much about the same time that the bounty was established.'
(WN IV.v.b.43)

45. Hont, I. and M. Ignatieff, 'Needs and Justice in the *Wealth of Nations*: An Introductory Essay' in Hont, I. and M. Ignatieff (eds.), *Wealth & Virtue. The Shaping of Political Economy in the Scottish Enlightenment*, Cambridge, 1983, pp. 1–44.
46. For a proper understanding of Smith's *utopia*, see WN IV.ii.43–44:

> 'To expect, ..., that the freedom of trade should ever be entirely restored in Great Britain, is as absurd as to expect that an Oceania or Utopia should ever be established in it. Not only the prejudices of the publick, but what is much more unconquerable, the private interests of many individuals, irresistibly oppose it. Were the officers of the army to oppose with the same zeal and unanimity any reduction in the number of forces, with which master manufacturers set themselves against every law that is likely to increase the number of their rivals in the home market; were the former to animate their soldiers, in the same manner as the latter enflame their workmen, to attack with violence and outrage the proposers of any such regulation; to attempt to reduce the army would be as dangerous as it has now become to attempt to diminish in any respect the monopoly which our manufacturers have obtained against us. This monopoly has so much increased the number of some particular tribes of them, that, like an overgrown standing army, they have become formidable to the government, and upon many occasions intimidate the legislature. The member of parliament who supports every proposal for strengthening this monopoly, is sure to acquire not only the reputation of understanding trade, but great popularity and influence with an order of men whose numbers and wealth render them of great importance. If he opposes them, on the contrary, and still more if he has great authority enough to be able to thwart them, neither the most acknowledged probity, nor the highest rank, nor the greatest publick services can protect him from the most infamous abuse and detraction, from personal insults, nor sometimes from real danger, arising from the insolent outrage of furious and disappointed monopolists.
>
> The undertaker of a great manufacture who, by the home markets being suddenly laid open to the competition of foreigners, should be obliged to abandon his trade, would no doubt suffer very considerably. That part of his capital which had usually been employed in purchasing materials and in paying his workmen, might, without much difficulty, perhaps, find another employment. But that part of it which was fixed in workhouses, and in the instruments of trade, could scarce be disposed of without considerable loss. The equitable regard, therefore, to his interest requires that changes of this kind should never be introduced suddenly, but slowly, gradually, and after a very long warning. The legislature, were it possible that its deliberations could be always directed, not by the clamorous importunity of partial interests, but by an extensive view of the general good, ought upon this very account, perhaps, to be particularly careful neither to establish any new monopolies of this kind, nor to extend further those which are already established. Every such regulation introduces some degree of real disorder into the constitution of the state, which it will be difficult afterwards to cure without occasioning another disorder.'

47. With regard to those two different streams in modern economic thought, see Letwin, W., *The Origins of Scientific Economics*, London, 1963, in particular pp. 79–98 and 207–228, and Hutchison, T.W., *Before Adam Smith: The Emergence of Political Economy, 1662–1776*, Oxford, 1988, pp. 10, 73, 215–218 and 280–289.
48. For a more extensive discussion, see Letwin, W., *The Origins of Scientific Economics*, London, 1963, among others pp. 79–146 and 182–228.
49. Goudzwaard, B., *Kapitalisme en vooruitgang*, Assen, 1978, p. 25.
50. WN IV.ii.9.
51. Schumpeter, J.A., *History of Economic Analysis*, New York, 1959, pp. 188–189 and 307–311. Although Schumpeter criticizes Smith's discussions of value and price, he

interprets these discussions benevolently as an anticipation of Marshall's theory of price, understood in accordance with the prevailing Walrasian view. Cf. Blaug, M., *Economic Theory in Retrospect*, Cambridge, 1985, p. 585 for this Walrasian interpretation of Marshall's theory of price.

52. In *A History of Marginal Utility Theory* (1965, p. 28) Kauder criticizes Smith sharply for his supposed objectivistic doctrine of value. Smith's doctrine, he says, was responsible for misleading English economic analysis to such a degree that it would have taken until the second half of the nineteenth century before English economists again reached the level of price and value analysis before Smith. See also Peil, J., 'A New Look at Adam Smith', in the *International Journal of Social Economics*, vol. 16, 1989, p. 68.

53. Hutchison, T.W., *Before Adam Smith: The Emergence of Political Economy, 1662–1776*, Oxford, 1988.

54. Id., pp. 192–199. For example:

   Thus, the general framework of Hutcheson's and Smith's conception and treatment of moral philosophy, political economy, and jurisprudence came from Pufendorf, via Carmichael. So also did their first treatments of the fundamental concepts of value and price.

55. Id., p. 100:

   'through Gershom Carmichael and Francis Hutcheson in Glasgow, Pufendorf's formulation of the economic concepts of the natural-law analysis passed on to Smith; while through Jean-Jacques Burlamaqui (an almost exact contemporary of Hutcheson) they passed to Auguste Walras, and so to his son Léon.'

56. Id.:

   'Burlamaqui's analysis of value and price should have helped to keep alive in France the Pufendorfian, natural-law tradition on the subject. ... More than half a century later, however, Auguste Walras was to complain, in his *De la nature de la richesse et de l'origine de la valeur* (1831), of the eclipse of the natural-law theory of Pufendorf and Burlamaqui.
   ... Walras (senior) proceeded to explain:

   'The doctrine, which I am about to present to my readers on the nature of wealth and the origin of value, is so little new or modern, that it has been set out a long time ago in a work on public law, written in French and published on the frontiers of France. I wish to mention the Élements du droit naturel, by Burlamaqui.'
   (1831, 209)

   Auguste Walras then went on to give a more than two-page quotation, much of which we have just reproduced. He then concluded with the claim that this passage from Burlamaqui 'is irrefutable. The reflections it contains are strikingly correct'. It provided a triumphant answer to J.B. Say:

   'After having read this passage, there is only one question to ask. How did such a doctrine remain buried in treatise of natural law? Why has it not already passed into the writings of economists? It would have produced the most valuable fruit.
      But I am saying that the doctrine of Burlamaqui is mine...'

   Subsequently, Auguste's son Léon was to complain that, while the English classical solution of Smith, Ricardo, and McCulloch, which traced the origin of value to labour was 'too narrow', the solution of Condillac and J.B. Say, in terms of *utility*, was too broad. The correct solution was 'that of Burlamaqui and my father' – and he might, of course, have added, of Pufendorf and Francis Hutcheson (though hardly, in *The*

Wealth of Nations, of Adam Smith). Léon then proceeded to re-quote from his father's quotation of Burlamaqui's chapter 11 (see 1954, 203–4). (pp. 323–324)

57. TMS VII.iii.1–4. Smith's point of view will be discussed in more detail in chapters III and IV.
58. Hutchison, T.W., *Before Adam Smith: The Emergence of Political Economy, 1662–1776*, Oxford, 1988, p. 378.
59. Id., p. 364.
60. Id., p. 378.
61. Id.:

> 'In breaking, ..., with the treatment of Pufendorf and Hutcheson, Smith both diminished or excluded the element of subjectivity and confused the relationship between utility and demand. Alfred Marshall's judicious conclusion seems unavoidable: "Adam Smith makes himself the judge of what is useful to other people and introduces unnecessary confusion".'

> 'It is not the case, ..., that Smith clearly and categorically put forward a general labour theory of exchange value. He did not. Nor did he entirely omit either the demand side, or the subjective element ... But his unhappy, tiresome, and awkward treatment of value-in-use, together with his introduction of a labour element both in the measurement of value and in the simplest case of exchange value, had confusing consequences which were very important for the subsequent history of value theory.'
> (pp. 364–365)

62. Cf. Medick, H., *Naturzustand und Naturgeschichte der bürgerlichen Gesellschaft*, Göttingen, 1973, 146–151. Since it is not our aim to reconsider the prevailing interpretation of the works of Grotius, Pufendorf, Locke and Hutcheson, secondary literature will frequently be referred to.
63. Euchner, W., *Naturrecht und Politik bei John Locke*, Frankfurt am Main, 1969, pp. 16, 19, 21–23, 29–31 and 37.
64. In Grotius' *De jure belli ac pacis*, we no longer find any reference to the *lex aeterna* regarding natural law. By focusing on human nature, man is supposed to be able to establish by means of his own ratio what the principles are of natural law.

> 'After all, the first principles of this law, for who observes well, are very clear in themselves, almost like the observations made by our senses',

according to Grotius (Eijffinger, A. and B. Vermeulen, *Hugo de Groot. Denken over oorlog en vrede*, 'Prolegomena', § 39, Baarn, 1991). Cf. Euchner, W., *Naturrecht und Politik bei John Locke*, Frankfurt am Main, 1969, p. 23.

65. 'All I have said so far, would in a certain sense retain its validity, even when I acknowledged – which I cannot acknowledge without committing the gravest sin – that there is no God or that He does not concern himself with the human affairs.'
(Eijffinger, A. and B. Vermeulen, *Hugo de Groot. Denken over oorlog en vrede*, 'Prolegomena', § 11, Baarn, 1991.)
Cf. Fortuin, H., *De Natuurlijke Grondslagen van De Groot's Volkenrecht*, The Hague, 1946, p. 119; Vermeulen, B., 'God, wil en rede in Hugo de Groots natuurrecht', *Wijsgerig Perspectief*, vol. 23, 1982, pp. 86–87; and Eijffinger, A. and B. Vermeulen, *Hugo de Groot. Denken over oorlog en vrede*, Baarn, 1991, p. 24.
66. Vermeulen, B., 'God, wil en rede in Hugo de Groots natuurrecht', *Wijsgerig Perspectief*, vol. 23, 1982, p. 57.
67. When discussing Grotius' rationalistic interpretation of natural order and law it is of interest to consider his frequently established affinity with the doctrine of the Stoics. Cf. Fortuin, H., *De natuurrechtelijke grondslagen van De Groots Volkenrecht*, The Hague, 1946, pp. 106–122 and Eijffinger, A. and B. Vermeulen, *Hugo de Groot. Denken over oorlog en vrede*, Baarn, 1991, p. 26.

68. Cf. some quotes from Grotius' *De Jure Belli ac Pacis*:

    'I mean his need for an ordered, peaceful living together with his fellow-men, attuned to his intelligence, a characteristic which the stoics called oikeioosis. For this reason I cannot confirm the assertion that nature and every animal creature are focused on self-interest, put in such general terms.'

    (Eijffinger, A. and B. Vermeulen, *Hugo de Groot. Denken over oorlog en vrede*, 'Prolegomena', § 6, Baarn, 1991)

    'Therefore, strictly speaking it is incorrect what not only Carneades, but also others claim: "Utility is as the mother of justice and fairness". For the mother of natural law is human nature itself, which would make us, even if we would not feel one single desire, strive for a mutual community.'

    (Id., 'Prolegomena', § 16)

    'from the fact that he *[the adult]* is capable of reacting equably in similar circumstances we may deduce that, beside this remarkable community spirit – for which he, solely among the living creatures, disposes over a special means, namely the language – he also has the ability to understand and to act according to general rules, as whatever comes together with this ability is not communal to all living creatures, but is specific for human nature.

    This care for the community, which I have now roughly outlined, and which suits the human mind, forms the source for that right, which may in actual sense be qualified thus. To this belongs the commandment not to violate other people's property and the obligation that whenever we have something belonging to someone else or have gained from this, we should return it; furthermore the obligation to fulfil promises, to refund damages caused by any fault of ours and the infliction of deserved punishment among the people.'

    (Id., 'Prolegomena', § 7–8)

    In his view of the community spirit Grotius is closer to the Stoics than to Aristotle. In Grotius, the community spirit goes beyond the society man lives in, and unites all people in one world community. The separate nation-states are conceived of as being subjected to an encompassing judicial system. (Id., pp. 26–27, 154). Euchner underlines the difference with Aristotle's view when he notices that in Aristotle:

    'das Naturrecht ist den Sitten und Satzungen der Polis immanent; es transzendiert sie nicht.'

    (Euchner, W., *Naturrecht und Politik bei John Locke*, Frankfurt am Main, 1969, p. 34; cf. Medick, H., *Naturzustand und Naturgeschichte der bürgerlichen Gesellschaft. Die Ursprünge der bürgerlichen Sozialtheorie als Geschichtsphilosophie und Sozialwissenschaft bei Samuel Pufendorf, John Locke und Adam Smith*, Göttingen, 1973, p. 31)

    While in Aristotle natural law is immanent to the morals and institutions of the nation-state, Grotius shares with the Stoics a rationalist and universalist approach in which natural law tends to become abstract.

69. In his renewal of scholastic moral philosophy in the thirteenth century, Thomas Aquinas gave more room to the subjective aspect of human action without relinquishing the idea that man was a social being, by which he meant that man was only given his due in the context of the community. While Thomas Aquinas upheld the idea that man has an unconditional right to the world as God's property to provide his basic needs, he recognized that individuation of possession, anchored in adequate property laws, suited human nature and was conducive to a proper management of the world, which would be advantageous to all.

    (Hont, I. and M. Ignatieff, 'Needs and Justice in the *Wealth of Nations*: An Introductory

Essay' in Hont, I. and M. Ignatieff (ed.), *Wealth & Virtue. The Shaping of Political Economy in the Scottish Enlightenment*, Cambridge, 1983, pp. 26–27).

Although in principle, Grotius had the same approach to property rights as Thomas Aquinas, the complementarity of distributive and commutative justice, which had been so characteristic for Thomas Aquinas is missing. In Grotius' view man had become an autonomous individual, albeit one with an innate need for social life, and with a faculty, namely ratio, to understand the natural order, intended by God. Therefore Grotius no longer wished to use the term property in the old, ambiguous meaning, and insisted upon the use of the term only in its modern meaning of exclusive authority over properties. As he himself remarked, this was entirely in concurrence with contemporary social developments (Eijffinger, A. and B. Vermeulen, *Hugo de Groot. Denken over oorlog en vrede*, 'Het Recht van Oorlog en Vrede', I.I. § X.4 and I.II. §1.5, Baarn, 1991).

Grotius attempted to dissolve the tension between commutative and distributive justice by pushing forward commutative justice and reducing the scope of distributive justice to exceptional situations. Only in times of direst need could people fall back on the original situation in which the world was still common property, and only then did the needy have the right to take possession of other people's property. Free trade, derived from natural law and only submitted to commutative justice, would then be permitted to be limited by the government for a product like corn, and could even be completely forbidden with the purpose of direct distribution among the needy. Cf. Hont, I. and M. Ignatieff, 'Needs and Justice in the *Wealth of Nations*: An Introductory Essay' in Hont, I. and M. Ignatieff (eds.), *Wealth & Virtue. The Shaping of Political Economy in the Scottish Enlightenment*, Cambridge, 1983, pp. 29–30.

70. Euchner, W., *Naturrecht und Politik bei John Locke*, Frankfurt am Main, 1969, pp. 17–18: Medick, H., *Naturzustand und Naturgeschichte der bürgerlichen Gesellschaft. Die Ursprünge der bürgerlichen Sozialtheorie als Geschichtsphilosophie und Sozialwissenschaft bei Samuel Pufendorf, John Locke und Adam Smith*, Göttingen, 1973, p. 37, and Wieacker, F. von, *Privatrechtsgeschichte der Neuzeit*, Göttingen, 1976, pp. 270–312.

71. Euchner, W., *Naturrecht und Politik bei John Locke*, Frankfurt am Main, 1969, pp. 17, 23–25.

72. Medick, H., *Naturzustand und Naturgeschichte der bürgerlichen Gesellschaft. Die Ursprünge der bürgerlichen Sozialtheorie als Geschichtsphilosophie und Sozialwissenschaft bei Samuel Pufendorf, John Locke und Adam Smith*, Göttingen, 1973, pp. 52–57.

73. Id.

74. See Hont, I. and M. Ignatieff, 'Needs and Justice in the *Wealth of Nations*: An Introductory Essay' in Hont, I. and M. Ignatieff (eds.), *Wealth & Virtue. The Shaping of Political Economy in the Scottish Enlightenment*, Cambridge, 1983, p. 32 with regard to Pufendorf, *Law of Nature*, 4.4.2, 4.4.14, and 4.6.6:

'Pufendorf had to explain both how individuation had occurred and whether it was consistent with God's original intentions when he granted the world to man's use. In thinking through these questions, Pufendorf made use of a distinction developed by the Spanish Jesuit Suarez between "preceptive" and "permissive" natural law. ... Pufendorf reduced the range of preceptive natural law to a minimum: "no man should hurt another", and no man should take what rightly belonged to another. Man had the liberty to initiate such forms of individuation as were consonant with these precepts.

This distinction between "preceptive" and "permissive" natural law entailed a rethinking of the nature of God's initial grant of the world to mankind. Using these concepts, Pufendorf argued that the "donation of God, described in the Sacred Scriptures, set forth not a definite form of dominion, but only an indefinite right to apply things to uses which are reasonable and necessary". Accordingly, in the beginning, things were lying '"open to any and every person", in the same sense [that] such things are said to be nobody's, more in a negative than in a positive sense; that is, they are not yet assigned to a particular person'. In the beginning, therefore, the world belonged to the community of mankind, but it was no one's in particular; it belonged neither to an individual Adam, nor to a primitive group of man. It was in a "negative" rather than a "positive" community, to use Pufendorf's terminology.'

See also Medick, H., *Naturzustand und Naturgeschichte der bürgerlichen Gesellschaft. Die Ursprünge der bürgerlichen Sozialtheorie als Geschichtsphilosophie und Sozialwissenschaft bei Samuel Pufendorf, John Locke und Adam Smith*, Göttingen, 1973, pp. 77–79, note 51.

75. Some statements by Locke, quoted from Stark, W., *The Ideal Foundations of Economic Thought*, London, 1944, pp. 4, 5, and 8:

'Nature ... has put into man a desire of happiness, and an aversion to misery: these indeed are innate practical principles, which (as practical principles ought) do continue constantly to operate and influence all our actions without ceasing: these may be observed in all persons and all ages, steady and universal; but these are inclinations of the appetite to good, not impressions of truth on the understanding.'
(Locke, J., *An Essay on Human Understanding*, I.iii.3)

'Things are good or evil, only in reference to pleasure or pain. That we call good, which is apt to cause or increase pleasure, or diminish pain in use; or else to procure or preserve us the possession of any other good, or absence of any evil. And on the contrary, we name that evil, which is apt to produce or increase any pain, or diminish any pleasure in us; or else to procure us any evil or deprive us of any good.'
(Locke, J., *An Essay on Human Understanding*, II.xx.2)

'the principal exercise of freedom is to stand still, open the eyes, look about, and take a view of the consequence of what we are going to do, as much as the weight of the matter requires.'
(Locke, J., *An Essay on Human Understanding*, II.xxi.67)

'were we determined by any thing but the last result of our minds, judging of the good or evil of any action, we were not free: the very end of our freedom being, that we may attain the good we choose. And therefore every man is put under a necessity by this constitution, as an intelligent being, to be determined in willing by his own thought and judgment what is best for him to do.'
(Locke, J., *An Essay on Human Understanding*, II.xxi.48)

See also Euchner, W., *Naturrecht und Politik bei John Locke*, Frankfurt am Main, 1969, pp. 92–109 and Medick, H., *Naturzustand und Naturgeschichte der bürgerlichen Gesellschaft*, Göttingen, 1973, pp. 69–72.

76. Medick, H., *Naturzustand und Naturgeschichte der bürgerlichen Gesellschaft. Die Ursprünge der bürgerlichen Sozialtheorie als Geschichtsphilosophie und Sozialwissenschaft bei Samuel Pufendorf, John Locke und Adam Smith*, Göttingen, 1973, pp. 75–87.

77. Dunn, J., *Locke*, Oxford, 1984, p. 84. See also pp. 84–85:

'But God had shown all men how he wished them to live by proclaiming to them the law of faith through the Messiah Jesus. ... Jesus himself proclaimed the law of faith, demanding obedience and promising salvation in return (R 71–5, W III 466).

... Faith is a form of trust, not against reason, but beyond reason. It demands effort (which is why infidelity can be a sin). But it makes truly open to every man the opportunity to live a good life.

This is not an inspiring conclusion to a philosophical quest that had covered three and a half decades. There is no reason to believe that Locke himself regarded it with enthusiasm; and he would scarcely have been happy to espouse it from the outset.'

Cf. Dunn, J., 'From Applied Theology to Social Analysis: The Break between John Locke and the Scottish Enlightenment' in Hont, I. and M. Ignatieff (eds.), *Wealth & Virtue*, Cambridge, 1983, pp. 119–137, and Euchner, W., *Naturrecht und Politik bei John Locke*, Frankfurt am Main, 1969, pp. 157–172.

78. For instance Hutcheson, F., 'An Inquiry concerning Moral Good and Evil', I.III, I.VI–VII, II.I–V and II.X in Raphael, D.D., *British Moralists. 1650–1800*, Oxford, 1969, pp. 266–268, 270–277 and 278–280.

79. Idem, I.I, I.VIII, V.III, and VII.I–VI, respectively pp. 264–265, 269–270, 291 and 294–298.

80. Hutcheson:

'But that our first ideas of moral good depend not on *laws*, may plainly appear from our constant inquiries into the *justice* of *laws themselves*; and that not only of human laws, but of the divine. What else can be the meaning of that universal opinion, "that the *laws* of God are *just*, and *holy*, and *good?*" Human laws may be called *good*, because of their conformity to the divine. But to call the laws of the supreme Deity *good*, or *holy*, or *just*, if all goodness, holiness, and justice be constituted by *laws*, or the *will* of a *superior* any way revealed, must be an insignificant tautology, amounting to no more than this, "that God *wills* what he *wills*. Or that his *will* is conformable to his *will*."

It must then first be supposed, that there is something in actions which is apprehended *absolutely good*; and this is *benevolence*, or desire of the *public natural happiness* of *rational agents*; and that our *moral sense* perceives this *excellence*: and then we call the *laws* of the Deity *good*, when we imagine that they are contrived to promote the *public good* in the most effectual and impartial manner. And the Deity is called *morally good*, when we apprehend that his *whole providence* tends to the universal happiness of his *creatures*; whence we conclude his *benevolence*, and *desire* in their happiness.

... when any sanctions co-operate with our moral sense, in exciting us to actions which we count morally good, we say we are *obliged*; but when sanctions of rewards or punishments oppose our moral sense, then we say we are *bribed* or *constrained*. In the former case we call the lawgiver *good*, as designing the public happiness; in the latter we call him *evil*, or *unjust*, for the supposed contrary intention. But were all our ideas of moral good or evil derived solely from opinions or private advantage or loss in actions, I see no possible difference which could be made in the meaning of these words.

VI. From this sense too we derive our ideas of RIGHTS. Whenever it appears to us, that a faculty of doing, demanding, or possessing anything, universally allowed in certain circumstances, would in the whole tend to the general good, we say, that one in such circumstances has a right to do, possess, or demand that thing. And according as this tendency to the public good is greater or less, the right is greater or less.

The *rights* called *perfect*, are of such necessity to the public good, that the universal violation of them would make human life intolerable; and it actually makes those miserable, whose rights are thus violated. On the contrary, to fulfil these rights in every instance, tends to the public good, either directly, or by promoting the innocent advantage of part. ... Instances of perfect rights are those to our lives; to the fruits of our labours; to demand performance of contracts upon valuable considerations, from men capable of performing them; to direct our own actions either for public, or innocent private good, before we have submitted them to the direction of others in any measure; and many others of like nature.

Imperfect rights are such as, when universally violated, would not necessarily make men miserable. These rights tend to the improvement and increase of positive good in any society, but are not absolutely necessary to prevent universal misery. The violation

of them only disappoints men of the happiness expected from the humanity or gratitude of others; but does not deprive men of any good which they had before. ... Instances of imperfect rights are those which the poor have to the charity of the wealthy; which all men have to offices of no trouble or expense to the performer; which benefactors have to returns of gratitude, and such-like.'
(Hutcheson, F., 'An Inquiry concerning Moral Good and Evil', VII.V–VI in Raphael, D.D., *British Moralists. 1650–1800*, part I, Oxford, 1969, pp. 296–298.

81. TMS VII.iii.2.7–9:

'But though reason is undoubtedly the source of the general rules of morality, and of all the moral judgements which we form by means of them, it is altogether absurd and unintelligible to suppose that the first perception of right and wrong can be derived from reason, even in those particular cases upon the experience of which the general rules are formed. These first perceptions, as well as all other experiments upon which any general rules are founded, cannot be the object of reason, but of immediate sense and feeling. ....

Pleasure and pain are the great objects of desire and aversion: but these are distinguished not by reason, but by immediate sense and feeling. If virtue, therefore, be desirable for its own sake, and if vice be, in the same manner, the object of aversion, it cannot be reason which originally distinguishes those different qualities, but immediate sense and feeling.

As reason, however, in a certain sense, may justly be considered as the principle of approbation and disapprobation, these sentiments were, through inattention, long regarded as originally flowing from the operations of this faculty. Dr. Hutcheson had the merit of being the first who distinguished with any degree of precision in what respect all moral distinctions may be said to arise from reason, and in what respect they are founded upon immediate sense and feeling. In his illustrations upon the moral sense he has explained this so fully, and, in my opinion, so unanswerably, that, if any controversy is still kept up about this subject, I can impute it to nothing, but either to inattention to what that gentleman has written, or to a superstitious attachment to certain forms of expression, a weakness not very uncommon among the learned, especially in subjects so deeply interesting as the present, in which a man of virtue is often loath to abandon, even the propriety of a single phrase which he has been accustomed to.'

82. Hutcheson, F., 'An Inquiry concerning Moral Good and Evil', III.VI in Raphael, D.D., *British Moralists. 1650–1800*, part I, Oxford, 1969, p. 282.

83. TMS I.i.I.5.

84. Footnote 1 in TMS I.i.I.

85. Seligman, B.B., 'Philosophic Perspectives in Economic Thought' in Samuels, W.J. (ed.), *The Methodology of Economic Thought*, New Brunswick, 1980, p. 252. In Screpanti, E. and S. Zamagni, *An Outline of the History of Economic Thought*, Oxford, 1993, pp. 55–56, we may find another example. As the next quote will indicate, Screpanti and Zamagni do not discuss *The Theory of Moral Sentiments*, but their discussion of the English and Scottish empiricists and 'moral sense' philosophers indicates that in their view Smith's *sympathy*-theory does not substantially differ from other *empiricists and 'moral sense' philosophers*:

'A different path *[i.e. to demonstrate that a free social life is possible even in the presence of selfish individuals]* was attempted by the English and Scottish empiricists and "moral sense" philosophers. Their approach was based on the assumption of the existence of a natural "benevolence", or "moral sentiment", which man experiences towards his fellows. If individuals are not naturally egoistic, they tend spontaneously to associate themselves and there is no need for external intervention to give sense to social life; neither God nor the State is necessary. It is sufficient to assume a particular structure of the human psyche. Now, apart from the fact that this way of thinking succeeds in solving the problem simply by ignoring its existence, the main difficulty with it is that the assumption on which it depends, benevolence, not only runs against common sense but also is not basically different from other metaphysical assumptions; nor is it less arbitrary and easier to demonstrate.

Both Hume and Hutcheson, Smith's teacher, and Smith himself moved in this direction. Smith's main contribution, however, the one which made him the father both of economic science and of modern liberalism, came precisely at the moment when he introduced innovations within that tradition. His stroke of genius consisted, not in the rejection of the empiricist position, but in taking it to its extreme logical conclusion, by leaving out even the arbitrary hypothesis of benevolence. With the "theorem of the invisible hand", Smith simply aimed at demonstrating that *individuals serve the collective interest precisely because they are guided by self-interest.*'

86. Clark, Ch.M.A., 'Adam Smith and Society as an Evolutionary Process', *Journal of Economic Issues*, volume 24, 1990, pp. 825–844.

87. Medick, H., *Naturzustand und Naturgeschichte der bürgerlichen Gesellschaft. Die Ursprünge der bürgerlichen Sozialtheorie als Geschichtphilosophie und Sozialwissenschaft bei Samuel Pufendorf, John Locke und Adam Smith*, Göttingen, 1973, p. 211.

88. Clark, Ch.M.A., 'Adam Smith and Society as an Evolutionary Process', *Journal of Economic Issues*, vol. 24, 1990, pp. 825–844, reprinted in Clark, Ch.M.A., *Economic Theory and Natural Philosophy: The Search for the Natural Laws of the Economy*, Aldershot, 1992, pp. 73-88.

89. Clark, Ch.M.A., 'Adam Smith and Society as an Evolutionary Process', *Journal of Economic Issues*, vol. 24, 1990, pp. 825–844, and 'Natural Law Influences on Adam Smith', *Quaderni di Storia dell' Economica Politica*, vol. 6, 1988, pp. 59–84 (in particular p. 80), reprinted in Clark, Ch.M.A., *Economic Theory and Natural Philosophy: The Search for the Natural Laws of the Economy*, Aldershot, 1992, pp. 35, 72.

90. LJ(B) 1–3:

'Jurisprudence is that science which inquires into the general principles which ought to be the foundation of the laws of all nations. Grotius seems to have been the first who attempted to give the world any thing like a regular system of natural jurisprudence, and his treatise on the laws of war and peace, with all its imperfections, is perhaps at this day the most compleat work on this subject. ... He determines war to be lawfull in every case where the state receives an injury which would be redress'd by an equitable civil magistrate. This naturally led him to inquire into the constitution of states, and the principles of civil laws; into the rights of sovereigns and subjects; into the nature of crimes, contracts, property, and whatever else was the object of law, so that the two first books of his treatise, which are upon this subject, are a compleat system of jurisprudence.

The next writer of note after Grotius was Mr. Hobbes. He had conceived an utter abhorrence of the ecclesiastics; and the bigottry of his times gave him occasion to think that the subjection of the consciences of men to ecclesiastic authority was the cause of the dissensions and civil wars that happened in England during the times of Charles the 1st and of Cromwell. In opposition to them he endeavoured to establish a system of morals by which the consciences of men might be subjected to the civil power, and which represented the will of the magistrate as the only proper rule of conduct. Before the establishment of civil society mankind according to him were in a state of war; and in order to avoid the ills of a natural state, men enter'd into contract to obey one common sovereign who should determine all disputes. Obedience to his will according to him constituted civil government, without which there could be no virtue, and consequently it too was the foundation and essence of virtue.

The divines thought themselves obliged to oppose this pernicious doctrine concerning virtue, and attacked it by endeavouring to shew that a state of nature was no state of war but that society might subsist, tho' not in so harmonious manner, without civil institutions. They endeavoured to shew that man in this state has certain rights belonging to him, such as a right to his body, to the fruits of his labour, and the fulfilling of contracts. With this design Puffendorf wrote his large treatise. The sole intention of the first part of it is to refute Hobbes, tho' it in reality serves no purpose to treat of the laws which would take place in a state of nature, or by what means succession to property was carried on, as there is no such state existing.'

91. TMS VII.iv.37:

'It might have been expected that the reasonings of lawyers, upon the different imperfections and improvements of the laws of different countries, should have given occasion to an inquiry into what were the natural rules of justice independent of all positive institution. It might have been expected that these reasonings should have led them to aim at establishing a system of what might properly be called natural jurisprudence, or a theory of the general principles which ought to run through and be the foundation of the laws of all nations. But though the reasonings of lawyers did produce something of this kind, and though no man has treated systematically of the laws of any particular country, without intermixing in his work many observations of this sort; it was very late in the world before any such general system was thought of, or before the philosophy of law was treated of by itself, and without regard to the particular institutions of any one nation. In none of the ancient moralists, do we find any attempt towards a particular enumeration of the rules of justice. Cicero in his Offices, and Aristotle in his Ethics, treat of justice in the same general manner in which they treat of all the other virtues. In the laws of Cicero and Plato, where we might naturally have expected some attempts towards an enumeration of those rules of natural equity, which ought to be enforced by the positive laws of every country, there is, however, nothing of this kind. Their laws are laws of police, not of justice. Grotius seems to have been the first who attempted to give the world anything like a system of those principles.'

See also the previous note.

92. LJ(A) ii.89–90:

'Now in all cases the measure of the punishment to be inflicted on the delinquent is the concurrence of the impartial spectator with the resentment of the injured. If the injury is so great as that the spectator can go along with the injured person in revenging himself by the death of the offender, this is the proper punishment, and what is to be exacted by the offended person or the magistrate in his place who acts in the character of an impartial spectator. ... In all cases a punishment appears equitable in the eyes of the rest of mankind when it is such that the spectator would concur with the offended person in exacting ‹it›.'

Cf. TMS, 'Appendix II', pp. 393 and 398.

93. TMS II.ii.3.4.

94. TMS VII.iv.37 and paragraph 2 of the 'Advertisement' of the sixth edition of TMS.

95. LJ, p. *30*.

'the four stages theory – i.e. the theory that society normally tends to develop through four successive stages based on hunting, pasturage, agriculture, and commerce'.

Cf. LJ(A) i.27–35 and WN III.

96. For instance WN I.vii.6, I.vii.30, I.x.a.1, I.x.c.1, IV.vii.c.44, IV.ix.17, and IV.ix.51.

97. That is, people living as isolated individuals in a state of poverty and fear.

III *Mutual Sympathy* and *Commerce*

Adam Smith's flash of genius was his recognition that the prices that emerged from voluntary transactions between buyers and sellers – for short, in a free market – could coordinate the activity of millions of people, each seeking his own interest, in such a way as to make everyone better off. It was a startling idea then, and it remains one today, that economic order can emerge as the unintended consequence of the actions of many people, each seeking his own interest.

(Friedman, M. and R., *Free to Choose: A Personal Statement*, New York, 1980, pp. 13–14)

Introduction

Smith repudiated mercantilism and physiocracy as explanations of the wealth of nations: it was not money or land, but labour which, he believed, should be considered the origin of wealth. A progressive division of labour in expanding markets would promote both the wealth of the individual and of society, he argued, referring to the idea of free exchange in the context of *natural liberty and equity*.

Accordingly Smith pleaded for a free market economy. This advocacy, however, has often been misunderstood as a plea for *laissez-faire* economics. Smith's discussion of the duties of the sovereign indicates the importance he attached to a measure of intervention. As we see in Book IV of *The Wealth of Nations*, Smith believed that more is required of the sovereign than the defence of society from internal and external enemies and the enforcement of the individual's respect for property and contractual obligations. According to Smith, the sovereign also holds a responsibility with respect to the wealth of his subjects; that is to take care of those facilities and services which are not supplied by the market, and to promote fairness and help his subjects achieve the level of competence necessary to live a decent life in the commercial society.

Some economists have tried to persuade us that Smith's ideas on the free market economy entail forced deregulation. Like the belief that Smith advocated *laissez-faire* economics, this too is fallacious. Smith thought of the free market economy as a utopian objective and he believed that deregulation should only become government policy when it accorded with the *communis opinio* in society.

Smith's discourse on the market economy does not refer to presupposed universal causal laws, as nineteenth and twentieth century economists believed when they modelled economics as the mechanics of self-interest. Rather Smith's view of the free market economy reflects his belief that the behaviour of the individual is ruled by values shared with other members of society, and that in a commercial society these values are increasingly produced and reproduced by free exchange.

As we have seen, Smith's economic analysis is based on his theory of *mutual sympathy*. In the present chapter we will consider this theory in greater detail and discuss its relationship to the idea of the *free market economy*. The first two sections are devoted to Smith's reinterpretation of the concept of *sympathy* and its role in his understanding of man and society. Sections 3 and 4 are concerned with Smith's reinterpretion of man's struggle for wealth and prestige as part of the struggle for *mutual sympathy* or *praiseworthiness*.

Section 1 focuses on Smith's reinterpretation of *sympathy*. In addition to considering Smith's new interpretation of this key concept we also look at the way in which its meaning is communicated, i.e. the style of his moral philosophy. His use of the dialogical style of argument, we suggest, reinforces the central point of Smith's reinterpretation of *sympathy*, namely that human feeling, action and thought is related to an intersubjectively shared world and life experience. Section 2 focuses on the processes of communication, competition and concurrence which Smith believed were an inevitable consequence of man's longing for *mutual sympathy*.

Smith's critique of contemporary utility-based explanations of economic behaviour forms the main topic of section 3. His reinterpretation of the notion of *utility* will be discussed and his proposal that we understand man's struggle for wealth and prestige as an element within the dynamics of communication, competition and concurrence driven by the desire for *mutual sympathy* will be explained. Section 4 investigates Smith's thesis that the corruption of moral sentiments will not be remedied by restraining free market exchange but by promoting it in order to strengthen the fair competition for praiseworthiness within society. When the *commercial society* is understood as a metaphor for a society directly regulated by the communication, competition and concurrence induced by the tendency to *mutual sympathy*, then the *free market economy* can be read as a complementary figure which illuminates the economic sphere of the commercial society.

1 Sympathy

The Theory of Moral Sentiments opens with the thesis that however selfish man may be, he nevertheless takes an interest in the well-being of others:

> 'How selfish soever man may be supposed, there are evidently some principles in his nature, which interest him in the fortune of others, and render their happiness necessary to him, though he derives nothing from it except the pleasure of seeing it.'[1]

In support of this thesis Smith invites us to imagine ourselves in various real-life situations and to reflect, through dialogue, upon the feelings we experience when contemplating the lives of other people.[2] In employing this dialogical form of argument Smith aims to convince us that our capacity for fellow-feeling is not limited to compassion and pity for the misfortune of others. On the basis of this conclusion he proposes widening and changing the meaning of *sympathy* to express 'our fellow-feeling with any passion whatever':

> 'Pity and compassion are words appropriated to signify our fellow-feeling with the sorrow of others. Sympathy, though its meaning was, perhaps, originally the same, may now, however, without much impropriety, be made use of to denote our fellow-feeling with any passion whatever.'[3]

Joining Smith in an investigation of various cases of fellow-feeling, we discover that *sympathy* involves observing the behaviour of other people and imagining oneself in their situation in order to share their feelings. Further, we discover that when we experience a concurrence of feelings with the object of our sympathy we are pleased and feel an urge to praise; where there is no concurrence we feel uneasy, which may sometimes lead to feelings of reproach or even revenge.

Other examples reveal that the dynamics of *sympathy* involve not only the praise(worthiness) of others but also our own praise(worthiness). We present ourselves to other people for acclaim, and hope to observe a fellow-feeling with our own passions. We imagine what other people would feel when they imagine themselves in our situation:

> 'But whatever may be the cause of sympathy, or however it may be excited, nothing pleases us more than to observe in other men a fellow-feeling with all the emotions of our own breast; nor are we ever so much shocked as by the appearance of the contrary.'[4]

> 'We suppose ourselves the spectators of our own behaviour, and endeavour to imagine what effect it would, in this light, produce upon us.'[5]

Thus our inclination to *sympathy* in fact contains a reflexive element and becomes an inclination towards *mutual sympathy*: not only do we experience an urge to identify with the fortunes of others, we also crave a reciprocal response from others to our own (mis)fortune.[6] This aspect of mutuality in man's yearning for *sympathy* plays a key role in Smith's moral philosophy, for it helps him explain why people live in societies and act according to shared rules and values.

In the previous chapter we suggested that Smith's re-interpretation of *sympathy* opened up a new vista in moral philosophy. The excerpts quoted above clearly show that Smith did not believe that man's behaviour could be conceived as exclusively motivated by selfishness. They also show that Smith's critique was not focused on demonstrating that human behaviour is also motivated by social passions such as pity or compassion. Instead Smith points out that we cannot hope to correctly comprehend human behaviour simply by nominating some specific human passions as fundamental. Rather, according to Smith, man's behaviour is governed by the pleasure and pain experienced in his dual need to sympathize and be the object of *sympathy*. For Smith, in other words, pleasure and pain are felt primarily in relation to a frame of values shared intersubjectively with other people.

The following passages indicate that Smith firmly believed that his *sympathetic* approach to social analysis was incompatible with other, 'passion-oriented', approaches. In the first passage Smith takes a stand against those authors who wanted to reduce all sentiments, including the feelings of pain and pleasure generated through *sympathy*, to selfishness or self-interest:

'Those who are fond of deducing all our sentiments from certain refinements of self-love, think themselves at no loss to account, according to their own principles, both for this pleasure and this pain. Man, say they, conscious of his own weakness, and of the need which he has for the assistance of others, rejoices whenever he observes that they adopt his own passions, because he is then assured of that assistance; and grieves whenever he observes the contrary, because he is then assured of their opposition. But both the pleasure and the pain are always felt so instantaneously, and often upon such frivolous occasions, that it seems evident, that neither of them can be derived from any such self-interested consideration.'[7]

The second passage deserves our attention because in it Smith expresses his belief that *sympathy* reflects an irreducible need in man to feel himself emotionally related to others:

'As the person who is principally interested in any event is pleased with our sympathy, and hurt by the want of it, so we, too, seem to be pleased when we are able to sympathize with him, and to be hurt when we are unable to do so. We run not only to congratulate the successful, but to condole with the afflicted; and the pleasure which we find in the conversation of one whom in all the passions of his heart we can entirely sympathize with, seems to do more than compensate the painfulness of that sorrow with which the view of his situation affects us. On the contrary, it is always disagreeable to feel that we cannot sympathize with him, and instead of being pleased with this exemption from sympathetic pain, it hurts us to find that we cannot share his uneasiness.'[8]

The third passage shows that Smith's *sympathy*-based interpretation of man's social nature differs fundamentally from the conventional interpretations according to which the term *social* refers to man's altruistic motives of behaviour and action:

'Were it possible that a human creature could grow up to manhood in some solitary place, without any communication with his own species, he could no more think of his own character, of the propriety or demerit of his own sentiments and conduct, of the beauty or deformity of his own mind, than of the beauty or deformity of his own face. All these are objects which he cannot easily see, which naturally he does not look at, and with regard to which he is provided with no mirror which can present them to his view. Bring him into society, and he is immediately provided with the mirror which he wanted before. It is placed in the countenance and behaviour of those he lives with, which always mark when they enter into, and when they disapprove of his sentiments; and it is here that he first views the propriety and impropriety of his own passions, the beauty and deformity of his own mind. To a man who from his birth was a stranger to society, the objects of his passions, the external bodies which either pleased or hurt him, would occupy his whole attention. The passions themselves, the desires or aversions, the joy or sorrows, which those objects excited, though of all things the most immediately present to him, could scarce ever be the objects of his thoughts. The idea of them could never interest him so much as to call upon his attentive consideration. The consideration of his joy in him excite no new joy, nor that of his sorrow any new sorrow, though the consideration of the causes of those passions might often excite both. Bring him into society, and all his own passions will immediately become the causes of new passions. He will observe that mankind approve of some of them, are disgusted by others. He will be elevated in the one case, and cast down in the other; his desires and aversions, his joys and sorrows, will now often become the causes of new desires and new aversions, new joys and new sorrows; they will now, therefore, interest him deeply, and often call upon his most attentive consideration.'[9]

This last passage clearly shows that Smith's conception of man as a social being differs radically from that of other contemporary moral philosophers.[10] For Smith the concept of *social being* means that man is an individual subject by virtue of his relationship with other human beings. In their tendency to *mutual sympathy* people effectively hold up a mirror to each other's faces in which they see themselves from the imagined perspective of others and therein discover the intersubjective values and rules which provide the frame of reference for their feeling, thought and action. In this view an act motivated by self-interest is equally as 'socially determined' as the altruistic promotion of the well-being of others. Macfie is right when he observes that for Smith, man was an *individual in society*.[11] In section 2 we will further discuss Smith's view of man and society. Here, it is important to note that Smith did not understand the individual subject as atomistic but as social – that is, as a subject whose individual subjectivity is formed in relation to the context of his society.

In the second part of this section we will consider the stylistic aspect of Smith's discussion of *sympathy*. In particular we will suggest that his use of the dialogical trope provides a further illustration of his fundamental belief that the individual's capacity for feeling, acting and thinking is related to an intersubjectively shared world and life experience.

As we have noted above, Smith discusses the meaning of *sympathy* by sketching a number of imaginary situations. Smith repeatedly invites his readers to imagine themselves in the situations described and to explore with him the phenomenon of *sympathy*. Critics who have commented on this distinctive dialogic style of argument have tended to explain it as a remnant of the lectures which Smith gave on this subject to very young students at the university of Glasgow.[12] This, we believe, is too simplistic.

In reading the various sketches we are invited to imagine ourselves in a variety of situations which will help us to better understand the true meaning of sympathy in real life situations.[13] It is important to recognize that, by employing this dialogic method, Smith avoids referring to innate ideas and empirical data. Instead he actively discusses the meaning of the phenomenon of *sympathy* with his readers. That is to say, that the meaning has to be produced by exchange and intersubjective exploration of experiences and concepts which the situations depicted elicit in the author and his reader. This dialogic approach to the practical interpretation of *sympathy* indicates that Smith envisioned a form of scientific discourse that was significantly different from the positivism of the nineteenth and twentieth centuries. In addition to criteria such as generality, coherence, familiarity and beauty, Smith's discursive style suggests that the theories of moral philosophy should also meet the criteria of propriety. That is to say, they should demonstrate their value through their contribution to the social processes that give sense and meaning to life.[14] In Smith's case this meant that his moral philosophy should reflect the debate about the substantial and functional rationality of the evolving commercial society.

It has often been suggested that Smith mixed and matched various methodologies. His oeuvre has been variously described as a mixture of science, metaphysics and natural theology.[15] Even Macfie asserts that in Smith theism and deism rub shoulders with the empirical-analytical approach of conventional science.[16] Smith allegedly refers on the one hand to God as the highest judge and the ultimate source of the order observed in man's behaviour and social processes, while on the other hand he seems to argue like a 'true' scientist who, on the basis of observation, sets up and tests hypotheses about human behaviour and social processes.

In the light of these traditional interpretations of Smith's style of argument our own account might at first sight seem questionable or at least partial. Against this objection we would argue that Smith did not adhere to the objectivism which has been presupposed in traditional readings. While the traditional dichotomous interpretation assumes that Smith supported the idea of an order previously given to man, we suggest that Smith understood the order observed as being conceived intersubjectively in man's longing for a meaningful life. In this view notions, such as *nature* and *God*, do not have the objectivist connotation of representing a previously given order, but are concepts used in various discourses intended to give sense and meaning to life-experiences.

Anticipating a more extensive discussion in Chapters IV and V, it is useful to very briefly consider Smith's view of philosophy and science as a preface to the fuller consideration of his *sympathetic* theory of man and society. We will begin by discussing briefly Smith's view of philosophy and science as it is presented in *The History of Astronomy*, after which Smith's understanding of *system* will be explicated with reference to Part IV of *The Theory of Moral Sentiments*: 'Of the Effect of Utility upon the Sentiment of Approbation'.

In *The History of Astronomy* Smith argues that the observation of order implies an instance of creative conceptualization. This contrasts with the traditional objectivist view of modern science according to which observations are simply representations of an ontologically prior reality. While science is traditionally supposed to use these representations in order to set up and test hypotheses about the order immanent within the 'real' world, Smith discusses philosophical or scientific discourse as no more than the professionalization of the ordinary, every-

day urge of modern man to give sense and meaning to his life experience in the
context of admirable systems of belief. Smith even warns his reader that a theory
– also called a *system* or *doctrine* – may mistakenly be understood as the image
of a previously given, 'real' order because of its familiarity. In discussing
Newton's astronomy, in particular his theory of gravitation, Smith reminds us that
every theory or system is virtual.[17]

Smith's remark about the tendency to objectify and ascribe an independent
reality to a familiar order is of particular interest in understanding his use of terms
such as *nature* and *God, creator and highest judge*. While these terms have been
traditionally understood in an objectivist sense, in Smith's discourse they are
interpreted as concepts generated by the belief-systems people share in order to
give meaning to their lives. In Smith's texts we even find tell-tale qualifiers such
as 'as it seems' and 'as if' which warn against the trap of objectivism into which
we may be betrayed by the familiarity of our current belief-system.[18]

In Part IV of *The Theory of Moral Sentiments*, titled: 'Of the effect of utility
upon the sentiment of approbation', we find an illustration of Smith's unorthodox
interpretation of modern man's admiration for systems, which is of particular importance to the discourse on economic behaviour and action. While economists generally
adhere to the common view that economic behaviour is caused by the desire to
satisfy needs, Smith argues that utility is of little importance as a motive for human
behaviour and action. An individual's desire for a well-appointed and pleasant house,
for example, is hardly motivated by a need for shelter, rather, that desire has its
roots in the house's expected contribution to an imagined well-ordered system of
conveniences and wealth, which will bring the individual social acclaim.[19]

This interpretation of the effect of utility upon the sentiment of approbation –
discussed more extensively below – shows that Smith considers well-orderedness,
system and functionality to be important in understanding human behaviour and
action without, however, falling into the functionalist-objectivist trap of later
social scientists and economists.[20] It also explains Smith's concern with demonstrating the beauty of his own theories and systems. Smith's understanding of
sympathy led him to believe that the acceptance of his theories depended on the
aesthetic pleasure and admiration people would feel in perceiving their life and
world in the mirror of his theories.[21]

2 *Mutual Sympathy*: The Intersubjective Basis of Thought and Action

Rephrasing our account of Smith's reinterpretation of *sympathy* we may argue that
mutual sympathy is the metaphor through which Smith expresses his fundamental
belief that our feelings, thoughts and behaviour are related to an intersubjectively
based framework of rules and values. In Smith's view, *sympathy* is not synonymous with *pity* or *compassion* but denotes the human urge to share the feelings
of other people by imagining oneself in another's shoes. However, closer inspec-
tion has revealed that this is only one side of the story. The urge to share the

feelings of others appears to be accompanied by a craving for the acclaim of others. This desire for acclaim implies the existence of a continuous exchange of *sympathy feelings* which at the same time constitutes an intersubjectively framed set of values and rules of behaviour.

In this section we will consider this idea of *mutual sympathy* in greater detail and examine some of its wider implications for Smith's view of man and society.

To date a number of studies have acknowledged that *sympathy* is not synonymous with *benevolence*, i.e. the antithesis of *self-interest*. So too, integral readings of *The Theory of Moral Sentiments* and *The Wealth of Nations* are no longer exceptional. However, as yet, many new readings of Smith do not give due weight to the role of *mutual sympathy* in his thought as a whole. Three examples taken from integral readings illustrate this deficiency.

- In *Adam Smith and His Legacy for Modern Capitalism*, Patricia Werhane correctly points out that according to Smith the maintenance of a *commercial society* is dependent on the principle of justice. Werhane seems, however, to misunderstand Smith's idea of the *natural order of liberty and equity* – and, more generally, Smith's idea of the market economy – when she limits the relevancy of the concept of *mutual sympathy* to *The Theory of Moral Sentiments*, suggesting that Smith's view of the natural order resembles contemporaneous deistic views of order.[22]
- In *Adam Smith in His Time and Ours*, Jerry Z. Muller rightly demands attention for the important role Smith allots to institutions in coordinating economic behaviour in a commercial society. Given the current rivalry between (neo-)institutionalists and new institutionalists it is, however, interesting to consider Smith's view of institutions in greater detail.[23] Did he understand institutions from the perspective of methodological individualism or did he endorse methodological collectivism? Alternatively, is it possible that he employed an entirely different interpretive model which transcends the traditional opposition of individualism and collectivism? Smith's understanding of *sympathy* encourages us to believe that the latter is the case. The discussion of this aspect of Smith's view of the coordination of economic behaviour in a commercial society has only just begun.[24]
- In *A Reconsideration of 'Das Adam Smith Problem'*, Jean-Pierre Dupuy confirms our impression that Smith depicts the moral and social world as resting on the single principle of *sympathy*.[25] However, this understanding of the world is, according to Dupuy, self-defeating because of the disposition implied in *sympathy* to admire the rich and the great, and to despise and neglect persons of poor and mean condition.[26] On the basis of our discussion thus far, we might ask, 'how convincing is the conclusion that Smith's *sympathetic* theory of man and society is self-defeating?' It seems that Dupuy feels that the argument that 'the only way to overcome self-love is through even more self-love', is incompatible with the idea of *sympathy*.[27] But this quite clearly ignores Smith's argument that we need to understand self-interest in the context of man's urge for *sympathy*.

A consideration of Smith's *sympathetic* view of man and society helps us arrive at a better understanding of the ways in which the *sympathy* exchange coordinates and regulates behaviour. We will begin this consideration by focusing on the exchange of *sympathy* sentiments as the intersubjective process that produces and reproduces the rules and values which give meaning and guidance to feelings, thoughts and behaviour. Secondly, we will explore the commitment to *sympathy* in order to explicate the basic structure of the values and rules implied by *sympathy* itself.

1 At its simplest, *sympathy* denotes the interest we show in the fortune of others.. We imagine ourselves in the situation of other people and are pleased when we feel that we share the same motivation to act, or agree with a particular course of action and appreciate its merits as richly deserved.[28] According to Smith, it is from this interest in other people that we first become acquainted with shared values and the rules of behaviour:

> 'Our first ideas of personal beauty and deformity are drawn from the shape and appearance of others, not from our own ...
>   In the same manner our first moral criticisms are exercised upon the characters and conduct of other people; and we are all very forward to observe how each of these affects us.'[29]

The experience that *sympathy* is mutual – that we judge and are judged – gives rise to an exchange of *sympathy* sentiments which fosters our commitment to intersubjectively shared values and rules:

> 'But soon we learn, that other people are equally frank with regard to our own. We become anxious to know how far we deserve their censure or applause, and whether to them we must necessarily appear those agreeable or disagreeable creatures which they represent us.'[30]

> 'We suppose ourselves the spectators of our own behaviour, and endeavour to imagine what effect it would, in this light, produce upon us.'[31]

At first, we might be inclined to try and understand the impact of *sympathy*-sentiments such as praise and hate, on feelings, thought and behaviour as a direct cause and effect relationship. According to Smith, however, the influence of these sentiments is mediated by the values and rules which are intersubjectively produced in the process of sentiment-exchange. Praise, for instance, is only truly welcome when it is the expression of praiseworthiness:

> 'Man naturally desires, not only to be loved, but to be lovely; or to be that thing which is the natural and proper object of love. He naturally dreads, not only to be hated, but to be hateful; or to be that thing which is the natural and proper object of hatred. He desires, not only praise, but praiseworthiness; or to be that thing which, though it should be praised by nobody, is, however, the natural and proper object of praise. He dreads, not only blame, but blame-worthiness; or to be that thing which, though it should be blamed by nobody, is, however, the natural and proper object of blame.

The most sincere praise can give little pleasure when it cannot be considered as some sort of proof of praise-worthiness'.[32]

Smith distinguishes between *praise* and *praiseworthiness*, *blame* and *blameworthiness* and by means of these distinctions he explains why the same amount of praise or blame do not always affect us to the same extent. Just as on the market, actual or de facto market prices differ from natural prices, so in the commerce of people, actual or de facto fellow-feeling – e.g. praise or blame – happens to diverge from feelings ruled by social values referred to by notions such as *praiseworthiness* and *blameworthiness*. From the social perspective our behaviour appears to be finally ruled by these values: for example, *praise* without *praiseworthiness* is as unsatisfactory as *market prices* which differ from *natural prices*. From the perspective of the individual it becomes clear why actual or de facto behaviour and fellow-feeling often deviates from the behaviour and fellow-feeling we expect from shared social values and rules: actual or de facto behaviour and fellow-feeling reflect the personal interpretation of these values and rules by the individual actor and his fellow-men.

The analogy between Smith's discussion of the *sympathy*-mechanism and the coordination of behaviour on markets – i.e. the market mechanism – confirms our view that Smith perceived the emerging commercial society and its market economy as the final chapter in the evolution of *sympathy*.[33] This means that the commercialization of society, including the expanding market economy, is understood as the last stage in the evolution of a society in which the principle of *sympathy* will reach its fulfilment. In this society man will be completely free to feel, think and act in accordance with intersubjectively generated values and rules.

This understanding of the commercial society reflects the analogical use of the idea of the (free) market economy and, indeed this idea can help us better understand Smith's thought on the commercial society. The key question, however, is 'What is meant by the idea of the free market economy?'. Although we have yet to deal with Smith's interpretation of the market economy, our discussion of *sympathy* indicates that it has little in common with the interpretation advanced by Walrasian theory. Four remarks, anticipating later discussions, may help illustrate this point.

(1)   Smith's theory of *sympathy* presupposes a different interpretation of exchange and competition than that used in Walrasian general equilibrium analysis.

In Walrasian economics, exchange and competition are viewed as the effects of action and reaction by atomistic individuals. Where Walrasian economics argues that exchange and competition are not chaotic but well-organized it is because Walrasian theory implicitly complements its individualism with a special kind of collectivism. That is to say, the explanation of how free exchange between atomistic individuals can give rise to a well-ordered system is dependent on such conditioning assumptions as the *auctioneer* and *ends-means rationality* explicated in such rules as maximization of utility and profit.

Smith's *sympathetic* model has no need for such supplemental assumptions in order to account for the well-orderedness of free exchange, as the rules of behaviour and action are immanent to the process of exchange itself. As we have seen, the idea of *mutual sympathy* implies that an individual's personal identity, ambition and needs are not antecedent to the exchange, but are produced in the continuous processes of exchange in which the individual is engaged. In his urge for praise(worthiness) the individual subject confirms his adherence to shared rules and values when he expresses his personal interpretation of these rules and values in performing the exchange.

Comparing Smith's *sympathetic* model with the Walrasian general equilibrium approach we may conclude that what Smith understood as a dialogical process has in the Walrasian approach been separated into two distinct unilateral relations. In accordance with its individualist view, Walrasian economics explains socio-economic phenomena by reducing them to the behaviour and actions of the individual subjects, while at the same time the collectivist metaphor of the auctioneer is used to provide the rules of behaviour and action, which ensure that these very socio-economic phenomena can be deduced from atomistic individuals' behaviour and action.

The differences between the Walrasian and Smithian understanding of individual behaviour and action and the social-economic process of exchange is mirrored in the respective interpretations of *competition* and *concurrence*. In Smith's text these terms remain close to the original meanings of the Latin verbs *competere* and *concurrere*, which together suggest a dialectical relationship between rivalry and convergence by combining both meanings.[34] The Walrasian use, on the other hand, reflects current usage in which competition has come to mean exclusively *rivalry* while the meaning of *concurrence* has been reduced to *convergence* or *consensus*.

(2) Neoclassical economics, exemplified by the Walrasian general equilibrium analysis, has often been criticized for its failure to discuss real-world economies. Smith's economic realism will be discussed more fully below but it should already be apparent that the *sympathy* model is particularly well suited to the analysis of real-world economies.

Because the *sympathy* model is rooted in the concrete social and economic exchanges of daily life it is evident that a *sympathy*-based understanding of the production and distribution of wealth must necessarily deal with real-world economies. However, while having its roots in the concrete social and economic exchanges of daily life, the sympathy model cannot be dismissed as being concerned with mere contingencies. Smith's concept of *sympathy*, we should remember, transcends accidental instances of praise or blame, considering instead such general notions as *praiseworthiness* and the *impartial spectator* as they are expressed in the prevailing social rules and values.[35]

At the same time, we should not allow the general character of social rules and values to lead us into regarding them as abstract or a priori. Because of the dual *sympathy*-based relation between these rules and values on the one hand, and concrete behaviour and action on the other hand, the rules and values have to be conceived as general and concrete. They only express their full meaning and significance in the context of daily life.

(3) Understanding the dynamics of the *sympathy* exchange enables us to explain society as a well-ordered system. The processes of that exchange – communication, competition and concurrence – allow us to understand society as a system organized solely by man's predisposition to *mutual sympathy*.[36] Although Smith's vision of society as structured by *sympathy* makes it appear to be a well-designed machine, we should not conclude that his theory of man and society is mechanistic or functionalistic. Such an interpretation, common in traditional readings of Smith, runs contrary to the true meaning of *sympathy*.

The desire to be *praiseworthy* consequent on the longing for *sympathy* is not analogous to the a priori imperative – presupposed in Walrasian economics – to maximize utility under given constraints. The longing for *sympathy* and the desire for *praiseworthiness* is like participating in a game in which the players are also engaged in a dialogue about the game's rules. Thus, from Smith's perspective society looks like a self-regulating system but not in the traditional mechanistic or functionalistic sense. Rather, in its capacity for self-regulation, society resembles a discourse. People give meaning and sense to their lives through reference to shared rules and values: by (inter)acting they express, on the one hand, their interpretation of these rules and values and contribute, on the other hand, to the dialogical evolution of the same frame of reference.

The idea that society has to be understood as an open system rooted in intersubjectively shared rules and values is illustrated in Smith's discussion of situations where people are seriously affected by unwarranted disapproval.

'In such cases *[in which the judgments of the man within, though not, perhaps, absolutely altered or perverted – by the violence and loudness, with which blame is sometimes poured upon us – are, however, so much shaken in the steadiness and firmness of their decision, that their natural effect, in securing the tranquillity of the mind, is frequently in a great measure destroyed]*, the only effectual consolation of humbled and afflicted man lies in an appeal to a still higher tribunal, to that of the all-seeing Judge of the world, whose eye can never be deceived, and whose judgements can never be perverted.'[37]

The fact that unwarranted disapproval is possible shows that people's behaviour is not determined by a priori laws as is assumed in, for example, the Walrasian general equilibrium theory which permits no exchange except exchange at general equilibrium prices established by the auctioneer.[38] It is also in the experience of undeserved disapproval that we realize most clearly that we depend on the commitment of others in producing and validating a frame of reference regarding meaning and sense.[39] The threat of loosening the bond with the other is unbearable since it is inconceivable. Thus we cannot but extend the dialogical exchange of values and rules beyond the exchange with the partial real and the impartial ideal spectator to an exchange with the ultimate other, the *all-seeing Judge of the world*, God:

'Our happiness in this life is ..., upon many occasions, dependent upon the humble
hope and expectation of a life to come: a hope and expectation deeply rooted in
human nature; which can alone support its lofty ideas of its own dignity; can alone
illumine the dreary prospect of its continually approaching mortality, and maintain
its cheerfulness under all the heaviest calamities to which, from the disorders of this
life, it may sometimes be exposed. That there is a world to come, where exact justice
will be done to every man, where every man will be ranked with those who, in the
moral and intellectual qualities, are really his equals; where ...; is a doctrine, in every
respect so venerable, so comfortable to the weakness, so flattering to the grandeur of
human nature, that the virtuous man who has the misfortune to doubt of it, cannot
possibly avoid wishing most earnestly and anxiously to believe it.'[40]

(4) To fully understand Smith's theological references we have to consider them
in relation to the meaning of *sympathy* discussed above. The following quote
dealing with the perversion of theological doctrine by 'some of its most zealous
assertors' provides a further illustration:

'It could never have been exposed to the derision of the scoffer, had not the distribu-
tions of rewards and punishments, which some of its most zealous assertors have
taught us was to be made in that world to come, been too frequently in direct
opposition to all our moral sentiments.'[41]

Smith speaks of a *doctrine* in order to remind us that our ideas about God have
a human authorship and have been conceived in order to render our experiences
meaningful by interpreting them as part of an admirable, Divine, order.[42] The
reference to *the derision of the scoffer* underlines Smith's belief that our understanding of the world is based in the dialogical exchange of moral sentiments. A
doctrine will be adhered to if it corresponds to our moral sentiments and makes
them representative of a system which demands our admiration.

2 *Sympathy* denotes our deepest feelings of a pre-rational interest in the well-
being of the other, including the want to be loved and respected by the other. Our
lives and social world appear to be constituted by our urge for *sympathy*. The
patterns of behaviour and the social order we are part of, reflect the rules and
values we share in the dialogical exchange of *sympathetic* feelings. In the very
urge for *sympathy* we can even recognize that *sympathy* gives rise to these rules
and values. This in turn helps explain why it is that some rules seem so natural
that we are inclined to forget that they are *sympathy*-based.
    In order to explicate the preformative nature of *sympathy* with respect to rules
and values, let us review Smith's discussions of *direct* and *indirect sympathy* and
the virtues of *self-command*, *benevolence*, *justice* and *prudence*.
    According to Smith, feelings of *sympathy* can be further divided into *direct
sympathy*, where we identify with the feelings of the actor and his intentions, and
indirect sympathy where we identify with the feelings of the affected.[43] Smith's
examples of *direct sympathy* demonstrate that the intensity of our *sympathetic*
feelings correlates with the extent to which sentiments can be the object of
dialogical exchange. We expect other people to show self-control and temperance

regarding sentiments which we ourselves find difficult to entertain. For example, we can only sympathize with somebody who is suffering physical pain insofar as we are able to imagine his pain. Consequently if the one who suffers expects our sympathy he will have to temper his expression of his pain to ensure that we can imagine his experience and approve of his motives and affections. Extravagant displays of suffering which exceed our capacity for imaginative identification are alienating and produce feelings of aversion.[44]

Other examples show that our feelings of fellowship are not solely dependent on our *direct sympathy* with the goal, motivation or manner of behaviour and action. We also recognize that our *sympathy* will, indirectly, be more intense when we feel that the affects induced by the action are agreeable and the affected are grateful to their benefactor.[45] Absence of gratitude or even of the motivation of benevolence with the actor tempers the feelings of *sympathy* but does not transform them into feelings of indignation, hatred or resentment. We even sympathize with people whose behaviour is motivated by prudence or proper self-interest.

Our feelings, however, are totally different in the case of injury – for example, when self-interested behaviour harms other people – and conflict with our feelings of what is fair.[46] In Smith's examples justice is presented as an attitude which, unlike benevolence or compassion is enforceable. In this respect it seems to be unique.[47] The principles of *justice* can be precisely translated into words which demand, in turn, to be strictly obeyed. Consequently, Smith compares the rules of justice to the rules of grammar. The rules of benevolence, self-command and prudence, by way of contrast, are compared to the stylistic advice a book reviewer may give to an author in order to improve the sublimity and elegance of a text.[48]

If we consider the normative pattern immanent to *sympathy* from a functional perspective it will be obvious that the pattern encourages social coherence. The principle of *sympathy* appears once again to be an admirable organizing principle. *Benevolence* and *gratitude* enlarge the beauty of a society, but in their absence, society loses only its polish. *Justice*, however, is indispensable. Society will disintegrate, when people deny each other the right to live a social life, i.e. the right to give a personal expression to the shared values and norms, or the right to be treated as equals in the dialogical exchange of *sympathy*.[49]

In Smith's account of social behaviour, general principles of conduct play a central role:

'The regard to those general rules of conduct *[i.e. the general Rules of Morality]*, is what is properly called a sense of duty, a principle of the greatest consequence in human life, and the only principle by which the bulk of mankind are capable of directing their actions.'[50]

With regard to the rules of *justice* Smith argues that,

'upon the tolerable observance of these duties, depends the very existence of human society, which would crumble into nothing if mankind were not generally impressed with a reverence for those important rules of conduct.'[51]

Religion and philosophy are understood as part of the framework which gave meaning and sense to these rules:

> 'religion, even in its rudest form, gave a sanction to the rules of morality, long before the age of artificial reasoning and philosophy. That the terrors of religion should thus enforce the natural sense of duty, was of too much importance to the happiness of mankind, for nature to leave it dependent upon the slowness and uncertainty of philosophical researches.'[52]

Smith, however, criticizes scholars who deal with the *general rules of conduct* as if they were absolute and ultimate laws. According to Smith, the very existence and efficacy of these rules has misled scholars into thinking of them as pre-given laws.[53] Smith agrees with these scholars with respect to the influence of such rules, and he even calls them *general rules*:

> 'There is scarce any man, however, who by discipline, education, and example, may not be so impressed with a regard to general rules, as to act upon almost every occasion with tolerable decency, and through the whole of his life to avoid any considerable degree of blame.'[54]

However, Smith disagrees with the interpretation of the general rules as absolute and ultimate laws. In the passage above Smith points out in his reference to man's tendency to avoid any considerable degree of blame, that all rules and principles end up in the dialogical exchange of *sympathy*.[55]

According to the sympathetic model, law and all other institutions by which 'the bulk of people are capable of directing their actions', are sedimentary products of the values and rules generated in the dialogical exchange of *sympathy* sentiments. Smith did not extensively discuss these *sediments* in *The Theory of Moral Sentiments*, since he planned to give an account of them in a later discourse.[56] In publishing *The Wealth of Nations* he executed this plan in so far as it concerned *police, revenue and arms*.[57]

In *The Theory of Moral Sentiments* Smith confined himself to explicating the *sympathetic* view of man and society. In the following section we will explore his *sympathy*-based account of man's continuous struggle for wealth, rank and distinction more extensively. Before discussing Smith's discourse of the free market economy in *The Wealth of Nations* we have to familiarize ourselves with his *sympathetic* interpretation of concepts such as *self-interest*, *utility* and *wealth*, i.e. concepts which are central to modern economic thought.

3 *Sympathy* and Wealth

Sympathetically understood society looks like a system regulated by an *invisible hand*: social activity is well-ordered because people share values and rules which are intersubjectively reproduced or transformed by behaviour and action.

In the previous section we highlighted the social aspect of the *sympathy* principle: we considered the way that people share values and rules in giving meaning and sense to their lives and world. In this section we will focus on the concept of *sympathy* as it relates to the individual. According to Smith, people intersubjectively reproduce or transform values and rules in their thoughts, feelings, and behaviour which in effect constitute their personal interpretation of these values and rules. In the dialogical exchange implicit in Smith's concept of *sympathy* we discover our individual identity against the background of a common frame of values and rules, and vice versa.

By means of various examples Smith tried to show that we sympathize with prudence or proper self-interest, and that we even expect people to take care of themselves. In our *sympathy* for prudence we feel, so to say, that,

'as he *[i.e. Every man]* is fitter to take care of himself than of any other person, it is fit and right that it should be so.'[58]

and further, that,

'The care of the health, of the fortune, of the rank and reputation of the individual, the objects upon which his comfort and happiness in this life are supposed principally to depend, is considered as the proper business of that virtue which is commonly called Prudence.'[59]

Comparing this *sympathetic* interpretation with, for example, Walrasian general equilibrium interpretations of man's care of his own comfort and happiness, it is clear that Smith did not anticipate the mechanics of rationalistic-individualistic economic behaviour. Passages such as these indicate that in Smith's view a discussion about wealth, fortune, rank and distinction is part of an all-encompassing discourse about man and society based in a dialogical exchange of *sympathetic* feelings. This does not mean that concepts such as *self-interest, utility* or a *well-ordered prosperous economy* are of no importance in Smith's discussions of economics and wealth, but rather that they are used within a different conceptual framework. In the following pages the incompatibility of Smith's and the well-known Walrasian general equilibrium theory will be illustrated through reference to Smith's discussion of utility.

In Smith's view the argument that economic behaviour is governed by self-interest does not contradict the idea that man is a social being. Self-interest is in fact a necessary part of our longing for *(mutual) sympathy*. Thus he writes that,

'Though it is in order to supply the necessities and conveniencies of the body, that the advantages of external fortune are originally recommended to us, yet we cannot live long in the world without perceiving that the respect of our equals, our credit and rank in the society we live in, depend very much upon the degree in which we possess, or are supposed to possess those advantages. The desire of becoming the proper objects of this respect, of deserving and obtaining this credit and rank among our equals is, perhaps, the strongest of all our desires, and our anxiety to obtain the advantages of fortune is accordingly much more excited and irritated by this desire, than by that of supplying all the necessities and conveniencies of the body, which are always very easily supplied.'[60]

Smith warns us against the fallacious idea, taken for granted in economic science, that people acquire things because of their expected utility. Referring to our daily-life experience, Smith argues that we strive for wealth and power not because we are hungry, thirsty or in need of shelter, but because we expect admiration and praise when people see our well-organized system of conveniencies and comfort:

> 'For to what purpose is all the toil and bustle of this world? what is the end of avarice and ambition, of the pursuit of wealth, of power, and preheminence? Is it to supply the necessities of nature? The wages of the meanest labourer can supply them. We see that they afford him food and clothing, the comfort of a house, and of a family. If we examined his oeconomy with rigour, we should find that he spends a great part of them upon conveniences, which may be regarded as superfluities, and that, upon extraordinary occasions, he can give something even to vanity and distinction. What then is the cause of our aversion to this situation, and why should those who have been educated in the higher ranks of life, regard it as worse than death, to be reduced to live, even without labour, upon the same simple fare with him, to dwell under the same lowly roof, and to be clothed in the same humble attire? Do they imagine that their stomach is better, or their sleep sounder in a palace than in a cottage? The contrary has been so often observed, and, indeed, is so very obvious, though it had never been observed, that there is nobody ignorant of it. From whence, then, arises that emulation which runs through all the different ranks of men, and what are the advantages which we propose by that great purpose of human life which we call bettering our condition? To be observed, to be attended to, to be taken notice of with sympathy, complacency, and approbation, are all the advantages which we can propose to derive from it.'[61]

If we imagine ourselves in the situations alternatively of the rich and of the poor, we will recognize that it is easier to *sympathize* with the rich than with the poor. This indicates that it is the dynamics of *sympathy* itself which encourages us to avoid poverty and to amass riches:

> 'It is because mankind are disposed to sympathize more entirely with our joy than with our sorrow, that we make parade of our riches, and conceal our poverty. Nothing is so mortifying as to be obliged to expose our distress to the view of the public and to feel, that though our situation is open to the eyes of all mankind, no mortal conceives for us the half of what we suffer. Nay, it is chiefly from this regard to the sentiments of mankind, that we pursue riches and avoid poverty.'[62]

Our recognition that fortune and riches more easily evoke the *sympathy* of others also helps us understand the *distinction of ranks* and the *order of society*:

> 'Upon this disposition of mankind, to go along with all the passions of the rich and the powerful, is founded the distinction of ranks, and the order of society. Our obsequiousness to our superiors more frequently arises from our admiration for the advantages of their situation, than from any private expectations of benefit from their good-will. Their benefits can extend but to a few; but their fortunes interest almost everybody. We are eager to assist them in completing a system of happiness that approaches so near to perfection; and we desire to serve them for their own sake, without any other recompense but the vanity or the honour of obliging them. Neither

is our deference to their inclinations founded chiefly, or altogether, upon a regard to the utility of such submission, and to the order of society, which is best supported by it. Even when the order of society seems to require that we should oppose them, we can hardly bring ourselves to do it. That kings are the servants of the people, to be obeyed, resisted, deposed, or punished, as the public conveniency may require, is the doctrine of reason and philosophy; but it is not the doctrine of Nature. Nature would teach us to submit to them for their own sake, to tremble and bow down before their exalted station, to regard their smile as a reward sufficient to compensate any services, and to dread their displeasure, though no other evil were to follow from it, as the severest of all mortifications.'[63]

This passage clearly illustrates Smith's understanding of the *order of society* – in particular its *distinction of ranks* – in relation to *sympathy*. The admiration of riches and power encourages people to become rich and powerful as well as to be loyal and devoted to the rich and mighty.[64] Smith thus subordinates utility in the traditional sense of private expectations of benefit to the fascination of the well-ordered system of comfort and happiness.

In Part IV of *The Theory of Moral Sentiments* Smith deals more extensively with what he calls 'the Effect of Utility upon the Sentiment of Approbation', explaining his view of the effect of wealth and power on the exchange of moral sentiments through a discussion of the meaning of *utility*. In line with other discussions about efficiency, order and system, Smith begins this reinterpretation of utility by calling attention to the agreeable feelings which the beauty and propriety of a system or machine evoke when it is fit to produce its intended end.

'That utility is one of the principal sources of beauty has been observed by every body, who has considered with any attention what constitutes the nature of beauty. The conveniency of a house gives pleasure to the spectator as well as its regularity, and he is as much hurt when he observes the contrary defect, as when he sees the correspondent windows of different forms, or the door not placed exactly in the middle of the building. That the fitness of any system or machine to produce the end for which it was intended, bestows a certain propriety and beauty upon the whole, and renders the very thought and contemplation of it agreeable, is so very obvious that nobody had overlooked it.'[65]

'The utility of any object, ..., pleases the master by perpetually suggesting to him the pleasure or conveniency which it is fitted to promote. Every time he looks at it, he is put in mind of this pleasure; and the object in this manner becomes a source of perpetual satisfaction and enjoyment. The spectator enters by sympathy into the sentiments of the master, and necessarily views the object under the same agreeable aspect. When we visit the palaces of the great, we cannot help conceiving the satisfaction we should enjoy if we ourselves were the masters, and were possessed of so much artful and ingeniously contrived accommodation.'[66]

According to Smith, this interpretation of the effect of utility from the perspective of beauty was not new, but nobody had previously noticed that in daily life the fitness of a system was more valued than the end for which it was intended:

'But that this fitness, this happy contrivance of any production of art, should often be more valued, than the very end for which it was intended; and that the exact adjustment of the means for attaining any conveniency or pleasure, should frequently be more regarded, than that very conveniency or pleasure, in the attainment of which their whole merit would seem to consist, has not, so far as I know, been yet taken notice of by any body. That this however is very frequently the case, may be observed in a thousand instances, both in the most frivolous and in the most important concerns of human life.'[67]

Thus Smith does not disagree with the economists' assertion that the notion of *utility* is important in explaining economic behaviour. However, he would criticize economists who reduce economic behaviour to a utilitarian calculus, expressed in a hypothesis such as maximizing utility under constraints.

'How many people ruin themselves by laying out money on trinkets of frivolous utility? What pleases these lovers of toys is not so much the utility, as the aptness of the machines which are fitted to promote it. All their pockets are stuffed with little conveniences.

Nor is it only with regard to such frivolous objects that our conduct is influenced by this principle; it is often the secret motive of the most serious and important pursuits of both private and public life.

The poor man's son, whom heaven in its anger has visited with ambition, when he begins to look around him, admires the condition of the rich. ... He thinks if he had attained all these, he would sit still contentedly, and be quiet, enjoying himself in the thought of the happiness and tranquillity of his situation. He is enchanted with the distant idea of this felicity. It appears in his fancy like the life of some superior rank of beings, and, in order to arrive at it, he devotes himself for ever to the pursuit of wealth and greatness.'[68]

Smith would disagree with those economists who, from a functionalist perspective, interpret *utility* exclusively according to intended ends. According to Smith, *utility* has to be understood from the perspective of people's longing for *sympathy*. Wealth and power suggest in their arrangement of things an agreeable order of comfort and happiness, which elicits the admiration and praise of fellow-men, and it is because of this impression that people compete with each other for wealth and power.

Concluding this section on *sympathy* and *wealth*, we again highlight three aspects of the difference between Smith's view and the Walrasian view of economic behaviour.

1 In contrast to Walrasian general equilibrium theorists, Smith did not deal with economics as a science separate from other philosophical or scientific discourses on man and society. We have argued that Smith's economics has to be understood as part of a wider, more encompassing moral philosophy. *The Theory of Moral Sentiments* shows that Smith discusses economic behaviour in relation to man's longing for *sympathy*. This, however, does not mean that Smith failed to distinguish between economics and other parts of moral philosophy. As we know, Smith published his discourse on law and government as a separate volume, i.e. *The Wealth of Nations*.

The following passage helps us to understand Smith's vision of economic behaviour as a competition for wealth and rank and distinction generated by man's longing for *sympathy*:

'Our imagination, which in pain and sorrow seems to be confined and cooped up within our own persons, in times of ease and prosperity expands itself to everything around us. We are then charmed with the beauty of that accommodation which reigns in the palaces and oeconomy of the great; and admire how every thing is adapted to promote their ease, to prevent their wants, to gratify their wishes, and to amuse and entertain their most frivolous desires. ... The pleasures of wealth and greatness, ..., strike the imagination as something grand and beautiful and noble, of which the attainment is well worth all the toil and anxiety which we are apt to bestow upon it. ... It is this deception which rouses and keeps in continual motion the industry of mankind. It is which first prompted them to cultivate the ground, to build houses, to found cities and commonwealths, and to invent and improve all the sciences and arts, which ennoble and embellish human life; which have entirely changed the whole face of the globe, have turned the rude forests of nature into agreeable and fertile plains, and made the trackless and barren ocean a new fund of subsistence, and the great high road of communication to the different nations of the earth. ... It is to no purpose, that the proud and unfeeling landlord views his extensive fields, and without a thought for the wants of his brethren, in imagination consumes himself the whole harvest that grows upon them. The homely and vulgar proverb, that the eye is larger than the belly, never was more fully verified than with regard to him. The capacity of his stomach bears no proportion to the immensity of his desires, and will receive no more than that of the meanest peasant. The rest he is obliged to distribute among those, who prepare, in the nicest manner, that little which he himself makes use of, among those who fit up the palace in which this little is to be consumed, among those who provide and keep in order all the different baubles and trinkets, which are employed in the oeconomy of greatness; all of whom thus derive from his luxury and caprice, that share of the necessaries of life, which they would in vain have expected from his humanity or his justice.'[69]

Competition for wealth, rank and distinction implies that people share a system of values and rules which distinguishes itself as economic from other systems of values and rules. From this point of view economics is the discourse of this economic system and is, as such, autonomous in relation to the encompassing discourse on *sympathy*.

2   Anticipating a more extensive explanation in Chapter IV, we may argue that Smith would also criticize the Walrasian general equilibrium theory for its exclusively abstract approach:

'When we consider virtue and vice in an abstract and general manner, the qualities by which they excite these several sentiments seem in a great measure to disappear, and the sentiments themselves become less obvious and discernible. On the contrary, the happy effects of the one and the fatal consequences of the other seem then to rise up to the view, and as it were to stand out and distinguish themselves from all the other qualities of either.'[70]

This mistrust of the abstract and general is further reflected in Smith's criticism of the philosopher who 'is ... contented with the vague and indeterminate idea which the general names ... suggest to him':

'When a philosopher goes to examine why humanity is approved of, or cruelty condemned, he does not always form to himself, in a very clear and distinct manner, the conception of any particular action either of cruelty or of humanity, but is commonly contented with the vague and indeterminate idea which the general names of those qualities suggest to him. But it is in particular instances only that the propriety or impropriety, the merit or demerit of actions is very obvious and discernible.'[71]

It is in line with this critique that Smith would expect the ideas presented in a discourse on economic behaviour to be concrete, i.e. interpreted and discussed in relation to real life situations. Only in relation to real life situations will they adequately contribute to the intersubjective exchange of values and rules in society.

3 In Smith's view the discourse of economics, as part of a more encompassing moral philosophy, is important for its role in backing-up the *sympathy*-induced competition in society for wealth, rank and distinction:

'if you would implant public virtue in the breast of him who seems heedless of the interest of his country, it will often be to no purpose to tell him, what superior advantages the subjects of a well-governed state enjoy; that they are better lodged, that they are better clothed, that they are better fed. These considerations will commonly make no great impression. You will be more likely to persuade, if you describe the great system of public police which procures these advantages, if you explain the connexions and dependencies of its several parts, their mutual subordination to one another, and their general subserviency to the happiness of the society; if you show how this system might be introduced into his own country, what it is that hinders it from taking place there at present, how those obstructions might be removed, and all the several wheels of the machine of government be made to move with more harmony and smoothness, without grating upon one another, or mutually retarding one another's motions. It is scarce possible that a man should listen to a discourse of this kind, and not feel himself animated to some degree of public spirit. He will, at least for the moment, feel some desire to remove those obstructions, and to put into motion so beautiful and so orderly a machine. Nothing tends so much to promote public spirit as the study of politics, of the several systems of civil government, their advantages and disadvantages, of the constitution of our own country, its situation, and interest with regard to foreign nations, its commerce, its defence, the disadvantages it labours under, the dangers to which it may be exposed, how to remove the one, and how to guard against the other. Upon this account political disquisitions, if just, and reasonable, and practicable, are of all the works of speculation the most useful. Even the weakest and the worst of them are not altogether without their utility. They serve at least to animate the public passions of men, and rouse them to seek out the means of promoting the happiness of the society.'[72]

The discourse of economics is important to society because it addresses the conceptions of order people adhere to in giving meaning and sense to their economic behaviour. However, in his critique of his learned friend Hume, Smith also warns us against considering virtue and vice in an abstract and general manner and degrading economics to a functionalistic discourse about efficiency in marrying means to ends:

'When we consider virtue and vice in an abstract and general manner, the qualities by which they excite these several sentiments seem in a great measure to disappear, and the sentiments themselves become less obvious and discernible. On the contrary, the happy effects of the one and the fatal consequences of the other seem then to rise up to the view, and as it were to stand out and distinguish themselves from all the other qualities of either.

The same ingenious and agreeable author who first explained why utility pleases, has been so struck with this view of things, as to resolve our whole approbation of virtue into a perception of this species of beauty which results from the appearance of utility. ... But still I affirm, that it is not the view of this utility or hurtfulness which is either the first or principal source of our approbation and disapprobation. These sentiments are no doubt enhanced and enlivened by the perception of the beauty or deformity which results from this utility or hurtfulness. But still, I say, they are originally and essentially different from this perception.'[73]

The discourse on the economic system will be a meaningful discourse insofar as it is related to the dialogical exchange of *sympathy*.

4 Society in the Age of Commerce

In discussing man's struggle for wealth, rank and distinction, Smith pointed to a bias in favour of the rich and powerful with whom we sympathize more readily than with the weak and poor. At first sight this seems to suggest there is a major flaw in Smith's *sympathetic* theory of man and society. According to Smith the care for the *bonum commune* can be entrusted to the free and fair exchange of moral sentiments. However, the bias in the *sympathy* exchange towards riches and power seems to provide proof to the contrary.

Smith devoted an entire chapter of *The Theory of Moral Sentiments* to this problem, namely,

'Of the corruption of our moral sentiments, which is occasioned by this disposition to admire the rich and the great, and to despise or neglect persons of poor and mean condition.'[74]

In this chapter Smith points out that although the bias in *sympathy* is essential to the order of society and prosperity, it is at the same time the great and most universal cause of the corruption of our moral sentiments:

'This disposition to admire, and almost to worship, the rich and the powerful, and to despise, or, at least, to neglect persons of poor and mean condition, though necessary both to establish and to maintain the distinction of ranks and the order of society, is, at the same time, the great and most universal cause of the corruption of our moral sentiments.'[75]

Smith mentions that moralists have complained of the corruption of moral sentiments by riches in all ages:

> 'That wealth and greatness are often regarded with the respect and admiration which
> are due only to wisdom and virtue; and that the contempt, of which vice and folly
> are the only proper objects, is often most unjustly bestowed upon poverty and
> weakness, has been the complaint of moralists in all ages.'[76]

Smith, however, disagrees with the moralists who claim that the *bonum commune*
has to be safeguarded by a priori laws which stimulate benevolence and restrict
self-interest. He acknowledges that the admiration of mere wealth and greatness
does not accord with traditional values and norms. At the same time, however, he
feels that we must acknowledge that people admire the rich and powerful. Thus,
admiration itself has to be interpreted as an indication that wealth and power are
also in some respects valuable:

> 'It is scarce agreeable to good morals, or even to good language, perhaps, to say, that
> mere wealth and greatness, abstracted from merit and virtue, deserve our respect. We
> must acknowledge, however, that they almost constantly obtain it; and that they may,
> therefore, be considered as, in some respects, the natural objects of it.'[77]

However persuasive a theory about the good life might be to the wise and
virtuous, we should always listen to the dialogical exchange of moral sentiments
in real life. When we discover that wealth and greatness are part of people's
sympathy-values, we have to respect this frame of reference in our dialogue about
values and norms. From the perspective of the wise and virtuous the acquisition
of wealth and greatness is by no means the ideal motivation for behaviour and
action. However, when we look at the great mob of mankind who admire and
worship these values, it is most frequently with a disinterestness which reminds
us of the impartial spectator:

> 'The great mob of mankind are the admirers and worshippers, and, what may seem
> more extraordinary, most frequently the disinterested admirers and worshippers, of
> wealth and greatness.'[78]

The virtuous and wise who try to live according to exalted ideas of the good life
might despise the way the greater part of humanity behave in their inferior and
middling stations of life. From Smith's perspective this is, however, not very
relevant to understanding and assessing the morals of society. Most people live
in inferior and middling stations of life and in these situations the road to virtue
almost coincides with the road to fortune:

> 'In the middling and inferior stations of life, the road to virtue and that to fortune,
> to such fortune, at least as men in such stations can reasonably expect to acquire, are,
> happily in most cases, very nearly the same. In all the middling and inferior pro-
> fessions, real and solid professional abilities, joined to prudent, just, firm, and
> temperate conduct, can very seldom fail of success. Abilities will even sometimes

prevail where the conduct is by no means correct. Either habitual imprudence, however, or injustice, or weakness, or profligacy, will always cloud, and sometimes depress altogether, the most splendid professional abilities. Men in the inferior and middling stations of life, besides, can never be great enough to be above the law, which must generally overawe them into some sort of respect for, at least, the more important rules of justice. The success of such people, too, almost always depends upon the favour and good opinion of their neighbours and equals; and without a tolerably regular conduct these can very seldom be obtained. The good old proverb, therefore, That honesty is the best policy, holds, in such situations, almost always perfectly true. In such situations, therefore, we may generally expect a considerable degree of virtue; and, fortunately for the good morals of society, these are the situations of by far the greater part of mankind.'[79]

There is no reason to fear that these people in their struggle for advancement will inevitably affect social morality. In their struggle for success people of inferior and middling stations of life actually recognize and express the importance of a proper exchange of moral sentiments:

'In the race for wealth, and honours, and preferments, he may run as hard as he can, and strain every nerve and every muscle, in order to outstrip all his competitors. But if he should justle, or throw down any of them, the indulgence of the spectators is entirely at an end. It is a violation of fair play, which they cannot admit of. This man is to them, in every respect, as good as he: they do not enter into that self-love by which he prefers himself so much to this other, and cannot go along with the motive from which he hurt him. They readily, therefore, sympathize with the natural resentment of the injured, and the offender becomes the object of their hatred and indignation. He is sensible that he becomes so, and feels that those sentiments are ready to burst out from all sides against him.'[80]

Not only does this interpretation of the people's interest in wealth explain why Smith disagreed with older moralists who had claimed that the *bonum commune* could only be safeguarded by laws which stimulate benevolence and restrict self-interest, it also suggests the explanation for Smith's plea in *The Wealth of Nations* for further expanding and improving the free market economy. The best safeguard against the corruption of moral sentiments is not to impede free and fair exchange, but to encourage the competition and concurrence of *sympathy* by generating a social context in which as many people as possible feel themselves committed to a direct, free and fair competition for praiseworthiness. This means that people who live in the inferior and middling stations of life, should not be obstructed in their struggle for wealth. On the contrary, their competence and will to compete has to be strengthened. Thus, when we return to Dupuy's argument that Smith's theory of *sympathy* is self-defeating because of its implied bias in favour of the rich and the great, we can see that it rests on an incomplete understanding of Smith's theory of sympathy.

Smith's argument in the *Lectures of Jurisprudence* and *The Wealth of Nations* that the commercial society of his day was superior to social structures of the past, does not contradict the *sympathy* theory of man and society advanced in *The Theory of Moral Sentiments*. However, we have to realize that Smith's interpretation of the term *commerce* differs significantly from present usage. While today the meaning of *commerce* is commonly reduced to 'trade intended to make a profit', Smith uses the term to describe an harmonious intercourse.[81] With reference to this interpretation of *commerce*, a society in the age of commerce – i.e. a commercial society – is understood as a society in which people, in free association with one another, express themselves freely in accordance with shared values and rules, or a society which is characterized by free, direct competition and concurrence according to the principle of *mutual sympathy*.

In the commercial society of his own time Smith saw that free exchange had become more than ever before the medium in which people found their values and rules for behaviour and action. The old feudal institutions and their legal expressions, such as the right of the first-born, which appeared to foster the corruption of the moral sentiments, were disappearing. It was becoming more difficult for the rich and powerful to escape the direct public competition and concurrence of *sympathy*. The bulk of people in the inferior and middling stations of life had become more involved in these processes of competition and concurrence, not just because of the new freedom of movement and action but also because of the greater prosperity in the new commercial societies. Greater prosperity renders people more sensitive to the opinion of others concerning their rank in society. Thus, free commerce is not a threat to *sympathy* and good morals; it reflects a new phase in the evolution of the *sympathy*-processes in which man gives sense and meaning to his life and world.[82]

Notes

1. TMS I.i.1.1.
2. For example:
    'Of this kind is pity or compassion, the emotion which we feel for the misery of others, when we either see it, or are made to conceive it in a very lively manner.'
    (TMS I.i.1.1)

    'When we see a stroke aimed and just ready to fall upon the leg or arm of another person, we naturally shrink and draw back our own leg or our own arm; and when it does fall, we feel it in some measure, and are hurt by it as well as the sufferer.'
    (TMS I.i.1.3)
3. TMS I.i.1.5. See also TMS I.iii.1.1 and VII.i.4.
4. TMS I.i.2.1.
5. TMS III.1.5.
6. See for instance TMS I.i.2.4:
    'How are the unfortunate relieved when they have found out a person to whom they can communicate the cause of their sorrow? Upon his sympathy they seem to disburthen themselves of a part of their distress; he is not improperly said to share it with them.'
7. See TMS I.i.2.1. See also TMS III.2.27:
    'Some splenetic philosophers, in judging of human nature, have done as peevish individuals are apt to do in judging of the conduct of one another, and have imputed to the love of praise, or to what they call vanity, every action which ought to be ascribed to

that of praise-worthiness. I shall hereafter have occasion to give an account of some of their systems, and shall not at present stop to examine them.'

In the last sentence, Smith refers to TMS VII.ii.4, in which he criticises the philosophy of Mandeville in particular.

8. TMS I.i.2.6.
9. TMS III.1.3. See also TMS III.3.4.
10. Altruism and altruistic behaviour were seen as the counterweight against selfishness and selfish behaviour, enabling men to naturally form a social community with others, without interference from the authorities. See TMS III.3.4 for Smith's rejection of this view.
11. Macfie, A.L., *The Individual in Society*, London, 1967, for instance pp. 3, 44 and 57. Cf. TMS II.iii.1.
12. See Raphael, D.D. and A.L. Macfie, 'Introduction' in *Adam Smith. The Theory of Moral Sentiments*, Oxford, 1976/1991, p. 5.
13. See also pp. 83–85.
14. Compare Lindgren, J., *The Social Philosophy of Adam Smith*, The Hague, 1973, pp. 15–19. For Smith's view of moral philosophy see TMS VII.ii.4.14.
15. Campbell, T., *Adam Smith's Science of Morals*, London, 1971, pp. 46 and 221–234.
16. Macfie, A.L., *The Individual in Society*, London, 1967, pp. 107–108.
17. EPS Astronomy, IV.76. Cf. Peil, J., 'Adam Smith en economische wetenschap' in Berns, E. (ed.), *Adam Smith. Ethiek, Politiek, Economie*, Tilburg, 1986, p. 301. In chapter V we take a closer look at Smith's view of science.
18. See also Lindgren, J., *The Social Philosophy of Adam Smith*, The Hague, 1973, p. 7.
19. Part IV of *The Theory of Moral Sentiments* consists of two sections:

    'Of the beauty which the appearance of *Utility* bestows upon all the production of art, and of the extensive influence of this species of Beauty.

    Of the beauty which the appearance of Utility bestows upon the characters and actions of men; and how far the perception of this beauty may be regarded as one of the original principles of approbation.'
20. See among others TMS IV.1.9–11 and TMS IV.2.3.
21. That Smith was conscious of this effect of functional beauty, appears also from the passage in *The Theory of Moral Sentiments* in which it is pointed out that somebody feels more directly addressed by the general interest, when it is pointed out to him what an impressive system his society forms:

    'if you would implant public virtue in the breast of him who seems heedless of the interest of his country, it will often be to no purpose to tell him, what superior advantages the subjects of a well-governed state enjoy; that they are better lodged, that they are better clothed, that they are better fed. These considerations will commonly make no great impression. You will be more likely to persuade, if you describe the great system of public police which procures these advantages, if you explain the connexions and dependencies of its several parts, their mutual subordination to one another, and their general subserviency to the happiness of the society; if you show how this system might be introduced into his own country, what it is that hinders it from taking place there at present, how those obstructions might be removed, and all the several wheels of the machine of government be made to move with more harmony and smoothness, without grating upon one another, or mutually retarding one another's motions. It is scarce possible that a man should listen to a discourse of this kind, and not feel himself animated to some degree of public spirit.'
    (TMS IV.1.11)
22. Werhane, P.H., *Adam Smith and His Legacy for Modern Capitalism*, New York, 1991, for instance pp. 17, 21, 46, 49–51, 53, 59, 68–69 and 96–100.

23. For a brief discussion of the *old* and *new* institutionalism see, for instance, Hodgson, G.M., 'Institutionalism, "Old" and "New"', in Hodgson, G.M., Samuels, W. and M. Tool (eds.), *The Elgar Companion to Institutional and Evolutionary Economics*, Brookfield, 1994, pp. 397–402.

24. Muller, J.Z., *Adam Smith in His Time and Ours: Designing the Decent Society*, New York, 1993, see among others pp. 2, 6, 106 and 115–116.

25. 'Smith himself, in The Theory of Moral Sentiments, depicts the moral and social world as resting on a single principle: sympathy.'

    (Dupuy, J.-P., 'A Reconsideration of *Das Adam Smith Problem*, *Stanford French Review*, 1993(17), p. 46)

26. Id., pp. 55–57.

27. Id., p. 48.

28. See, for instance, TMS I.i.3–4.

29. TMS III.1.4–5.

30. TMS III.1.5. Compare also the following passage:

    'As the love and admiration which we naturally conceive for some characters, dispose us to wish to become ourselves the proper objects of such agreeable sentiments; so the hatred and contempt which we as naturally conceive for others, dispose us, perhaps still more strongly, to dread the very thought of resembling them in any respect.'
    (TMS III.2.9)

31. TMS III.1.5. Compare also the following passage:

    'When I endeavour to examine my own conduct, when I endeavour to pass sentence upon it, and either to approve or condemn it, it is evident that, in all such cases, I divide myself, as it were, into two persons; and that I, the examiner and judge, represent a different character from that other I, the person whose conduct is examined into and judged of. The first is the spectator, whose sentiments with regard to my own conduct I endeavour to enter into, by placing myself in his situation, and by considering how it would appear to me, when seen from that particular point of view. The second is the agent, the person whom I properly call myself, and of whose conduct, under the character of a spectator, I was endeavouring to form some opinion.'
    (TMS III.1.6)

32. TMS III.2.1 and III.2.4. See also the following passage:

    'As ignorant and groundless praise can give no solid joy, no satisfaction that will bear any serious examination, so, on the contrary, it often gives real comfort to reflect, that though no praise should actually be bestowed upon us, our conduct, however, has been such as to deserve it, and has been in every respect suitable to those measures and rules by which praise and approbation are naturally and commonly bestowed. We are pleased, not only with praise, but with having done what is praise-worthy. We are pleased to think that we have rendered ourselves the natural objects of approbation, though no approbation should ever actually be bestowed upon us: and we are mortified to reflect that we have justly merited the blame of those we live with, though that sentiment should never actually be exerted against us.'
    (TMS III.2.5)

33. Cf. TMS II.ii.3.1–2:

    'It is thus that man, who can subsist only in society, was fitted by nature to that situation for which he was made. All the members of human society stand in need of each others assistance, and are likewise exposed to mutual injuries. Where the neccessary assistance is reciprocally afforded from love, from gratitude, from friendship, and esteem, the society flourishes and is happy. All the different members of it are bound together by the agreeable bands of love and affection, and are, as it were, drawn to one common centre of mutual good offices.

But though the necessary assistance should not be afforded from such generous and disinterested motives, though among the different members of the society there should be no mutual love and affection, the society, though less happy and agreeable, will not necessarily be dissolved. Society may subsist among different men, as among different merchants, from a sense of its utility, without any mutual love or affection; and though no man in it should owe any obligation, or be bound in gratitude to any other, it may still be upheld by mercenary exchange of good offices according to an agreed valuation.'

34. Cf. TMS I.i.5.10, II.ii.2.1, III.3.7, IV.1.8, VI.iii.23; II.iii.2.2, III.6.1.
35. Cf., for example,

'The love of praise-worthiness is by no means derived altogether from the love of praise. Those two principles, though they resemble one another, though they are connected, and often blended with one another, are yet, in many respects, distinct and independent of one another.'
(TMS III.2.2)

'The propriety of our moral sentiments is never so apt to be corrupted, as when the indulgent and partial spectator is at hand, while the indifferent and impartial one is at a great distance.'
(TMS III.3.41)

36. Cf. TMS III.2.6–7:

'Nature, when she formed man for society, endowed him with an original desire to please, and an original aversion to offend his brethren. She taught him to feel pleasure in their favourable, and pain in their unfavourable regard. She rendered their approbation most flattering and most agreeable to him for its own sake; and their disapprobation most mortifying and most offensive.

But this desire of the approbation, and this aversion to this disapprobation of his brethren, would not alone have rendered him fit for that society for which he was made. Nature, accordingly, has endowed him, not only with a desire of being approved of, but with a desire of being what ought to be approved of; or of being what he himself approves of in other men.'

37. TMS III.2.32–33.
38. Cf. Schumpeter, J.A. *History of Economic Analyses*, New York, 1954, pp. 1002 and 1008.
39. Cf. TMS III.2.29–30:

'A wise man may frequently neglect praise, even when he has best deserved it; but, in all matters of serious consequence, he will most carefully endeavour so to regulate his conduct as to avoid, not only blame-worthiness, but, as much as possible, every probable imputation of blame. He will never, indeed, avoid blame by doing any thing which he judges blame-worthy; by omitting any part of his duty, or by neglecting any opportunity of doing any thing which he judges to be really and greatly praise-worthy. But, with these modifications, he will most anxiously and carefully avoid it. To show much anxiety about praise, even for praise-worthy actions, is seldom a mark of great wisdom, but generally of some degree of weakness. But, in being anxious to avoid the shadow of blame or reproach, there may be no weakness, but frequently the most praise-worthy prudence.

'Many people,' says Cicero, 'despise glory, who are yet most severely mortified by unjust reproach; and that most inconsistently.' This inconsistency, however, seems to be founded in the unalterable principles of human nature.'

40. TMS III.2.33.
41. Id. See also TMS III.5.3–4.

42. Cf. TMS III.2.33.
43. Cf. TMS I.i.3.5, II.i.1–2 and II.i.5.1.
44. Cf. TMS I.ii.1–2.
45. Cf. TMS II.i.3.1–3 and II.i.5.11.
46. TMS II.ii.1 in particular TMS II.ii.1.1–4 and TMS II.ii.1.7.
47. TMS II.i.5.8 and TMS II.ii.1 in particular II.ii.1.4–5 and II.ii.1.9–10.
48.   'The rules of justice may be compared to the rules of grammar; the rules of the other virtues, to the rules which critics lay down for the attainment of what is sublime and elegant in composition. The one, are precise, accurate, and indispensable. The other, are loose, vague, and indeterminate, and present us rather with a general idea of the perfection we ought to aim at, than afford us any certain and infallible directions for acquiring it. A man may learn to write grammatically by rule, with the most absolute infallibility; and so, perhaps, he may be taught to act justly. But there are no rules whose observance will infallibly lead us to the attainment of elegance or sublimity in writing; though there are some which may help us, in some measure, to correct and ascertain the vague ideas which we might otherwise have entertained of those perfections. And there are no rules by the knowledge of which we can infallibly be taught to act upon all occasions with prudence, with just magnanimity, or proper beneficence: though there are some which may enable us to correct and ascertain, in several respects, the imperfect ideas which we might otherwise have entertained of those virtues.'
       (TMS III.6.11)
49. Cf. TMS II.ii.3.
50. TMS III.5.1.
51. TMS III.5.2.
52. TMS III.5.4. See also TMS II.i.5.9.
53. TMS III.4.11:
       'When these general rules, indeed, have been formed, when they are universally acknowledged and established, by the concurring sentiments of mankind, we frequently appeal to them as to the standards of judgment, in debating concerning the degree of praise or blame that is due to certain actions of a complicated and dubious nature. They are upon these occasions commonly cited as the ultimate foundations of what is just and unjust in human conduct; and this circumstance seems to have misled several very eminent authors, to draw up their systems in such a manner, as if they had supposed that the original judgments of mankind with regard to right and wrong, were formed like the decisions of a court of judicatory, by considering first the general rule, and then, secondly, whether the particular action under consideration fell properly within its comprehension.'
       See also TMS II.ii.3.5–9.
54. TMS III.5.1.
55. Cf. TMS III.4.7–8:
       'Our continual observations upon the conduct of others, insensibly lead us to form to ourselves certain general rules concerning what is fit and proper either to be done or to be avoided. Some of their actions shock all our natural sentiments. We hear every body about us express the like detestation against them. This still further confirms, and even exasperates our natural sense of their deformity. It satisfies us that we view them in the proper light, when we see other people view them in the same light. We resolve never to be guilty of the like, nor ever, upon any account, to render ourselves in this manner the objects of universal disapprobation. We thus naturally lay down to ourselves a general rule, that all such actions are to be avoided, as tending to render us odious, contemptible, or punishable, the objects of all those sentiments for which we

have the greatest dread and aversion. Other actions, on the contrary, call forth our approbation, and we hear every body around us express the same favourable opinion concerning them. Every body is eager to honour and reward them. They excite all those sentiments for which we have by nature the strongest desire; the love, the gratitude, the admiration of mankind. We become ambitious of performing the like; and thus naturally lay down to ourselves a rule of another kind, that every opportunity of acting in this manner is carefully to be sought after.

It is thus that the general rules of morality are formed. They are ultimately founded upon experience of what, in particular instances, our moral faculties, our natural sense of merit and propriety, approve, or disapprove of. We do not originally approve or condemn particular actions; because, upon examination, they appear to be agreeable or inconsistent with a certain general rule. The general rule, on the contrary, is formed, by finding from experience, that all actions of a certain kind, or circumstanced in a certain manner, are approved or disapproved of.'

56. TMS VII.iv.37:

'I shall in another discourse endeavour to give an account of the general principles of law and government, and of the different revolutions they have undergone in the different ages and periods of society, not only in what concerns justice, but in what concerns police, revenue, and arms, and whatever else is the object of law.'

57. TMS Advertisement, 2:

'In the last paragraph of the first Edition of the present work, I said, that I should in another discourse endeavour to give an account of the general principles of law and government, and of the different revolutions which they had undergone in the different ages and periods of society; not only in what concerns justice, but in what concerns police, revenue, and arms, and whatever else is the object of law. In the *Enquiry concerning the Nature and Causes of the Wealth of Nations*, I have partly executed this promise; at least so far as concerns police, revenue, and arms. What remains, the theory of jurisprudence, which I have long projected, I have hitherto been hindered from executing'

58. TMS II.ii.2.1. See also

'Every man is, no doubt, by nature, first and principally recommended to his own care' (TMS II.ii.2.1)

59. TMS VI.i.5.
60. TMS VI.i.3.
61. TMS I.iii.2.1. To gain a fuller understanding of Smith's view of the struggle for wealth we should also take note of the rest of the citation.

'It is the vanity, not the ease, or the pleasure, which interests us. But vanity is always founded upon the belief of our being the object of attention and approbation. The rich man glories in his riches, because he feels that they naturally draw upon him the attention of the world, and that mankind are disposed to go along with him in all those agreeable emotions with which the advantages of his situation so readily inspire him. At the thought of this, his heart seems to swell and dilate itself within him, and he is fonder of his wealth, upon this account, than for all the other advantages it procures him. The poor man, on the contrary, is ashamed of his poverty. He feels that it either places him out of the sight of mankind, or, that if they take any notice of him, they have, however, scarce any fellow-feeling with the misery and distress which he suffers. He is mortified upon both accounts; for though to be overlooked, and to be disapproved of, are things entirely different, yet as obscurity covers us from the daylight of honour and approbation, to feel that we are taken no notice of, necessarily damps the most agreeable hope, and disappoints the most ardent desire, of human nature. The poor man goes out and comes in unheeded, and when in the midst of a crowd is in the same obscurity as if shut up in his own hovel. Those humble cares and painful attentions which occupy those in his situation, afford no amusement to the dissipated and the gay. They turn away their eyes from him, or if the extremity of his distress forces them to look at him, it is only to spurn so disagreeable an object from among them. The fortunate and the proud wonder at the insolence of human wretchedness, that it should dare to present itself before them, and with the loathsome aspect of its misery presume to disturb the serenity of their happiness. The man of rank and distinction, on the contrary, is observed by all of the world. Every body is eager to look at him, and to conceive, at least by sympathy, that joy and exultation with which his circumstances naturally inspire him. ... and if his behaviour is not altogether absurd, he has, every moment, an opportunity of interesting mankind, and of rendering himself the object of the observation and fellow-feeling of every body about him.'

62. TMS I.iii.2.1.
63. TMS I.iii.2.3.
64. See also Smith's analysis of how gratitude and benevolence reinforce one another: TMS II.iii.intro.1 and TMS II.iii.1.4.
65. TMS IV.1.1.
66. TMS IV.1.2.
67. TMS IV.1.3.
68. TMS IV.1.6–8.
69. TMS IV.1.9–10.
70. TMS IV.2.2.
71. Id.
72. TMS IV.1.11.
73. TMS IV.2.2–3.
74. TMS I.iii.3.
75. Id.
76. Id.
77. TMS I.iii.3.4.
78. TMS I.iii.3.2.
79. TMS I.iii.3.5.
80. TMS II.ii.2.1. See further:
    'Man, it has been said, has a natural love for society, and desires that the union of mankind should be preserved for its own sake, and though he himself was to derive no benefit from it. ... He is sensible too that his own interest is connected with the prosperity of society, and that the happiness, perhaps the preservation of his existence, depends upon its preservation.'
    (TMS II.ii.3.6)

    'But though it commonly requires no great discernment to see the destructive tendency of all licentious practices to the welfare of society, it is seldom this consideration which first animates us against them. All men, even the most stupid and unthinking, abhor fraud, perfidy, and injustice, and delight to see them punished. But few men have reflected upon the necessity of justice to the existence of society, how obvious soever that necessity may appear to be.'
    (TMS II.ii.3.9)
81. Cf. TMS I.ii.4.1, III.3.4, IV.1.11, VI.ii.2.3, especially TMS I.ii.4.1:
    'We have always, ..., the strongest disposition to sympathize with the benevolent affec-tions. They appear in every respect agreeable to us. We enter into the satisfaction both of the person who feels them, and of the person who is the object of them. ... What character is so detestable as that of one who takes pleasure to sow dissension among friends, and to turn their most tender love into mortal hatred? Yet wherein does the

atrocity of this so much abhorred injury consist? Is it in depriving them of the frivolous good offices, which, had their friendship continued, they might have expected from one another? It is in depriving them of that friendship itself, in robbing them of each other's affections, from which both derived so much satisfaction; it is in disturbing the harmony of their hearts, and putting an end to that happy *commerce [emphasis mine]* which had before subsisted between them. These affections, that harmony, this *commerce [emphasis mine]*, are felt, not only by the tender and the delicate, but by the rudest vulgar mankind, to be of more importance to happiness than all the little services which could be expected to flow from them.'

82. Cf. TMS V.2.7–9:

'Every age and country look upon that degree of each quality, which is commonly to be met with in those who are esteemed among themselves, as the golden mean of that particular talent or virtue. And as this varies, according as their different circumstances render different qualities more or less habitual to them, their sentiments concerning the exact propriety of character and behaviour vary accordingly.

Among civilized nations, the virtues which are founded upon humanity, are more cultivated than those which are founded upon self-denial and the command of the passions. Among rude and barbarous nations, it is quite otherwise, the virtues of self-denial are more cultivated than those of humanity. The general security and happiness which prevail in ages of civility and politeness, afford little exercise to the contempt of danger, to patience in enduring labour, hunger, and pain. Poverty may easily be avoided, and the contempt of it therefore almost ceases to be a virtue. The abstinence from pleasure becomes less necessary, and the mind is more at liberty to unbend itself, and to indulge its natural inclinations in all those particular respects.

Among savages and barbarians it is quite otherwise. Every savage undergoes a sort of Spartan discipline, and by the necessity of his situation is inured to every sort of hardship. He is in continual danger: he is often exposed to the greatest extremities of hunger, and frequently dies of pure want. His circumstances not only habituate him to every sort of distress, but teach him to give way to none of the passions which that distress is apt to excite. He can expect from his countrymen no sympathy or indulgence for such weakness. Before we can feel much for others, we must in some measure be at ease ourselves. If our own misery pinches us very severely, we have no leisure to attend to that of our neighbour: and all savages are too much occupied with their own wants and necessities, to give much attention to those of another person. A savage, therefore, whatever be the nature of his distress, expects no sympathy from those about him, and disdains, upon that account, to expose himself, by allowing the least weakness to escape him. His passions, how furious and violent soever, are never permitted to disturb the serenity of his countenance or the composure of his conduct and behaviour.'

IV The *Invisible Hand and Mutual Sympathy*

In the eighteenth century, students of government sought to devise policies that would achieve a pre-ordained social pattern and lead to an increase in national wealth. Adam Smith altered the nature of the inquiry by asking a different question. He speculated on how a nation of autonomous individuals, each seeking to increase his own wealth and well-being, could produce an overall order that was no part of anyone's intention. The answers to this question spawned what we now recognise as economic science.

(G.P. O'Driscoll jr., and M.J. Rizzo, *The Economics of Time & Ignorance*, Oxford, 1985, pp. 229–230)

Introduction

The idea of the *invisible hand* and the twin concepts of *natural* and *market price* have encouraged economists to interpret Smith's economics as a general equilibrium theory *in nucleo*. However, in the preceding chapter we argued that Smith's *sympathetic* model of man and society differs substantially from the economists' rational choice approach exemplified by the Walrasian general equilibrium analysis. We have also seen that Smith understood competition for wealth, rank and distinction as being motivated by the human desire for *praise(worthiness)*. Economics as a discourse on the production and distribution of wealth is, according to the *sympathetic* model, an integral part of moral philosophy.

In this chapter we consider some of the failings of the traditional interpretation of Smith's idea of the *invisible hand* advanced by economists, in particular as it relates to the twin concepts of *natural* and *market price*.

Section 1 briefly considers whether the proof by Walrasian economists that Smith's idea of the self-coordinating market economy is scientifically valid has been achieved at too high a price. We know that in his economic discourse Smith addressed real-world economies. However, the Walrasian demonstration of the effectiveness of the *invisible hand* in realizing general equilibrium is based on economic models which run counter to our real-world experience. We consider Smith's call for realism and discuss his understanding of the claim that science has to be in touch with reality.

In sections 2 and 3 the idea of the *invisible hand* is considered in detail. In section 2 the Walrasian and the older theistic/deistic interpretations are contrasted with an interpretation based on Smith's *sympathetic* view of man and society. In section 3 this interpretation provides the point of departure for a reinterpretation of the *price mechanism*.

Sections 4 and 5 consider Smith's use of the ideas of *natural price* and *market price*. Section 4 presents a survey of Chapter VII of Book I of *The Wealth of Nations*. According to Schumpeter 'the rudimentary equilibrium theory' outlined in this chapter is 'by far the best piece of economic theory turned out by Smith' and anticipates Walras. We will discuss how Smith describes *natural* and *market prices* as concepts of a self-coordinating economic system. In section 5 a new interpretation of *natural* and *market price* is presented in accordance with Smith's *sympathetic* theory of man's competition for wealth, rank and distinction.

1 The Price of Being a Golden Boy in Economic Science

In *Theoretical Issues in Macroeconomics* the Nobel Prize winner James Tobin asserts that Smith's *invisible hand* is one of the 'great ideas of intellectual history'. According to Tobin, we have Smith to thank for our acquaintance with the idea that self-interest in the context of competition in interrelated markets is efficient in enlarging individual and social wealth. As Tobin writes,

> 'The invisible hand is one of the Great Ideas of intellectual history. According to Adam Smith, market competition transmutes selfish and myopic individual actions into the wealth of nations ... Central direction is not necessary. The system demands of its participants neither altruism nor omniscience. Natural self-interest is enough motivation; everyday local observation is enough information. All that is required of the participants is respect for property rights and contractual obligations. All that is required of government is to establish and enforce those laws and to defend the society against internal and external enemies. Government interferences in markets are generally inefficient because they prevent individuals from making mutually and socially beneficial trades and contracts.'[1]

Later general equilibrium theorists are supposed to have demonstrated that Smith's intuitions about the efficiency of market economies are scientifically sound. That is to say that they can be rigorously formulated and proven. However, the research of general equilibrium theorists such as Léon Walras, Vilfredo Pareto, John R. Hicks and Gerard Debreu has according to Tobin also shown that Smith's idea of the *invisible hand* only holds true in a world that contradicts real-world economies:

> The task of giving rigour and precision to the relation of our individual actions and aggregate outcomes has engaged the best minds of our profession, including Walras, Pareto, Hicks, Samuelson, Debreu and Arrow. The propositions that survived this process are more complicated and more limited than the conjectures of earlier writers and the extravagant claims of the ideology. ... Where does the modern version of the theory *[i.e. the Walrasian general equilibrium theory]* leave the Invisible Hand? Two quite opposite responses are conceivable. On the one hand there is the good news: the intuitions of Adam Smith and many later writers can indeed be rigorously formulated and proved. The bad news is that the theorems depend on a host of conditions, many of dubious realism. ... The modern version might be taken to refute, not to support, the applicability of invisible hand propositions to real-world economies.'[2]

This last point should give anyone who is even remotely acquainted with Smith's work pause for thought. An economist such as Gerard Debreu has made significant contributions to the explication of the Walrasian general equilibrium model of the market economy. But what are the grounds for thinking that this model relates to Smith's idea of the self-coordinating market economy? Why should we applaud a model which is irrelevant to Smith's discussion of phenomena of self-coordination in real-world market economies?

In this section we will discuss four excerpts from Smith's works in order to demonstrate that the *invisible hand* should properly be understood as a metaphor expressing the real-world experience that behaviour and action, despite being motivated by self-interest, reflect social rules and values. The first excerpt is taken from Smith's discussion in the *Lectures on Jurisprudence* (1766) of Pufendorf's attempt to refute Hobbes' idea of *homo homini lupus*. Smith criticizes Pufendorf's argument based on the idea of the *state of nature*, on the grounds that *there is no such state existing*:

> 'The divines thought themselves obliged to oppose this *[i.e. Hobbes']* pernicious doctrine concerning virtue, and attacked it by endeavouring to shew that a state of nature was not a state of war but that society might subsist, ..., without civil institutions. They endeavoured to shew that man in this state has certain rights belonging to him, such as a right to his body, to the fruits of his labour, and the fullfilling of contracts. With this design Puffendorf wrote his large treatise. The sole intention of the first part of it is to confute Hobbes, tho' it in reality serves no purpose to treat of the laws which would take place in a state of nature, or by what means succession to property was carried on, as there is no such state existing.'[3]

Instead of abstract reasoning about laws and property rights, Smith believed that these institutions should be understood in relation to the real societies of which they are a part. From Smith's perspective, laws and property rights are, like every other institution, related to the *sympathy* exchanges which govern the real-life interaction of man as a social being. Accordingly, Smith's references to past and present economies in *The Wealth of Nations* should not be seen as simply illustrative: it is only in discussing these concrete situations, he believes, that we will develop a true understanding of economic processes and its institutions. Consequently we have to reject the assertion of Samuel Hollander and others, that those references are irrelevant to true economic analysis and can be separated from it.[4]

The second excerpt is from *The History of Astronomy* and describes the consequences of becoming too deeply engrossed in the process of theorizing:

> 'And even we, while we have been endeavouring to represent all philosophical systems as mere inventions of the imagination, to connect together the otherwise disjointed and discordant phaenomena of nature, have insensibly been drawn in, to make use of language expressing the connecting principles of this one, as if they were the real chains which Nature makes use of to bind together her several operations. Can we wonder then, that it should have gained the general and complete approbation of mankind, and that it should now be considered, not as an attempt to connect in the imagination the phaenomena of the Heavens, but as the greatest

discovery that ever was made by man, the discovery of an immense chain of the most important and sublime truths, all closely connected together, by one capital fact, of the reality of which we have daily experience.'[5]

Here Smith warns us that excessive theorizing may result in us becoming the dupes of our own imagination. He reminds us that we may become so impressed by, or familiar with, our images of the world that we forget that the conceived order is merely virtual. Theories which began as inventions whose purpose was to give sense and meaning to our real-world experiences become substitutes of the real world in the sense of being representations of an a priori world-order. When this occurs and a theory is no longer discussed in relation to real-world experiences, the dialogical relation between theory and real-world experience is broken. The imagined order assumes an ontological priority and man's real-world experiences are dealt with as manifestations of that order.

The third excerpt, from *The Wealth of Nations*, highlights the importance of maintaining the dialogical relation between theory and real-world experiences from another perspective:

'Some speculative physicians seem to have imagined that the health of the human body could be preserved only by a certain precise regimen of diet and exercise, of which every, the smallest, violation necessarily occasioned some degree of disease or disorder proportioned to the degree of the violation. Experience, however, would seem to show that the human body frequently preserves, to all appearance at least, the most perfect state of health under a vast variety of different regimens; even under some which are generally believed to be very far from perfectly wholesome. But the healthful state of the human body, it would seem, contains in itself some unknown principle of preservation, capable either of preventing or of correcting, in many respects, the bad effects even of a very faulty regimen. Mr. Quesnai, who was himself a physician, and a very speculative physician, seems to have entertained a notion of the same kind concerning the political body, and to have imagined that it would thrive and prosper only under a certain precise regimen, the exact regimen of perfect liberty and perfect justice. He seems not to have considered that in the political body, the natural effort which every man is continually making to better his own condition, is a principle of preservation capable of preventing and correcting, in many respects, the bad effects of a political oeconomy, in some degree, both partial and oppressive. Such a political oeconomy, though it no doubt retards more or less, is not always capable of stopping altogether the natural progress of a nation towards wealth and prosperity, and still less making it to go backwards. If a nation could not prosper without the enjoyment of perfect liberty and perfect justice, there is not in the world a nation which could ever have prospered. In the political body, however, the wisdom of nature has fortunately made ample provision for remedying many of the bad effects of the folly and injustice of man; in the same manner as it has done in the natural body, for remedying those of his sloth and intemperance.'[6]

Here Smith cautions us against the dangers of misunderstanding and misinterpretation inherent in theorizing by analogy. Instead of using the idea of healing a sick body metaphorically in theorizing about economic phenomena, François Quesnay transposed a specific idea of healing almost literally from the field of medicine to the field of economics.

The fourth passage is taken from *The Theory of Moral Sentiments* and concerns another form of estrangement incipient in the distorted relation between theory and real-word experience. Theorizing about the efficiency of behaviour may seduce us into substituting sentiments for reason, Smith suggests:

'In every part of the universe we observe means adjusted with the nicest artifice to the ends which they are intended to produce; and in the mechanism of a plant, or animal body, admire how every thing is contrived for advancing the two great purposes of nature, the support of the individual, and the propagation of the species. But in these, and in all such objects, we still distinguish the efficient from the final cause of their several motions and organisations. ... But though, in accounting for the operations of bodies, we never fail to distinguish in this manner the efficient from the final cause, in accounting for those of the mind we are very apt to confound these two different things with one another. When by natural principles we are led to advance those ends, which a refined and enlightened reason would recommend to us, we are very apt to impute to that reason, ..., the sentiments and actions by which we advance those ends'[7]

In this passage Smith points to the categorical mistake which can arise from theorizing about the well-ordered effects of behaviour when the analysis is not firmly embedded in a dialogue between theory and experience. Our admiration for the well-orderedness of the effects may seduce us into substituting a rational choice explanation for an understanding of behaviour in its relation to (moral) sentiments. From the rational choice perspective, man's tendency to *sympathy* would be nothing but one of the means in the actors' repertoire of means-ends calculations.

Smith's realism has been noted and discussed by other scholars.[8] We, however, want to emphasize that Smith's approach cannot be subsumed within the conceptual frames of traditional debates such as realism versus nominalism, realism versus positivism, or empiricism versus rationalism. Consequently we will avoid single-term qualifications of Smith's view of philosophy and science, and refer the reader instead to the fuller description presented earlier in Chapter III.[9] As a general pointer to understanding Smith's theory of philosophy and science, it is important to note that, for Smith, the end of philosophy and science does not differ substantially from that attained by everyday knowledge. In Smith's perspective philosophy and science are rooted in man's existential need to give meaning and sense to experience by referring to generally accepted principles. From this point of view the essential problem of the so-called unrealistic assumptions of Walrasian general equilibrium analysis is that Walrasian general equilibrium analysis is divorced from the true purpose of science. Instead of understanding and evaluating itself as a contribution to the public discourse on real-world economies it has isolated itself, and claimed the sovereign status of an autonomous science.

In Smith's view science has to prove itself in contributing to discussions of the principles which people actually use to give sense and meaning to their lives and world. Walrasian general equilibrium analysis denies this guiding relation with the public discourse in both its method and content.[10] It insists on explaining efficiency by postulating efficiency in terms of an ends-means calculus and reducing behaviour and action to this type of functionalism.

At the same time, however, it should be emphasized that Smith would certainly not have opposed the Walrasian attempt to explain economic behaviour and action in interrelated markets as a well-ordered, self-regulating system. In Smith's view theory is even synonymous with system.[11] He also recognizes that theorizing implies contemplation in 'a certain abstract and philosophical light':

'That the tendency of virtue to promote, and of vice to disturb the order of society, when we consider it coolly and philosophically, reflects a very great beauty on the one, and a very great deformity upon the other, cannot, ..., be called in question. Human society, when we contemplate it in a certain abstract and philosophical light, appears like a great, an immense machine, whose regular and harmonious movements produce a thousand agreeable effects.'[12]

As the passage shows, even contemplation in a *certain abstract and philosophical light* is not, in Smith's approach, isolated from real-world experience. Smith would in the first place have criticized Walrasian general equilibrium analysis for not distinguishing between understanding human behaviour, on the one hand, and discussing the effects of this behaviour, on the other. In Smith's view the effects have, so to say, misled economists into adopting a rationalistic interpretation of man and society. As we have seen, Smith would have opposed an approach which reduces human behaviour to the effects of the ends-means calculations of atomistic individuals. He writes:

'That whole account of human nature, ..., which deduces all sentiments and affections from self-love, which has made so much noise in the world, but which, so far as I know, has never yet been fully and distinctly explained, seems to me to have arisen from some confused misapprehension of the system of sympathy.'[13]

The central premise of Smith's discourse on *sympathy* is that we have to understand man's feelings, thoughts, behaviour and actions in relation to real-world situations that arise in the competition and concurrence for *sympathy*. In short, Smith would have opposed the functionalistic and atomistic view of Walrasian general equilibrium theory, which denies the relationship between efficiency and *sympathy*.

2 The *Invisible Hand*: Two current Interpretations Reassessed

In discussing Smith's notion of the *invisible hand* we have to consider at least two current interpretations of the concept. Firstly, the Walrasian interpretation which is very common among economists and which we have already discussed in some detail. Secondly, the theistic/deistic interpretation which is favoured by scholars approaching Smith from an historical-philosophical perspective.

We have already noted that Smith's discourse concerns self-coordination in real-world market economies, while the Walrasian general equilibrium interpretation appears to make sense only as a sophisticated but alienating piece of 'science fiction'. Given Smith's view of science, this problem is critical, but the Walrasian general equilibrium interpretation also raises a number of additional questions. A brief excursion into Schumpeter's discussion of Smith and Walras in his *History of Economic Analysis* illustrates this point.

As we have seen, Schumpeter regards Smith as a predecessor of Walras:

> 'The rudimentary equilibrium theory of Chapter 7, by far the best piece of economic theory turned out by A. Smith, in fact points toward Say and, through the latter's work, to Walras. The purely theoretical developments of the nineteenth century consist to a considerable degree in improvements upon it.'[14]

Schumpeter regards Walras' general equilibrium theory as the *Magna Charta of economic theory*.[15] However, he also distances himself from Walras on precisely the issue which is at stake in the interpretation of Smith's discussion of the so-called price mechanism: namely, the question whether the theory is or is not true for real-world economies.

Dealing with Walras' discussion of the price mechanism, Schumpeter notes on the one hand that,

> 'Like Clark J.B., he *[i.e. Walras]* used the analogy with the "level" of a lake in order to convey his idea – the old idea of A. Smith.'[16]

On the other hand, Schumpeter also suggests that this resemblance between Smith and Walras is irrelevant when he explicitly distances himself from Walras' contention that he was discussing real-world economies:

> 'I have spoken of prices "that would be paid in perfect equilibrium and pure competition." This manner of speaking is not Walrasian: Walras, much like J.B. Clark, conceived these equilibrium prices to be, normally, the actual level around which prices oscillate in real life, which involves a claim that I do not wish to make.'[17]

So, what does Schumpeter mean when he argues that Smith's rudimentary equilibrium theory anticipates Walras? Is it not more accurate to contend that in the *History of Economic Analysis* Smith is read with a distinctively twentieth-century understanding of Walrasian general equilibrium theory? That is to say, an understanding generated by the acknowledgement that Walras' theory of general equilibrium is not about explaining the auto-coordination of real-world market economies?

In this context it is important to note that Tobin was mistaken in suggesting that the work of later economists, including Walras, might be taken as a proof that Smith's *invisible hand* does not help explain real-world economies. Walras also believed that he was explaining real-world economies when he conceived his general equilibrium theory.[18] Whether or not Pareto, Hicks, Samuelson, Debreu and Arrow believed that Smith anticipated Walras, their elaborations on Walrasian general equilibrium primarily refer to Walras and not to Smith. Consequently, if today's Walrasian general equilibrium analysis is supposed to prove something, it will be primarily about the Walrasian concept of general equilibrium and not about Smith's idea of the *invisible hand*.

That Schumpeter hardly mentions Smith's *invisible hand* in the *History of Economic Analysis* is probably due to the fact that he does not consider it a scientific concept, referring to it dismissively as the *doctrine of the invisible hand*.[19] A mere *doctrine* clearly has no part in Schumpeter's positivistic model of scientific knowledge. He does, however, discuss Walras' *auctioneer* metaphor in some detail. In the following passage Walras' *auctioneer* is described as *some agent in the market*:

'he *[i.e. Walras]* tried to build up an equilibrium state ab ovo in the manner in which it would be built, if smooth and instantaneous adaptation of all existing goods and processes, to the conditions obtaining at the moment, were feasible. His households do not purchase consumers' goods or sell productive services outright. Nor do his firms (entrepreneurs) purchase productive services and offer products outright. They all merely declare what they *would* respectively buy and sell (produce) at prices *criés au hasard*, that is, announced experimentally by some agent in the market, and are free to change their minds if these prices do not turn out to be the equilibrium prices: other prices are thereupon announced, other declarations of willingness to buy or sell (and to produce) are written down on *bons* – pieces of paper that do not carry any obligation – until equilibrium values emerge, namely prices such that no demand willing to pay them and no supply willing to accept them remain unsatisfied. And the only mechanism of reaction to these variations of experimental prices that Walras recognizes is to raise the prices of commodities or services, the demand for which at these prices is greater than the supply, and to reduce the prices of commodities or services, the supply of which at these prices is greater than the demand.'[20]

Later, when discussing Smith's discourse on the *market* and *natural price*, we will consider Walras' use of the *auctioneer* in more detail. For now it is sufficient to note that in the last excerpt the *auctioneer* is more than a metaphor which serves to indicate the phenomenon of self-coordination in market economies. In Walrasian theory the *auctioneer* is a *real agent* without whom order and stability are unthinkable. Order and stability exist only because the atomistic, rationalistic actors are supposed to sell and buy against equilibrium prices discovered and announced by the *auctioneer*.

This contrasts explicitly with Smith's discourse on *market* and *natural price*. In Smith's narrative, actors share social values, including *natural prices*, and exchange commodities against *market prices* which often differ from the *natural prices*. In Smith's market economy, individuals unintentionally serve the public interest *as if* they are being directed by an invisible hand.

What arguments might lead us to conclude that Smith anticipated the Walrasian model where individual actors are atomistic and rationalistic, and the general equilibrium prices have to be enforced from the outside by an actor standing above the trading parties? Can we dispose of Smith's idea of the *invisible hand* by ascribing it to the naivety of a science still in its infancy? In the last section of this chapter it will be shown that Smith's *sympathetic* understanding of man and society may provide an insight into the idea metaphorically expressed by the figure of the *invisible hand*, namely that market economies produce their own well-orderedness.

The second, theistic/deistic, interpretation is less commonly employed by economists. It is a contextual interpretation which presupposes that Smith continued to work within a theistic/deistic frame of reference and thus used the term *invisible hand* to allude to the invisible power of God. That is to say, that Smith believed that the world was directed by God directly or indirectly through the agency of pre-given natural laws.[21]

It will be clear that we sympathize with contextual approaches of Smith's work. However, taking Syed Ahmad's article, *Adam Smith's Four Invisible Hands*, as an example, we will question whether the theistic/deistic interpretation is really based in a contextual reading.[22]

In his study Ahmad answers the criticism that Smith was inconsistent in his use of the notion of the *invisible hand* thus:

'No doubt the functions performed by all these invisible hands are different, but they are not inconsistent, since none of these functions is precluded by any other. All the four invisible hands could, therefore, without inconsistency belong to the same Invisible Power.'[23]

He concludes his article with the remark that,

'the argument of this paper does not lend support to those looking for inconsistencies in Smith's writings.'[24]

We agree with Ahmad that there is no inconsistency in Smith's use of the *invisible hand* in *The Theory of Moral Sentiment* or *The Wealth of Nations*, as will be demonstrated in the following section. However, we disagree with Ahmad's argument insofar as it continues the theistic/deistic misinterpretation of Smith.

For the sake of clarity, we are not concerned with whether or not Smith lived in a time in which the theistic or deistic worldview was still predominant. The important point is that even if this is true of the worldview in Smith's time, it would not be a sufficient argument to conclude that Smith himself held theistic or deistic views. Contextual reading of a text means that the reader acknowledges the relatedness of the author to the ideas of his own time without losing sight of the autonomy of the author in that relationship.

In his commentary on the *invisible hand* passages, Ahmad presupposes that Smith's frame of reference is theistic or deistic.[25] However, at a number of points he seems less than confident on this score as is indicated by the following three passages.

In the first passage Ahmad describes the philosophical outlook of Smith's time in the course of commenting on the *invisible hand of Jupiter* passage in *The History of Astronomy*:

'Here the role directly ascribed to the invisible hand, that of causing "irregular" events, supposedly represents polytheists' beliefs; and Smith clearly wishes to distance himself from them. Hence in Smith's own view, the appropriate role of the invisible hand here is not as a stopper, thwarter, or disturber of the natural order; on the contrary, it is what Smith chastises the polytheists for their inability to see, that of the preserver and enforcer of that order. Would Smith thus exclude the "irregular" events of nature from the domain of the invisible hand? Since the apparently "irregular" events themselves result from the regular laws of nature, it seems reasonable to suggest that the answer would be in the negative.

The philosophical position that God's will is expressed essentially through nature and its laws dates back to antiquity. Nearer Smith's time, one can find it in the opening sentence of Hobbes (1651), in deistic writings, and in Spinoza (1737). For instance, Spinoza writes that "the vulgar believe Gods Power and Providence do most plainly, appear, when they see anything strange and unusual happen in nature" (125). He had earlier presented his own, in contrast to the vulgar, view on the relationship between God and Nature: "I take Gods disposing or direction, to be the fixed order and immutable course of Nature" (59). The parallel is almost exact.'[26]

Here it is merely suggested that theism or deism was Smith's primary frame of reference.

The second passage concerns 'the core, or common features, of these invisible hands':

'let us consider the core, or the common features, of these invisible hands – a question of particular importance for those who ascribe an invisible-hand doctrine or philosophy to Smith. It seems that there is little of substance in the core; in fact there does not appear to be *any* feature common to all of them, except, possibly, their theistic origin.'[27]

Ahmad does not explicitly state that the primary meaning of the *invisible hands* is theistic, nor that their meaning is theistic in origin. Rather he argues that there is a possibility that they share a theistic origin.

The third example relates to the concluding words of Ahmad's paper quoted earlier in this section.

'All the four invisible hands could, ..., without inconsistency belong to the same Invisible Power. Hence the argument of this paper does not lend support to those looking for inconsistencies in Smith's writings.'[28]

Once again Ahmad presents his idea that Smith referred to the *Invisible Power*, as a possibility. Nor does the footnote supplied by Ahmad do anything to clarify the meaning of the *invisible hands*:

'Although not quite in the above sense, Smith does use the phrase "invisible and designing power" only a few sentences before the passage we have quoted from his "History of Astronomy." In fact the word "invisible" appears several times in this essay in expressions such as "invisible causes", "chain of invisible objects", "invisible chains", and "invisible beings."'[29]

Ahmad does not elaborate any further on the appearance of the word *invisible* in *The History of Astronomy*, nor does he explain in what way the meaning of

Smith's phrase *invisible and designing power* differs from his own *Invisible Power*.

Reviewing these three excerpts from Ahmad's interpretation of Smith's *invisible hands* the question arises: 'Why all these vague conjectures?' Anticipating our own reinterpretation of the *invisible hand* passages, it will be shown that Smith's texts are not ambiguous when the theistic or deistic view is not presupposed. We will now focus on Smith's *History of Astronomy* to gain a better understanding of such aforementioned phrases as *invisible chains* and *invisible beings*.

The full title of Smith's essay is *The Principles which lead and direct Philosophical Enquiries; illustrated by the History of Astronomy*. It is in this essay that Smith uses the expressions: *invisible and designing power, invisible causes, chain of invisible objects, invisible chains,* and *invisible beings.* Just as in his discussion of *sympathy* in *The Theory of Moral Sentiments*, Smith's *History of Astronomy* deals with the principles of philosophical enquiries by reflecting on common daily-life experience and its corresponding language:

> 'Wonder, Surprise, and Admiration, are words which, though often confounded, denote, in our language, sentiments that are indeed allies, but that are in some respects different also, and distinct from one another. What is new and singular, excites that sentiment which, in strict propriety, is called Wonder; what is unexpected, Surprise; and what is great or beautiful, Admiration.'

> 'It is the design of this Essay to consider particularly the nature and causes of each of these sentiments, whose influence is of far wider extent than we should be apt upon a careless view to imagine.'[30]

According to Smith, there is no essential difference between learning in daily life, and scientific research. Science is simply a more professional form of enquiry and thus, more systematic, explicit and critical. Through their education and profession, scientists are intent on asking questions about phenomena which in daily life are too quickly experienced as self-evident:

> 'as in those sounds, which to the greater part of men seem perfectly agreeable to measure and harmony, the nicer ear of a musician will discover a want, both of the most exact time, and of the most perfect coincidence: so the more practised thought of a philosopher, who has spent his whole life in the study of the connecting principles of nature, will often feel an interval betwixt two objects, which, to more careless observers, seem very strictly conjoined. By long attention to all the connections which have ever been presented to his observation, by having often compared them with one another, he has, like the musician, acquired, if one may say so, a nicer ear, and a more delicate feeling with regard to things of this nature. And as to the one, that music seems dissonance which falls short of the most perfect harmony; so to the other, those events seem altogether separated and disjointed, which fall short of the strictest and most perfect connection.'[31]

Smith understands learning as an integral part of life, it is simply a part of human nature which affects man's perception of the world. Repetition of experiences results in the observation of patterns which are understood as the ordinary course of things:

> 'When two objects, however unlike, have often been observed to follow each other, and have constantly presented themselves to the senses in that order, they come to be so connected together in the fancy, that the idea of the one seems, of its own accord, to call up and introduce that of the other. If the objects are still observed to succeed each other as before, this connection, or, as it has been called, this association of their ideas, becomes stricter and stricter, and the habit of the imagination to pass from the conception of the one to that of the other, grows more and more rivetted and confirmed. As its ideas move more rapidly than external objects, it is continually running before them, and therefore anticipates, before it happens, every event which falls out according to this ordinary course of things.'[32]

Effectively, Smith distinguishes between what Thomas S. Kuhn was later to term *normal science* and *scientific revolutions*. Where normal learning comprises the accumulation of knowledge within the same, familiar, frame of reference, scientific revolution is characterized by anomalies and crisis.[33]

> 'Whatever, ..., occurs to us we are fond of referring to some species or class of things, with all of which it has a nearly exact resemblance; and though we often know no more about them than about it, yet we are apt to fancy that by being able to do so, we show ourselves to be better acquainted with it, and to have a more thorough insight into its nature.'

> 'When objects succeed each other in the same train in which the ideas of the imagination have thus been accustomed to move, and in which, though not conducted by that chain of events presented to the senses, they have acquired a tendency to go on of their own accord, such objects appear all closely connected with one another, and the thought glides easily along them, without effort and without interruption. They fall in with the natural career of the imagination; and as the ideas which represented such a train of things would seem all mutually to introduce each other, every last thought to be called up by the foregoing, and to call up the succeeding; so when the objects themselves occur, every last event seems, in the same manner, to be introduced by the foregoing, and to introduce the succeeding. There is no break, no stop, no gap, no interval. The ideas excited by so coherent a chain of things seem, as it were, to float through the mind of their own accord, without obliging it to exert itself, or to make any effort in order to pass from one of them to another.'[34]

A disagreeable feeling of *wonder* or *surprise* arises when experiences do not conform to the familiar train of thoughts. At first we try to make the experience conform to the familiar frame of thought. When this fails the problem escalates into a crisis. The explanatory system, which had previously seemed so cogent, no longer convinces and is thrown open to debate. In this period of revolution we search for a new unifying framework which will once more lend coherence to our experiences and thus evoke feelings of *admiration*. It is in this context, while discussing how people develop a new framework to give sense and meaning to their experiences, that Smith speaks of the *invisible*:

'The supposition of a chain of intermediate, though invisible events, which succeed
each other in a train similar to that in which the imagination has been accustomed to
move, and which link together those two disjointed appearances, is the only means
by which the imagination can fill up this interval, is the only bridge which, if one
may say so, can smooth its passage from the one object to the other.'[35]

This passage demonstrates that, contrary to Ahmad's contention, there is no
reason to conclude that in speaking of the *chain of intermediate, though invisible
events* Smith refers to causal connections preordained by an Invisible Power. On
the contrary, the presupposition that Smith's frame of thought was theistic or
deistic, conceals the fact that Smith presents a totally different account of causa-
tion, law and the natural, i.e. ordinary, order of things. The principles according
to which man perceives the world as a meaningful whole are virtually created by
man himself, as Smith illustrates through the example of the phenomenon of
magnetism:

'Thus, when we observe the motion of the iron, in consequence of that of the loadstone, we gaze and hesitate, and feel a want of connection betwixt two events which
follow one another in so unusual a train. But when, with Des Cartes, we imagine
certain invisible effluvia to circulate round one of them, and by their repeated
impulses to impel the other, both to move towards it, and to follow its motion, we
fill up the interval betwixt them, we join them together by a sort of bridge, and thus
take off that hesitation and difficulty which the imagination felt in passing from the
one to the other. That the iron should move after the loadstone seems, upon this
hypothesis, in some measure according to the ordinary course of things. Motion after
impulse is an order of succession with which of all things we are the most familiar.
Two objects which are so connected seem no longer to be disjoined, and the imagination flows smoothly and easily along them.'[36]

Here, Smith explains how a new ordering principle for initially inexplicable
phenomena is imagined by drawing an analogy with a principle which has been
successful and hence become familiar in a different field of experience. The
principle makes the impression of a *chain of intermediate, though invisible events*
because of its analogical transference from a familiar to an unfamiliar world of
experiences. Thus, once again we can see that Smith's invocation of *invisible
chains* and *chains of invisible objects* has nothing to do with the theistic or deistic
belief that an *Invisible Power* governs the world.

Our excursion into *The Principles which lead and direct Philosophical
Enquiries* confirms our interpretation of the central themes of Smith's view of
human interaction established in Chapter III: people themselves produce both their
social order and corresponding worldview in the course of interacting with each
other in a context of *sympathetic* communication, competition and concurrence.

In the following section we will reread the various *invisible hand* passages
against the background of our reinterpretation of Smith's view of *sympathy* and
his theory of philosophy and science.

3 The *Invisible Hand* in the *sympathy* model

The expression *invisible hand* occurs three times in Smith's work, and on one of these occasions Smith speaks of the 'invisible hand of Jupiter'.[37] At first sight the *invisible hand of Jupiter* passage may not seem very relevant to economists. Nevertheless we shall begin by looking at this passage before examining the *invisible hand* passages in *The Theory of Moral Sentiments* and *The Wealth of Nations*.

Smith uses the phrase the *invisible hand of Jupiter* in 'Section III' of *The History of Astronomy*, titled 'Of the Origin of Philosophy'.[38] Referring to ancient Greece, Smith distinguishes two stages in the history of mankind: a stage without order, law and prosperity – Greece before the city states – and a stage with order, law and prosperity – the classical Greece of the city states, the colonies, etc.

In Smith's stadialist account of man's social evolution, the ancient Greeks lived like savages before the advent of the well-organized and prosperous city state. Completely taken up with the battle for survival, they had no time for philosophy. The lack of a clear system of law, and the continual battle for survival meant that they felt themselves to be at the mercy of events. They experienced their own actions as an intervention in the natural course of events, and when they were confronted with events or phenomena which departed from the normal pattern, they imagined them to be the work of more powerful creatures who resembled themselves – the gods:

'it may be observed, that in all Polytheistic religions, among savages, as well as in the early ages of Heathen antiquity, it is the irregular events of nature only that are ascribed to the agency and power of their gods. Fire burns, and water refreshes; heavy bodies descend, and lighter substances fly upwards, by the necessity of their own nature; nor was the *invisible hand of Jupiter [emphasis mine]* ever apprehended to be employed in those matters. But thunder and lightning, storms and sunshine, those more irregular events, were ascribed to his favour, or his anger. Man, the only designing power with which they were acquainted, never acts but either to stop, or to alter the course, which natural events would take, if left to themselves. Those other intelligent beings, whom they imagined, but knew not, were naturally supposed to act in the same manner; not to employ themselves in supporting the ordinary course of things, which went on of its own accord, but to stop, to thwart, and to disturb it. And thus, in the first ages of the world, the lowest and most pusillanimous superstition supplied the place of philosophy.'[39]

As we can see, Smith uses the *invisible hand of Jupiter* as a figure of speech to suggest the way people in the so-called first stage of history, explained disruptions of the familiar image of the natural course of things. It is important to note that the *invisible hand of Jupiter* passage provides no support for Ahmad's comment that

'Smith clearly wishes to distance himself from them *[i.e. polytheistic beliefs]*. Hence in Smith's own view, the appropriate role of the invisible hand here is not as a stopper, thwarter, or disturber of the natural order; on the contrary, it is what Smith chastises the polytheists for their inability to see, that of the preserver and enforcer of that order.'[40]

Smith does not criticize the savages living in the first ages of the world for substituting the *invisible hand of Jupiter* as the disturber of order for the *invisible hand of God*, the preserver and enforcer of order. The *invisible hand of Jupiter* passage even contradicts Ahmad's exegesis insofar as Smith considered the savages' explanation of the world as natural, that is to say, in accordance with their particular stage of social evolution:

'Those other intelligent beings, whom they imagined, but knew not, were *naturally [emphasis mine]* supposed to act in the same manner; not to employ themselves in supporting the ordinary course of things, which went on of its own accord, but to stop, to thwart, and to disturb it.'[41]

Smith's discussion of the second stage of man's social evolution provides further evidence that he understood knowledge and science as systems of belief people use in order to give sense and meaning to their experiences.

According to Smith the second stage of human history dawned in ancient Greece when prosperous and well-organized city states came into being:

'But when law has established order and security, and subsistence ceases to be precarious, the curiosity of mankind is increased, and their fears are diminished. The leisure which they then can enjoy renders them more attentive to the appearances of nature, more observant of her smallest irregularities, and more desirous to know what is the chain which links them all together.'[42]

It is to the second stage of history, in which order, security and prosperity develop in line with people's confidence to act and organize social life according to certain ordering principles, that Smith dates the birth of philosophy.

Just as Smith had made a connection between the general feeling of powerlessness and insecurity and the view of gods disturbing the ordinary course of things, so he relates people's growing belief that they can order life and society according to their own principles, to their need to conceive of observed irregularities as elements of regularities as yet unimagined:

'That some such chain subsists betwixt all her seemingly disjointed phaenomena, they are necessarily led to conceive; and that magnanimity, and cheerfulness, which all generous natures acquire who are bred in civilized societies, where they have so few occasions to feel their weakness, and so many to be conscious of their strength and security, renders them less disposed to employ, for this connecting chain, those invisible beings whom the fear and ignorance of their rude forefathers had engendered.'[43]

Smith finally presents an illustration of how the processes of constructing and reconstructing systems of belief in civil society had developed since the beginning of the Greek city states in his discussion of the history of astronomy.[44] We will deal with that discussion later in Chapter V. For now this brief review of 'Section III' – *'Of the origin of philosophy'* – will suffice.

Two conclusions important for understanding Smith's idea of the *invisible hand*, can be drawn:

1 Irrespective of the model of people's understanding of the world, Smith interprets all the various kinds of knowledge as belief systems. Smith would not subscribe to any single explanative system whether theistic or deistic, since all of them presuppose a pre-given order behind the observed phenomena of which man is trying to make representations in his theories.
2 The search for principles to explain the world is understood by Smith as a process of analogical thinking. Savages, for example, give meaning to the irregularities in their experience by imagining gods acting in analogy to their own actions which are perceived as disrupting the ordinary course of things. The disturbing *invisible hand of Jupiter* is analogous to man's own hand which is also the instrument of disruption.

Having discussed Smith's use of the *invisible hand of Jupiter* to explain how *savages* give sense and meaning to their world, we can now examine his use of the *invisible hand* in, successively, *The Theory of Moral Sentiments* and *The Wealth of Nations*. In both these texts the figure relates to the second stage of human history.

The *invisible hand* passage in *The Theory of Moral Sentiments* occurs in a story about a rich landlord whose actions are governed solely by selfishness and avarice. At first sight, judged from a strictly humanitarian standpoint, the landlord's behaviour would clearly deserve censure. We might even conclude that this sort of behaviour should be subject to legal sanction or be the object of some other institutional devices of behavioural control. Smith, however, advises us that we should not attach too much importance to these selfish passions. That the landlord, upon seeing his estates, already enjoys the prospect of the harvest, does no imply that this harvest will ultimately be consumed by him alone:

> 'It is to no purpose, that the proud and unfeeling landlord views his extensive fields, and without a thought for the wants of his brethren, in imagination consumes himself the whole harvest that grows upon them. The homely and vulgar proverb, that the eye is larger than the belly, never was more fully verified than with regard to him. The capacity of his stomach bears no proportion to the immensity of his desires, and will receive no more than that of the meanest peasant.'[45]

According to Smith, the selfishness of the landlord is not in conflict with the public interest as might initially be supposed. In the actual feudal context, to be rich and powerful means to live as a great landlord on a prosperous estate with as many servants as possible providing the desired luxury. In other words, striving for wealth according to the prevailing social values and the accompanying means of wealth production, means that the selfish landlord must strive to produce the richest possible harvests and must then share these harvests with his serfs, peasants and servants.

'The capacity of his [i.e. the landlord's] stomach bears no proportion to the immensity of his desires, and will receive no more than that of the meanest peasant. The rest he is obliged to distribute among those, who prepare, in the nicest manner, that little which he himself makes use of, among those who fit up the palace in which this little is to be consumed, among those who provide and keep in order all the different baubles and trinkets which are employed in the oeconomy of greatness; all of whom thus derive from his luxury and caprice, that share of the necessaries of life, which they would in vain have expected from his humanity or his justice. The produce of the soil maintains at all times nearly that number of inhabitants which it is capable of maintaining. The rich only select from the heap what is most precious and agreeable. They consume little more than the poor, and in spite of their natural selfishness and rapacity, though they mean only their own conveniency, though the sole end which they propose from the labours of all the thousands whom they employ, be the gratification of their own vain and insatiable desires, they divide with the poor the produce of all their improvements.'[46]

Since the selfish landlord depends on his serfs, peasants and servants in order toestablish his wealth and power, he also has to provide them with the necessaries of life. So, considering the distribution of these necessaries, it is apparent that a more equable division of the land would hardly change the distribution of its produce. Or, looking at the selfishness of the landlord, we might say with Smith:

'They [i.e. the rich] are led by an invisible hand [emphasis mine] to make nearly the same distribution of the necessaries of life, which would have been made, had the earth been divided into equal portions among all its inhabitants, and thus without intending it, without knowing it, advance the interest of society, and afford means to the multiplication of the species.'[47]

Given the feudal context of the example, it is also easy to understand that according to Smith, the

'produce of the soil maintains at all times nearly that number of inhabitants which it is capable of maintaining.'[48]

Trade and industry were very limited and closely regulated in a feudal society where the estates functioned as virtually closed economic systems. In such an environment the landlords' desire to distinguish themselves through their wealth and power in order to be praised, naturally expressed itself in exhibiting as much pomp and circumstance as the soil can bear serfs, peasants and servants.[49]

Unlike Ahmad's reading of the invisible hand passage from The Theory of Moral Sentiments, we give a metaphorical rather than a literal interpretation to the phrase. The passage indicates, contrary to the arguments of the traditional moralists, that selfishness does not necessarily conflict with, but may even contribute to the public interest. The invisible hand is a metaphor used to communicate the image of order to people who, used to the perspective of the traditional moralist, see a contradiction between self-interest and public interest. Our interpretation, drawing on Smith's understanding of sympathy, shows that we do not need to presuppose a theistic or deistic model of the world to make the text persuasive in demonstrating the well-orderedness of an economy based on self-interest.

Ahmad's interpretation of this excerpt takes no account of Smith's discourse on *sympathy*, despite the fact that Smith argues at length that it is the longing for *sympathy* which encourages man to strive for wealth and power beyond the necessaries of life. Instead, Ahmad presupposes a theistic or deistic frame of reference which was actually not shared by Smith himself.[50] Effectively, Ahmad begins by assuming the existence of an *invisible hand* and thereafter enquires about its function. He claims that the *invisible hand* has been assigned two different functions, but in discussing these functions he assumes two different invisible hands:

> 'the first invisible hand suppresses the harmful effect of selfishness by limiting the size of the stomach, the second uses the residual selfishness for distributing among Mandeville's "Million" the food that has been saved by the first.'[51]

This introduction of a second invisible hand following his earlier argument about one hand with two functions points to one weakness in Ahmad's account. More seriously Ahmad's interpretation ignores Smith's remarks in *The Theory of Moral Sentiments* concerning man's striving for wealth and power:

1 man is an *individual in society*, his behaviour is *sympathetically* based which means that it is an expression of his interpretation of the values and rules he shares with other people in his society,
2 in his striving for wealth and power he interacts with other people according to the prevailing social values and rules, which ensures that supposedly self-interested motives usually do not conflict with the public interest.

Smith's use of the *invisible hand* in *The Wealth of Nations* accords with his use of the phrase in *The Theory of Moral Sentiments*. Here too, Smith points out that it is a fallacy to think that self-interest necessarily contradicts with public interest. Just as in *The Theory of Moral Sentiments*, he presents in *The Wealth of Nations* an example of behaviour which serves the public interest, even though the actor was motivated purely by self-interest. Here, however, the context of the example shifts from feudal to commercial society.

The *invisible hand* passage from *The Wealth of Nations* is to be found in Smith's critique of two leading doctrines current in the political economy of his time: the *mercantile* and *agricultural systems of political oeconomy*. Both systems endorsed the principle of free commercial exchange, unlike the older doctrines. Referring, however, to the actual economic situation, Smith stressed the point that they were still selective. From Smith's historical perspective both doctrines were anachronistic: they no longer made sense in the commercial society Smith believed to be characteristic of his own time.

Mercantilist pamphlets and essays on economic problems generally presupposed a world in which free commercial exchange was almost completely restricted to the king and a small privileged group of merchants. Wealth was still supposed to consist in money – i.e. gold and silver – amassed in international trade:

'That wealth consists in money, or in gold and silver, is a popular notion which naturally arises from the double function of money, as the instrument of commerce and as a measure of value.'

'A rich country, in the same manner as a rich man, is supposed to be a country abounding in money; and to heap up gold and silver in any country is supposed to be the readiest way to enrich it.'[52]

Free commercial exchange was discussed in relation to its role in the accumulation of gold and silver while the behaviour and actions of various orders of people were still largely determined by old feudal rules.

The *system of agriculture*, in particular the doctrine of physiocracy, was a more progressive doctrine in the sense that it contributed to a rethinking of the origin of wealth by focusing on

'the Produce of Land as either the sole or the principal Source of the Revenue and Wealth of every Country.'[53]

Smith praised this system, since

'in representing the wealth of nations as consisting, not in the unconsumable riches of money, but in the consumable goods annually reproduced by the labour of the society; and in representing perfect liberty as the only effectual expedient for rendering this annual reproduction the greatest possible, its doctrine seems to be in every respect as just as it is generous and liberal.'[54]

The system of agriculture contributed to the emancipation of the farmers and peasantry. However, by exaggerating the importance of agriculture in the production of wealth, the system threatened to hamper the process of emancipation in general. Smith argued in favour of the development of commercial societies according to their own historical dynamics towards the *obvious and simple system of natural liberty.*[55]

The *invisible hand* passage from *The Wealth of Nations* highlights the free commercial exchange of capital to illustrate this argument[56]:

'But the annual revenue of every society is always precisely equal to the exchangeable value of the whole annual produce of its industry, or rather is precisely the same thing with that exchangeable value. As every individual, therefore, endeavours as much as he can both to employ his capital in the support of the domestick industry, and so to direct that industry that its produce may be of the greatest value; every individual necessarily labours to render the annual revenue of the society as great as he can. He generally, indeed, neither intends to promote the publick interest, nor knows how much he is promoting it. By preferring the support of domestick to that of foreign industry, he intends only his own security; and by directing that industry in such a manner as its produce may be of the greatest value, he intends only his own gain, and he is in this, as in many other cases, led by an *invisible hand [emphasis mine]* to promote an end which was no part of his intention. Nor is it always the worse for the society that it was no part of it. By pursuing his own interest he frequently promotes that of the society more effectually than when he really intends to promote it. I have never known much good done by those who affected to trade for the publick good.'[57]

Ahmad's exegesis of this passage is brief. He concludes that in *The Wealth of Nations* the role Smith attributes to the *invisible hand* is completely different from either of the two roles it assumes in *The Theory of Moral Sentiments*. Having described the effect of selfishness on demand in *The Theory of Moral Sentiments* as *Keynesian*, the issue raised by the passage from *The Wealth of Nations* is called *neoclassical*, since it relates selfishness to 'optimizing the use of productive resources'.[58]

Clearly the passage is indeed concerned with the allocation of one of the productive resources – i.e. capital. However, it is debatable whether this in itself is sufficient reason to describe Smith's discussion as *neoclassical*. For example, we might ask, in what way does this passage encourage us to believe that Smith espoused the rationalistic and atomistic view of man presupposed in neoclassical economic analysis? Furthermore, is there any reason to conclude that Smith's reference to selfishness or self-interest in *The Wealth of Nations* contradicts the discussion in *The Theory of Moral Sentiments*, as the opposition between neoclassical and Keynesian economics suggests?

Before demonstrating that the passage from *The Wealth of Nations* conforms with the *sympathy* theory of the earlier work, there is a related point to make with regard to Ahmad's neoclassical interpretation of the *invisible hand* passage from *The Wealth of Nations*. Ahmad writes:

'this was the first occasion when self-interest was assigned to the *specific* role of optimizing the use of productive resources. The disagreement has been in the more general area of the role of self-interest in establishing equilibrium in the system as a whole. Although given considerable prominence in economists' discussions of the invisible hand, this is a somewhat exaggerated view of its function in the passage quoted above; clearer statements can be found elsewhere in *The Wealth of Nations*. I have nothing to add to this debate except to draw attention to a significant piece of evidence which does not seem to have been cited. In a letter to Adam Smith dated April 1759, the year of the publication of *The Theory of Moral Sentiments* and long before that of *The Wealth of Nations*, David Hume congratulates him on the enthusiastic reception of his just-published book and then goes on to say, "I believe I have mentioned to you already Helvetius's book of *De l'Esprit*. It is worth your reading, not for its philosophy, which I do not highly value, but for its agreeable composition" ... Hume's reason for recommendation appears rather unusual for a book of this kind, but given its contents, is not surprising; Helvetius's work is as much a collection of semifictional historical and mythological anecdotes as a treatise on philosophy. However, it does contain a famous statement mentioning the role of self-interest in creating a general social equilibrium: "Si l'univers physique est soumis au loix du mouvement, l'univers moral ne l'est pas moins à celle de l'interest".'[59]

How significant is this quote from Helvetius' book *De l'Esprit* and does it really support the general equilibrium interpretation of Smith's economics? Firstly we should note that the phrase from Helvetius, quoted by Ahmad, cannot be found in Hume's letter. Hume only mentioned Helvetius' book because Smith had told him that he

'was curious of literary Anecdotes.'[60]

Secondly, Ahmad gives no proof that Smith agreed with Helvetius'

'famous statement mentioning the role of self-interest in creating a general social equilibrium: "Si l'univers physique est soumis au loix du mouvement, l'univers moral ne l'est pas moins à celle de l'interest".'[61]

Smith used some ideas from Newton's astronomy analogically to elucidate the well-orderedness of a market economy based on self-interest. This fact in itself, however, is not sufficient to lead us to conclude that Smith anticipated the general equilibrium analysis. To repeat our earlier point: the fact that Smith used a particular notion is far less important than the perspective from which he interpreted it. In the last chapter we will deal in detail with the interpretation of Smith's analogical use of Newton's astronomy, in this section we confine ourselves to an interpretation of the *invisible hand* passage from *The Wealth of Nations* from the perspective of the *sympathetic* model outlined above in Chapter III.

As we have noted, in *The Wealth of Nations* the *invisible hand* serves as an illustration of the effects on the accumulation of wealth which would be realized if production and distribution were coordinated by free commercial exchange. In *The Wealth of Nations* Smith does not explicitly refer to his *sympathetic* theory of man and society. However, the essential elements of his theory of *sympathy* are present in Smith's discussion of the origin of the division of labour:

'This division of labour, from which so many advantages are derived, is not original-ly the effect of any human wisdom, which foresees and intends that general opulence to which it gives occasion. It is the necessary, though very slow and gradual con-sequence of a certain propensity in human nature which has in view no such exten-sive utility; the propensity to truck, barter, and exchange one thing for another.

Whether this propensity be one of those original principles in human nature, of which no further account can be given; or whether, as seems more probable, it be the necessary consequence of the faculties of reason and speech, it belongs not to our present subject to enquire. It is common to all men, and to be found in no other race of animals, which seem to know neither this nor any other species of contracts.'[62]

Elsewhere, for example in the *Lectures of Jurisprudence*, Smith relates the *propensity to truck, barter and exchange* to the *natural inclination* of man *to persuade*:

'If we should enquire into the principle in the human mind on which this disposition of trucking is founded, it is clearly the naturall inclination every one has to persuade.

The offering of a shilling, which to us appears to have so plain and simple a meaning, is in reality offering an argument to persuade one to do so and so as it is for his interest. Men always endeavour to persuade others to be of their opinion even when the matter is of no consequence to them. If one advances any thing concerning China or the *more distant moon* which contradicts what you imagine to be true, you immediately try to persuade him to alter his opinion. And in this manner every one is practising oratory on others thro the whole of his life. – You are uneasy whenever one differs from you, and you endeavour to persuade him to be of your mind; or if you do not it is a certain degree of self command, and to this every one is breeding thro their whole lives. In this manner they acquire a certain dexterity and address in managing their affairs, or in other words in managing of men; and this is altogether the practise of every man in the most ordinary affairs. – This being the constant employment or trade of every man, in the same manner as the artizans invent simple methods of doing their work, so will each one here endeavour to do this work in the simplest manner. That is bartering, by which they adress themselves to the self interest of the person and seldom fail immediately to gain their end. The brutes have no notion of this; the dogs, as I mentiond, by having the same object in their view sometimes unite their labours, but never from contract. The same is seen still more strongly in the manner in which the monkeys rob an orchard at the Cape of Good Hope. – But after they have very ingeniously conveyd away the apples, as they have no contract they fight (even unto death) and leave after many dead upon the spot. They have no other way of gaining their end but by gaining ones favour by fawning and flattering. Men when necessitated do also, but generally apply to the stronger string of self interest.'[63]

When interpreting the *propensity to truck, barter, and exchange* as one of the various manifestations of the communication, competition and concurrence of people's pre-rational longing for mutual sympathy, Smith's argument in favour of free commercial exchange points to an economic order which agrees with a new phase in the evolution of sympathy. As Smith's expression *society in the age of commerce* indicates, a new order is envisioned in which the production of wealth will be as much as possible organized as a free and fair game in which the accumulation and distribution of wealth and power are regulated by direct communication, competition and concurrence of *sympathy*.

As in *The Theory of Moral Sentiments*, so in *The Wealth of Nations*, the *invisible hand* is used as a metaphor to illustrate the point that, contrary to traditional thought, self-interest is not necessarily in conflict with public interest. Embedded in the social context of *mutual sympathy*, behaviour and action motivated by self-interest reflect the interests of society. However, the usage here does differ from that in *The Theory of Moral Sentiments* insofar as the passage in the earlier work refers to a feudal situation in which the communication, competition and concurrence of *sympathy* are severely regulated in accordance with the prevailing aprioristic understanding of social rules and values. *The Wealth of Nations* refers to the commercial society, characterized by the ever growing need of people to act, think and believe according to principles derived from their own experience and reasoning.

Viewed through the lens of Smith's *sympathetic* theory it is a society in which, on the one hand, people want increasingly to interpret values and rules for themselves, and on the other hand, a society where the values and rules are more than ever an expression of the actual free play of *mutual sympathy*. The background of the *invisible hand* passage is the utopian situation in which individual actors freely express their own interpretation of the social values and rules, while these values and rules simultaneously evolve according to the competition and concurrence between these interpretations.

With this context of sound competition and concurrence in mind, it is clear that any interference of the government in the *sympathy* games for wealth and power will have sub-optimal results:

> 'What is the species of domestick industry which his capital can employ, and of which the produce is likely to be of the greatest value, every individual, it is evident, can, in his local situation, judge much better than any statesman or lawgiver can do for him. The statesman, who should attempt to direct private people in what manner they ought to employ their capitals, would not only load himself with a most unnecessary attention, but assume an authority which could safely be trusted, not only to no single person, but to no council or senate whatever, and which would nowhere be so dangerous as in the hands of a man who had folly and presumption enough to fancy himself fit to exercise it.'[64]

However, not only does Smith oppose the government's intervention in the *sympathy* games for wealth and power, it is clear he would also oppose any government intervention in the economy intended to force the transformation towards the utopian situation of completely free commercial exchange. This is not to say that Smith did not object to the obstruction of free commerce where it occurred in various orders of society, nor that he argued for laissez-faire. Instead Smith opposes any institutional change which will be forced against the actual prevailing social beliefs. He argues in favour of the *natural system of perfect liberty and justice* but fears the *man of system*, as he explains in *The Theory of Moral Sentiments*:

> 'The man of system, ..., is apt to be very wise in his own conceit; and is often so enamoured with the supposed beauty of his own ideal plan of government, that he cannot suffer the smallest deviation from any part of it. He goes on to establish it completely and in all its parts, without any regard either to the great interests, or to the strong prejudices which may oppose it. He seems to imagine that he can arrange the different members of a great society with as much ease as the hand arranges the different pieces upon a chess-board.'[65]

The *man of system* is so obsessed with the beauty of his system that in his view man and society are no more than elements within a system which can be manipulated according to his blueprints. Smith criticizes this functionalistic view of man and society thus,

> 'He [*i.e. the man of system*] does not consider that the pieces upon the chess-board have no other principle of motion besides that which the hand impresses upon them; but that, in the great chess-board of human society, every single piece has a principle

of motion of its own, altogether different from that which the legislature might chuse to impress upon it. If those two principles coincide and act in the same direction, the game of human society will go on easily and harmoniously, and is very likely to be happy and successful. If they are opposite and different, the game will go on miserably, and the society must be at all times in the highest degree of disorder.'[66]

The functionalist view effectively denies what really moves people: the communication, competition and concurrence of *sympathy*.

4 *Natural Price*: A Walrasian General Equilibrium Price?

Having discussed Smith's idea of the *invisible hand* we can now turn our attention to the interpretation of the *natural* and *market price* in Book I, Chapter VII of *The Wealth of Nations*.

In this section we begin by considering the comments of Samuel Hollander and Rory O'Donnell on the Walrasian general equilibrium interpretation presented by Schumpeter in his *History of Economic Analysis*. In the second part, an outline of Book I, Chapter VII will provide the background for the reinterpretation advanced in the closing section of this chapter.

As we have noted, Schumpeter regarded Chapter VII of Book I as containing a *rudimentary equilibrium theory* which he described as 'by far the best piece of economic theory turned out by A. Smith'.[67] We have also noted that on the basis of this *rudimentary equilibrium theory* Schumpeter believed Smith should be regarded as a predecessor of Walras. According to Schumpeter, Smith's analysis

'points ... to Walras. The purely theoretical developments of the nineteenth century consist to a considerable degree in improvements upon it.'[68]

In his *Reader's Guide* to Book I, Chapter VII, Schumpeter explains the substance of Smith's equilibrium theory thus:

'Market price, defined in terms of short-run demand and supply, is treated as fluctuating around a "natural" price – J.S Mill's "necessary" price, A. Marshall's "normal" price – which is the price that is sufficient and not more than sufficient to cover "the whole value of the rent, wages, and profit, which must be paid in order to bring" to market that quantity of every commodity "which will supply the effectual demand," that is, the demand effective at that price. There is no theory of monopoly price beyond the meaningless (or even false) sentence that the "price of monopoly is upon every occasion the highest which can be got," whereas "the price of free competition ... is the lowest which can be got," whereas "the price of free competition ... the lowest which can be taken" in the long run – an important theorem though Smith does not seem to have had any notion of the difficulties of a satisfactory proof.'[69]

Later, referring back to his *Reader's Guide*, Schumpeter elucidated his understanding of the equilibrium theory and Smith's concept of *natural price* in a discourse on value and money. This further explanation, however, does little to extend his earlier remarks. That is to say, Schumpeter discussed Smith's economic analysis as a landmark in the growth of economic science towards a maturity most fully represented by Walras' general equilibrium theory without any demonstration that Smith's economics can really be accommodated by the Walrasian general equilibrium frame of reference.[70] Samuel Hollander dealt with this question some twenty years later in *The Economics of Adam Smith*. He concerned himself with

'the relationship between Smith's analyses of economic development and "general equilibrium".'[71]

Discussing the question whether it is legitimate to use

'modern analytical tools, concepts and procedures ... in an analysis of the work of an early writer,'

Hollander contends that

'we believe that there is justification for the utilization of the current state of knowledge regarding the general equilibrium process in a study of the economics of Adam Smith insofar as he adopted the position that the price mechanism can be relied upon to clear product and factor markets.'[72]

However, in discussing the analytic sections of *The Wealth of Nations* in which Smith was supposed to anticipate Walras, Hollander concluded that there is no general equilibrium theory unless we accept the proposition that the analysis is a simplified one, constrained by restrictive assumptions.[73] Describing these parts of *The Wealth of Nations* as a *formal analysis*, Hollander fails to consider the possibility that these findings indicate that Smith's approach does not correspond with the Walrasian general equilibrium view. Instead, he argues that Smith in his main object – discussing real contemporary economic problems – was not restricting himself to the limiting cases of competition and market coordination, implied by the formal analysis:

'The main purpose of the *Wealth of Nations* was evidently not to provide an analytic framework for its own sake. ... It is, ..., not merely the elaboration of the mechanisms of resource allocation which requires attention, but also the particular uses to which the analysis was put, and it is in the course of Smith's treatment of the historical sequence of investment priorities according to the principle of profit-rate equalisation, that a fundamental equilibrating mechanism is utilised, namely, resource allocation governed by the differential pattern of factor endowments between economies. Despite the overwhelming significance of the mechanism, the reader of the Wealth of Nations will find no hint thereof in the First Book. It is rather in the "applied" chapters, dealing with contemporary restraints on importation and with colonial trade, that full and skilful use is made of the mechanism, casting a new light upon Smith's contribution to both theoretical and applied economics.'[74]

Hollander is of course correct to insist that we avoid concentrating exclusively on the so-called formal parts of *The Wealth of Nations* – i.e. Book I – and read the text as a whole. However, reference to the other parts of Smith's discourse does not in itself provide the evidence that Smith's economics is framed in accordance with the Walrasian general equilibrium theory – as has been demonstrated by Rory O'Donnell.[75] O'Donnell's conclusion is devastating:

'In evaluating this influential book every passage from the *Wealth of Nations* cited by Hollander has been examined and it has been found that none of these offers support for the radical new interpretation of Smith as a general equilibrium theorist.'[76]

O'Donnell's discussion of Hollander's *The Economics of Adam Smith* is instructive in the sense that it helps to deconstruct the Walrasian interpretation of Smith's text. It demonstrates how this interpretation is based on a reading in which the resistance of the text against an infusion of the Walrasian general equilibrium frame is neutralized by additional assumptions about the author and his oeuvre.[77] O'Donnell also makes an important contribution to the deconstruction of other traditions in Smith interpretation where Smith is similarly presented, retrospectively, as the source of both the classical surplus and the (neo)classical cost of production approaches.[78] However, O'Donnell is less useful in the search for a new interpretation which recognizes that Smith may have worked within a conceptual framework which differs fundamentally from that of modern nineteenth- and twentieth-century economics.

Implicitly, O'Donnell supports the objectivistic view of interpretation according to which a text is supposed to have an immanent meaning which is discovered by careful and meticulous reading. He aims to let the text speak for itself in order to reveal the correspondence between Smith's economics and later schools of modern economics. O'Donnell does not attempt a hermeneutic interpretation of the text which incorporates the horizon of the author as well as the horizon of the interpreter. Because he fails to consider Smith's own horizon and reviews the text solely from the perspective of modern economics, O'Donnell inevitably concludes that Smith's discourse resembles a mosaic of fragments taken from different lines of thought.[79]

As outlined in Chapter I, the present study aims to contribute to a better understanding of the market economy through a dialogue with Smith on that subject. Focusing on the notions of *natural* and *market price*, we will start with a review of Smith's discussion of these notions in Book I of *The Wealth of Nations* which is described as *analytic* by Schumpeter and as *formal* by Hollander.

Book I is devoted to

'the Causes of Improvement in the productive Powers of Labour, and of the Order according to which its Produce is naturally distributed among the different Ranks of the People.'[80]

It comprises eleven chapters. The first three chapters discuss successively (1) the effects of the division of labour, particularly its contribution to the improvement of labour productivity, (2) the division of labour explained by man's propensity to truck, barter and exchange, and (3) the extent of the market as a limit to the division of labour. Chapters IV, V, VI and VII deal with (4) the origin and use of money, (5) the real and nominal price of commodities, (6) the component parts of the price of commodities, and, (7) the natural and market price of commodities. Finally, Chapters VIII through XI focus on understanding the different levels of wages, profit and rent.

Reviewing these chapters it is clear why Schumpeter isolates Chapter VII for special consideration. In interpreting the concepts of *natural* and *market price*, Smith also deals with the way in which markets coordinate economic behaviour, in the sense that actors are ruled by *natural* and *market prices*. We will now turn our attention to this chapter and Smith's remarks on this so-called price mechanism.

Chapter VII opens with two paragraphs in which it is established that every society or neighbourhood is acquainted with an ordinary rate of wages, profit and rent and that these rates relate to the socio-historical context:

'There is in every society or neighbourhood an ordinary or average rate both of wages and profit in every different employment of labour and stock. This rate is naturally regulated, ..., partly by the general circumstances of the society, their riches or poverty, their advancing, stationary, or declining condition; and partly by the particular nature of each employment.

There is likewise in every society or neighbourhood an ordinary or average rate of rent, which is regulated too, ..., partly by the general circumstances of the society or neighbourhood in which the land is situated, and partly by the natural or improved fertility of the land.'[81]

As these opening lines demonstrate, it is clear from the very outset of the discussion that Smith is concerned with prices as real-world phenomena which are related to the contemporary socio-historical situations. There is no evidence here or elsewhere in Chapter VII of Book I to support the assumption that Smith intended to engage in a formal analysis such as the Walrasian analysis of general equilibrium. Smith points to the fact that every society has its own value patterns varying according to its current socio-historical situation.

In the third paragraph Smith suggests we use the expression *natural rates* for these rates of wages, profit and rent which are central to the prevailing value patterns:

'These ordinary or average rates may be called the natural rates of wages, profit, and rent, at the time and place in which they commonly prevail.'[82]

Here, as elsewhere, *natural* refers to the rates which people experience as normal in the actual social situation.[83] In the fourth paragraph, which focuses on the price of commodities, he introduces the term *natural price* to indicate the value which is experienced in society to be in accordance with the prevailing value patterns:

'When the price of any commodity is neither more nor less than what is sufficient to pay the rent of the land, the wages of the labour, and the profits of stock employed in raising, preparing, and bringing it to market, according to their natural rates, the commodity is then sold for what may be called its natural price.'[84]

The *natural price* indicates the rate of exchange which is believed to be normal, that is to say in accordance with the value patterns prevailing in the society under consideration. Every other price is understood as abnormal and encourages the actors to modify their behaviour.

The actual price at which a commodity is commonly sold, Smith calls the *market price*:

'The actual price at which any commodity is commonly sold is called its market price. It may either be above, or below, or exactly the same with its natural price.'[85]

By using a separate expression, i.e. *market price*, to express the prices realized on the market, Smith emphasizes that the *natural price* has a different connotation. This difference has, however, nothing in common with the Walrasian distinction between general equilibrium prices and other non-equilibrium prices used by the auctioneer in order to discover the general equilibrium prices at which the actors are allowed to trade.[86]

The notion *natural price* refers to the value patterns people share as a frame of reference in their personal interpretations and evaluations of behaviour and action; *market prices* reflect the effects of these personal interpretations and evaluations in the actual exchange:

'The market price of every particular commodity is regulated by the proportion between the quantity which is actually brought to market, and the demand of those who are willing to pay the natural price of the commodity, or the whole value of the rent, labour, and profit, which must be paid in order to bring it thither. Such people may be called the effectual demanders, and their demand the effectual demand; since it may be sufficient to effectuate the bringing of the commodity to market. It is different from the absolute demand. A very poor man may be said in some sense to have a demand for a coach and six; he might like to have it; but his demand is not an effectual demand, as the commodity can never be brought to market in order to satisfy it.'[87]

By pointing to the difference between absolute and effectual demand Smith presents a further illustration of how social value patterns embodied in people's relative position in terms of wealth and power regulate the economy. A very poor man may be said to have a certain absolute demand for a certain commodity – i.e. a certain demand irrespective of his wealth and power in society – however, this demand will not be effective when the actor does not have the appropriate relative wealth and power.

Arguments that Smith anticipated Walrasian general equilibrium theory, often refer to passages from Chapter VII of Book I in which the effect of a difference between *market price* and *natural price* on behaviour and actions is discussed:

'When the quantity of any commodity which is brought to market falls short of the effectual demand, all those who are willing to pay the whole value of the rent, wages, and profit, which must be paid in order to bring it thither, cannot be supplied with the quantity which they want. Rather than want it altogether, some of them will be willing to give more. A competition will immediately begin among them, and the market price will rise more or less above the natural price, according as either the greatness of the deficiency, or the wealth and wanton luxury of the competitors, happen to animate more or less the eagerness of the competition.'

'If, ..., the quantity brought to market should at any time fall short of the effectual demand, some of the component parts of its price must rise above their natural rate. If it is rent, the interest of all other landlords will naturally prompt them to prepare more land for the raising of this commodity; if it is wages or profit, the interest of all other labourers and dealers will soon prompt them to employ more labour and stock in preparing and bringing it to market. The quantity brought thither will soon be sufficient to supply the effectual demand. All the different parts of its price will soon sink to their natural rate, and the whole price to its natural price.'[88]

Schumpeter's argument that the *market price* is essentially a short-run phenomenon and the *natural price* a long-run phenomenon, – i.e. Marshall's long-run normal – may seem, at first sight, to gain some credibility from the following passage[89]:

'The natural price, ..., is, as it were, in the central place, to which the prices of all commodities are continually gravitating. Different accidents may sometimes keep them suspended a good deal above it, and sometimes force them down even somewhat below it. But whatever may be the obstacles which hinder them from settling in this center of repose and continuance, they are constantly tending towards it.'[90]

However, Smith's description of the *natural price* should remind us that this price is not the long run market price caused by ongoing interaction on the market. It is of a different order than the *market price*. That is to say that the *natural price* is part of society's prevailing value patterns which provide the orientation of people's behaviour and action, while the *market price* – irrespective of whether its level differs from or corresponds with the level of the *natural price* – reflects the actual social values, produced in the actual exchange of the personal interpretations which the actors gave to the value patterns in their local situation.

5 *Natural Price* from the *Mutual Sympathy* Perspective

Reading the *invisible hand* passages from the *mutual sympathy* perspective, we concluded in section 3 that we do not need a *deus ex machina* to understand that self-interested behaviour promotes both private and public welfare. When behaviour and action is embedded in the communication, competition and concurrence of *mutual sympathy*, self-interest reflects the actor's intention to take good care of himself against the background of prevailing social values and rules. Thus, self-interested behaviour and action mirrors a well-orderedness which calls for the metaphor of the *invisible hand*, stressing the unintendedness of the order by the actors.

In line with the metaphorical interpretation of the *invisible hand*, we reject the mechanistic interpretation of the idea that *market prices* gravitate towards *natural prices* when people are motivated by self-interest in producing and distributing wealth. In the perspective of the *sympathy* theory of man and society economic behaviour and action is not law-governed but rule-governed. People in a market economy compete for rank and distinction against the horizon of prevailing social values and rules. *Natural prices*, as part of this frame of reference, contribute to the sense and meaning of economic behaviour and evolve with the real exchange on the market.

In order to elucidate this interpretation of the *natural price*, we will confront it with some aspects of the conventional understanding of the market economy, exemplified by Schumpeter's Walrasian general equilibrium theory.[91]

1 Just like modern economists, Smith explains economic behaviour through reference to man's self-love, selfishness or self-interest:

> 'It is not from the benevolence of the butcher, the brewer, or the baker, that we expect our dinner, but from their regard to their own interest. We address ourselves, not to their humanity but to their self-love, and never talk to them of our own necessities but of their advantages.'[92]

Smith's reference to self-love, selfishness or self-interest is not, however, identical with the modern economists's understanding of economic behaviour, modelled according to the idea of the *homo economicus* – an atomistic individual whose behaviour is determined by the rationalistic calculus of expected pain and pleasure. Close reading of the quoted passage from *The Wealth of Nations* reveals that the argument only makes sense when we understand that man is a social being, as is indicated in, respectively, *The Theory of Moral Sentiments* by means of the notion of *sympathy* and in *The Wealth of Nations* by the related idea of man's propensity to truck, barter and exchange.[93]

According to the last passage cited,

> 'We address ourselves ... to their self-love, and never talk to them of our own necessities but of their advantages.'

But how do we know where these advantages lie, when we are atomistic individuals – i.e. entities separated from each other and isolated in our pre-given selves? How can we persuade or even communicate with the butcher, the brewer and the baker, if we do not participate with them in language games such as those dealt with by Smith in his discourse on *sympathy*? Just as in *The Theory of Moral Sentiments* the identity of a person was discussed as related to the communication, competition and concurrence of *sympathy*, so in *The Wealth of Nations*, every individual, even a beggar, looks after exchange to give his life shape and substance:

'Nobody but a beggar chuses to depend chiefly upon the benevolence of his fellow-citizens. Even a beggar does not depend upon it entirely. The charity of well-disposed people, indeed, supplies him with the whole fund of his subsistence. But though this principle ultimately provides him with all the necessaries of life which he has occasion for, it neither does nor can provide him with them as he has occasion for them. The greater part of his occasional wants are supplied in the same manner as those of other people, by treaty, by barter, and by purchase. With the money which one man gives him he purchases food. The old cloaths which another bestows upon him he exchanges for.'[94]

Nobody, not even a beggar, wants to be dependent on human kindness. We seek to give our individual lives shape and substance by means of exchange against the background of current values. In the performance of free exchange we look for mutual appreciation and produce simultaneously an awareness of social values and personal identity.

2 In both *The Theory of Moral Sentiment* and *The Wealth of Nations* we may find many passages in which people view their behaviour from a functional perspective. This could be called rational behaviour if we are careful to avoid confusion with the same expression in modern economics.

To stress the difference we have used the expression *rationalistic* to character-ize the meaning of rational behaviour in modern economics. The tendency in modern economic analysis to reduce behaviour and action to ends-means calcula-tions by atomistic actors is a rationalistic fallacy when viewed from Smith's *sympathetic* perspective on utility:

'When by natural principles we are led to advance those ends, which a refined and enlightened reason would recommend to us, we are very apt to impute to that reason, as to their efficient cause, the sentiments and actions by which we advance those ends, and to imagine that to be the wisdom of man.'[95]

So too, in *The Wealth of Nations* we find further indications that Smith under-stood his discussions of the functional aspects of the market economy to be related to the more encompassing project, i.e. to give sense and meaning – substantial rationality – to the evolving *commercial society*. A first example occurs in his discussion of the division of labour. While explicating the effects of the division of labour on wealth, Smith emphasizes that the division of labour is not the effect of ends-means calculations but the consequence of man's propensity to truck, barter and exchange. That is to say, it reflects the tendency to communi-cate, compete and concur for *mutual sympathy* in the context of producing and distributing wealth:

'This division of labour, from which so many advantages are derived, is not original-ly the effect of any human wisdom, which foresees and intends that general opulence to which it gives occasion. It is the necessary, though very slow and gradual con-sequence of a certain propensity in human nature which has in view no such exten-sive utility; the propensity to truck, barter, and exchange one thing for another.

Whether this propensity be one of these original principles in human nature, of which no further account can be given; or whether, as seems more probable, it be the necessary consequence of the faculties of reason and speech, it belongs not to our present subject to enquire.'[96]

A different example may be found in Chapter X of Book I: *Of Wages and Profit in the Different Employments of Labour and Stock*:

'Honour makes a great part of the reward of all honourable professions. In point of pecuniary gain, all things considered, they are generally under-recompensed.'[97]

This passage concerning honour is not only reminiscent of Smith's discussion in *The Theory of Moral Sentiments* about man's tendency to seek *mutual sympathy*. It also reminds us of what Smith said about the bulk of people who do not catch the eye in public commerce and just follow the rules.[98] By analogy the quote can be read as suggesting that labour which is not honourable, will only be commanded by rules expressing the rates at which the value of labour is fully recompensed in money.

3 While arguing for the free market economy, Friedrich A. Hayek repeated in *Economics and Knowledge* Smith's claim that the individual actor knows much better than the government what he has to do in his particular situation in order to produce wealth.[99] From this perspective, the system of interrelated markets is vital to the continued prosperity of a society because the communication, competition and concurrence of the exchange transmits the fragmented and context-specific knowledge of the actors throughout the economy in the sense of transforming that knowledge through the various webs of exchanges into the more general knowledge that cumulates in *market* and *natural price* signals.

Smith's *sympathy* based theory of man and society reminds us not to reduce the multidimensional jumble of all the different webs of exchanges that comprise a market economy to a mechanism driven by general and abstract price signals. It is important to note that from Smith's *sympathetic* perspective the transmission of knowledge reflects the simultaneous involvement of people in various kinds of exchanges. Smith's observation that the tendency to be involved in another person's well-being becomes less intense and less tuned to the characteristics particular of this well-being as people become less closely related, is illuminating in this respect:

'We expect less sympathy from a common acquaintance than from a friend: we cannot open to the former all those little circumstances which we can unfold to the latter: we assume, therefore, more tranquillity before him, and endeavour to fix our thoughts upon those general outlines of our situation which he is willing to consider. We expect still less sympathy from an assembly of strangers, and we assume, therefore, still more tranquillity before them, and always endeavour to bring down our passion to that pitch, which the particular company we are in may be expected to go along with.'

'... a certain reserve is necessary when we talk of our friends, our own studies, our own professions. All these are objects which we cannot expect should interest our companions in the same degree in which they interest us. ... A philosopher is company to a philosopher only; the member of a club, to his own little knot of companions.'

'As to the eye of the body, objects appear great or small, not so much according to their real dimensions, as according to the nearness or distance of their situation; so do they likewise to what may be called the natural eye of the mind: and we remedy the defects of both these organs pretty much in the same manner.
... to the selfish and original passions of human nature, the loss or gain of a very small interest of our own, appears to be of vastly more importance, excites a much more passionate joy or sorrow, a much more ardent desire or aversion, than the greatest concern of another with whom we have no particular connexion. ...
... how comes it that our active principles should so often be so generous and so noble? ... It is reason, principle, conscience, the inhabitant of the breast, the man within, the great judge and arbiter of our conduct.'[100]

By analogy, the market economy consists of a multitude of interrelated webs of exchanges reflecting the fact that the actors are simultaneously engaged in various kinds of exchanges and interpret behaviour, actions and their results differently according to varying commitments and perspectives. Thus, when we discuss the importance of *natural* and *market prices* in coordinating behaviour and action, we must always be fully aware that these general and abstract values, expressed in an artificial means of exchange, are effective in relation to the multitude of exchanges in which these general and abstract values are related to and interfere with more local, and personal valuations.

From this *sympathy*-based perspective of value, it is clearly inappropriate to ask whether Smith adhered to either a subjective or an objective theory of value, to either a demand theory of value, or a labour or a cost-of-production theory of value. What in modern economics are interpreted as conflicting causal explanations of value, are in the *sympathetic* view a set of complementary rational reconstructions, each elucidating current value patterns from a different perspective.

4 With reference to Smith's *sympathy*-based view of man and society, *natural prices* have been interpreted as social values which people recognize as being adhered to in producing and distributing wealth. The auto-coordination of the market economy, expressed in *market prices* gravitating to *natural prices*, has been understood as the effect of the communication, competition and concurrence by people longing for praise(worthiness) in the context of the production and distribution of wealth.

This interpretation of Smith's discussion of the auto-coordinating market economy sheds new light on Tobin's assessment of the *invisible hand*, dealt with in section 1. In that section we considered Tobin's 'bad news' that Smith's idea of the *invisible hand* is inappropriate to understanding real-world economies. We considered various passages from Smith's work in which, each time from a different perspective, a serious concern for realism is expressed, and argued that Tobin's assessment referred to models of the market economy which refer to a view of man and society which Smith would have rejected.

Our *sympathy*-based reinterpretation of Smith's discussion of the *invisible hand*, of the *natural* and *market price* not only shows that Tobin's observation does not in fact relate to Smith, but also indicates that the problem of modern economics with understanding the phenomenon of auto-coordination relates to its atomistic and rationalistic interpretation of man and society.

Against the background of Smith's *sympathy*-based view of man and society, auto-coordination is the reflection of well-orderedness produced in the communication, competition and concurrence of people longing for praise(worthiness) in the context of the production and distribution of wealth. But what does auto-coordination mean in a model in which man is conceived as an atomistic and rational individual: an individual whose self-understanding is not based in pre-rational intercourse? This problem also raises questions about Tobin's more positive verdict on Smith's *invisible hand*, namely that his intuitions can be rigorously formulated and proven. What does Walrasian economics really prove?

Close reading of Schumpeter's discussion of Walras' general equilibrium analysis suggests that the Walrasian causal explanation of auto-coordination based on the idea of atomistic and rationalistic actors cannot be successful: it assumes what it sets out to prove, and comes close to circular reasoning. That is to say, the well-ordered whole – general equilibrium – is not explained as the effect of interaction between individuals conceived as rationally reacting to subjectively perceived opportunities. General equilibrium – the explanandum – is presupposed by an apriori application of specific laws to the behaviour of the individual actors – the explanans. The actors are assumed to know their general equilibrium behaviour and to realize it.

> 'It is one of the greatest merits of Walras to have distinguished between the 'existence' and the 'stability' problems and to have paralleled the argument about the former by an elaborate argument of the latter. However, he treated the problem of stability in a peculiar way, because it posed itself to him in connection with what in strict logic is an entirely different problem, namely, the problem of the relation between the mathematical solution of his equations and the processes of any actual market: first and foremost he was anxious to show that the people in the market, though evidently not solving any equations, do by a different method the same thing that the theorist does by solving equations; or, to put it differently, that the 'empirical' method used in perfectly competitive markets and the 'theoretical' or 'scientific' method of the observer tend to produce the same equilibrium configuration.'[101]

Limitation to the so-called scientific case of solving mathematical equations – the so-called existential proof – does not alter the conclusion, since the equilibrium is preprogrammed in the equations of the model.

Notes

1. See Tobin, J., 'Theoretical Issues in Macroeconomics' in Feiwel, G.R. (ed.), *Issues in Contemporary Macroeconomics and Distribution*, London, 1985, p. 105.
2. Id., pp. 105–106. We remark here, albeit superfluously, that Tobin considers the Walrasian general equilibrium theory as the basic paradigm of economic science:
   > '*Walrasian general equilibrium theory* – the basic paradigm of our discipline and as it happens, the scientific counterpart of the common central theme of the conservative counter-revolutions, The Invisible Hand.'
   > (Id., p. 104)
3. LJ(B) 3.
4. Hollander, S., 'The Historical Dimension of the Wealth of Nations', *Transactions of the Royal Society of Canada*, Series IV, vol. 14, 1976, pp. 277–292.
5. EPS Astronomy, IV.76.
6. WN IV.ix.28. See also Myers, M.L., *The Soul of Modern Economic Man*. Ideas of Self-interest. *Thomas Hobbes to Adam Smith*, Chicago, 1983, pp. 98–99.
7. TMS II.ii.3.5.
8. For example Bitterman, H.J., 'Adam Smith's Empiricism and the Law of Nature', *Journal of Political Economy*, vol. 48, 1940, pp. 487–520 and 703–734, Mirowski, Ph.E., 'Adam Smith, Empiricism, and the Rate of Profit in Eighteenth-Century England', *History of Political Economy*, vol. 14, 1982, pp. 178–198, Myers, M.L., *The Soul of Modern Economic Man*. Ideas of Self-Interest. *Thomas Hobbes to Adam Smith*, Chicago, 1983.
9. Smith's view of science will be more extensively discussed below in the following two sections on the *invisible hand*.
10. See for a similar critique, for instance, Kuttner, R., 'On the State of Economics', *Dialogue*, 1986, pp. 65–71.
11. See also chapter III, p. 88.
12. TMS VII.iii.I.2. For further discussion of the educative function of science in respect to society, see also TMS IV.1.11.
13. TMS VII.iii.1.4.
14. Schumpeter, J.A., *History of Economic Analysis*, London, 1954/1972, p. 189. Schumpeter describes the Walrasian general equilibrium theory as the
    > 'system of the conditions or relations (equations) that are to determine the equilibrium values of all the economic variables, to wit: the prices of all products and factors and the quantities of these products and factors that would be bought, in perfect equilibrium and pure competition, by all the households and firms.'
    > (Schumpeter, J.A., *History of Economic Analysis*, London, 1954/1972, pp. 998–999)
15. Schumpeter, J.A., *History of Economic Analysis*, New York, 1954/1959, p. 968.
16. Schumpeter, J.A., *History of Economic Analysis*, London, 1954/1972, p. 999, footnote 1. See also p. 1008:
    > 'it is clear from the outset that the markets of real life never do attain equilibrium,'
    and p. 1000, footnote 4:
    > 'These views *[concerning the oscillations that occur around the equilibrium state]* do not differ essentially from those of Adam Smith. Walras' analogy of market equilibrium with a *lac agité par le vent*, which is so characteristic for his belief in the reality – normality even – of the equilibrium level of values, has been repeated by J.B. Clark. It should be emphasized once more that this uncritical belief, undoubtedly held widely at that time, is untenable; but that this fact does not render analysis of the properties of those equilibrium levels either superfluous or practically useless ... It should also be emphasized that Walras ..., though he did underestimate the distance

between his theory and the facts of capitalist reality, was by no means unaware of its existence.'

17. Schumpeter, J.A., *History of Economic Analysis*, London, 1954/1972, p. 999. See also p. 1008:

'it is clear from the outset that the markets of real life never do attain equilibrium.'

18. Cf. In *Money, Interest, and Prices. An Integration of Monetary and Value Theory*, Patinkin also points out that Walras did not understand his theories as a purely formal analysis. Patinkin criticises Goodwin in this matter:

'Goodwin ... basing himself on p. 106 of the Elements, says: "Walras disavowed in advance the use of this kind of market adjustment [i.e., the tâtonnement] as a practical device. ... He explicitly states that it is only a mathematical method of solution and not the practical one exemplified in the behavior of real markets." Actually, the passage on p. 106 says just the opposite – as do all the other passages just cited. Goodwin's statement must accordingly be rejected as a fundamental misinterpretation of Walras' conceptual framework.'

(p. 532)

19. Schumpeter, J.A., *History of Economic Analysis*, London, 1954/1972, p. 371.

20. Id., p. 1002. See also pp. 1008–1009.

21. Both in the theist and in the deist worldview, by means of referring to God, it is assumed that the course of events is previously given to mankind. Theism however, sees in the events the direct hand of God, while deism places God at a distance by presuming that God is not directly active in the world, but has given his order in the form of natural laws to the world at creation. Cf. Manenschijn, G., *Moraal en eigenbelang bij Thomas Hobbes en Adam Smith*, Amsterdam, 1979, pp. 196–197.

22. Ahmad, S., 'Adam Smith's Four Invisible Hands', *History of Political Economy*, vol. 22, 1990, pp. 137–144.

23. Ahmad, S., 'Adam Smith's Four Invisible Hands', *History of Political Economy*, vol. 22, 1990, p. 143.

24. Id.

25. The author makes no distinction between theism and deism. He remarks in a note on page 143:

'Here "theistic" includes "deistic", instead of being considered its opposite.'

26. Ahmad, S., 'Adam Smith's Four Invisible Hands', *History of Political Economy*, vol. 22, 1990, p. 142.

27. Id., pp. 142–143. As we mentioned above, in Ahmad theism includes deism.

28. Id., p. 143.

29. Id., p. 143.

30. EPS Astronomy, Intro. 1 en 7.

31. EPS Astronomy, II.11.

32. EPS Astronomy, II.7.

33. See also Thompson, H.F., 'Adam Smith's Philosophy of Science', *The Quarterly Journal of Economics*, vol. 79, 1965, pp. 213–233 and Skinner, A.S., 'Adam Smith: An Aspect of Modern Economics?', *Scottish Journal of Political Economy*, vol. 26, 1979, pp. 109–125.

34. EPS Astronomy, II.3 and 7; see also EPS Astronomy, II.11.

35. EPS Astronomy, II.8.

36. Id.

37. Cf. Ahmad, S., 'Adam Smith's four invisible hands', *History of Political Economy*, 1990 (22), p. 137:

'a catchy phrase, ... used by Smith on only three occasions: once in *The theory of moral sentiments* (1759), once in *The Wealth of Nations* (1776), and once in his "History of astronomy" (1795).'

Ahmad still counts four *invisible hands*, because he claims

> 'that on at least one occasion *[i.e. in The Theory of Moral Sentiments]* the hand has been assigned two different functions.'

(Ahmad, S., 'Adam Smith's four invisible hands', *History of Political Economy*, 1990 (22), p. 138)

38. EPS Astronomy, III.2.
39. EPS Astronomy, III.2. Cf. Macfie, A.L., 'The Invisible Hand of Jupiter', *Journal of the History of Ideas*, 1971(32), p. 595.
40. Ahmad, S., 'Adam Smith's Four Invisible Hands', *History of Political Economy*, vol. 22, 1990, p. 142.
41. EPS Astronomy, III.2.
42. EPS Astronomy, III.3. Cf. TMS V.2.9.
43. EPS Astronomy, III.3.
44. See Section IV of *The History of Astronomy*.
45. TMS IV.1.10.
46. Id.
47. Id.
48. Id.
49. See also WN III.iv.5 and WN V.i.b.
50. Those who are not yet completely convinced that theism or deism was not Smith's frame of reference, might consider the closing lines of the paragraph from which the *invisible hand* excerpt was taken:

> 'When Providence divided the earth among a few landly masters, it neither forgot nor abandoned those who seemed to have been left out in the partition. These last too enjoy their share of all that it produces. In what constitutes the real happiness of human life, they are in no respect inferior to those who would seem so much above them. In ease of body and peace of mind, all the different ranks of life are nearly upon a level, and the beggar, who suns himself by the side of the highway, possesses that security which kings are fighting for.'

Should we interpret the first line literally, assuming that Smith believed the world to be ordered by God as the real, pre-ordained, cause of things which man can only try to represent as correctly as possible in his theories and models of the world? This interpretation seems inconsistent with the rest of Smith's oeuvre. Not only does his view of knowledge and science contradict this interpretation, but also his *sympathy*-based evolutionary-historical discussions of law, government and other institutions of human society in various epochs. In particular Book III of *The Wealth of Nations* should be mentioned, anticipated in for example the *Report of 1762–1763* of the *Lectures of Jurisprudence*. There Smith deals extensively with the landlords – the subject of the *invisible hand* quote – discussing the revolutions law and government had undergone after the fall of the Roman Empire. Cf. WN III.ii and LJ(A), for instance, pp. 49–54.

Referring to other passages in *The Theory of Moral Sentiments* in which the figure of *Providence* is used, the conclusion has to be that Smith speaks of *Providence* in a metaphorical sense, thus using an image which was still common in the contemporary *commercial society* which was not yet fully emancipated from the feudal past. Cf. TMS III.5.7.

51. Ahmad, S., 'Adam Smith's four invisible hands', *History of Political Economy*, 1990 (22:1), pp. 138–140.
52. WN IV.i.1 and 2.
53. WN IV.ix.
54. WN IV.ix.38.
55. Cf. WN IV.ix.38, IV.ix.28–29, IV.ix.49–51.
56. See also WN IV.vii.c.44 for Smith's critique of the regulation of the allocation of capital.

57. WN IV.ii.9. See also WN IV.ii.4:
    'Every individual is continually exerting himself to find out the most advantageous employment for whatever capital he can command. It is his own advantage, indeed, not that of the society, which he has in view. But the study of his own advantage naturally, or rather necessarily, leads him to prefer that employment which is most advantageous to the society.'

58. Ahmad, S., 'Adam Smith's four invisible hands', *History of Political Economy*, 1990 (22:1), p. 140.

59. Id., p. 141.

60. The reference to Helvetius in the letter relates to a conversation between Hume and a 'man of Letters' who interrupted him while he was writing that letter.
    'But to return to your Book *[after being interrupted by the visit]* and its Success in this Town, I must tell you – – A Plague of Interruptions! I orderd myself to be deny'd; and yet here is one that has broke in upon me again. He is a man of Letters, and we have had a good deal of literary Conversation. You told me, that you was curious of literary Anecdotes, and therefore I shall inform you of a few, that have come to my knowledge. I believe I have mentiond to you already Helvetius's Book *de l'Esprit*. It is worth your reading, not for its philsophy, which I do not highly value, but for its agreeable composition'
    (Corr. p. 34)

61. Id., p. 141.

62. WN I.ii.1–2.

63. LJ(A) vi.56. Also LJ(B) 221–222:
    'If a person asserts any thing about the moon, tho' it should not be true, he will feel a kind of uneasiness in being contradicted, and would be very glad that the person he is endeavouring to perswade should be of the same way of thinking with himself. We ought then mainly to cultivate the power of perswasion, and indeed we do so without intending it.'
    See further ED 2.20–21; LJ(A) vi.44, 48 and 54–56, and LJ(B) 219–222 and 300–301.

64. WN IV.ii.10. We also find the same idea elsewhere.
    'It is thus that the private interests and passions of individuals naturally dispose them to turn their stocks towards the employments which in ordinary cases are most advantageous to the society. But if from this natural preference they should turn too much of it towards those employments, the fall of profit in them and the rise of it in all others immediately dispose them to alter this faulty distribution. Without any intervention of law, therefore, the private interests and passions of men naturally lead them to divide and distribute the stock of every society, among all the different employments carried on in it, as nearly as possible in the proportion which is most agreeable to the interest of the whole society.'
    (WN IV.vii.c.88)
    'All systems either of preference or of restraint, therefore, being thus completely taken away, the obvious and simple system of natural liberty establishes itself of its own accord. Every man, as long as he does not violate the laws of justice, is left perfectly free to pursue his own interest his own way, and to bring both his industry and capital into competition with those of any other man, or order of men. The sovereign is completely discharged from a duty, in attempting to perform which he must always be exposed to innumerable delusions, and for the proper performance of which no human wisdom or knowledge could ever be sufficient; the duty of superintending the industry of private people, and of directing it towards the employments most suitable to the interest of the society. According to the system of natural liberty, the sovereign has only three duties to attend to; three duties of great importance, indeed, but plain and

intelligible to common understandings: first, the duty of protecting the society from the violence and invasion of other independent societies; secondly, the duty of protecting, as far as possible, every member of the society from the injustice or oppression of every other member of it, or the duty of establishing an exact administration of justice; and thirdly, the duty of erecting and maintaining certain publick works and certain publick institutions, which it can never be for the interest of any individual, or small number of individuals, to erect and maintain; because the profit could never repay the expence to any individual or small number of individuals, though it may frequently do much more than repay it to a great society.'

(WN IV.ix.51)

WN IV.vii.c.44 gives an example of the regulations for the capital allocation criticised by Smith.

65. TMS VI.ii.2.17.
66. Id.
67. Schumpeter, J.A., *History of Economic Analysis*, London, New York, 1954/1959/1972, p. 189.
68. Id., p. 189.
69. Id.
70. Id., pp. 308–309:

'The reader should refresh his recollection of the Reader's Guide presented above. A. Smith's exposition in the first Book surges purposefully up to the phenomenon of price and down again into the component parts of commodity prices, which components are the cost and income categories, wages, profit, and rent. This is, to repeat, a primitive way of describing the universal interdependence of the magnitudes that constitute the economic cosmos; but it is an effective way. Critics who did not understand that the theory of price is but another name for theory of economic logic – including, among other things, all the principles of allocation of resources and of formation of incomes – blamed him for having adopted the narrow point of view of the businessman. Other critics who did not understand the nature of a system of interdependent magnitudes accused him of circular reasoning. ... It is this part of his performance that constitutes his chief merit in this field. There are others. As primitive but as distinctly visible as is his concept of universal interdependence is his concept of equilibrium or "natural" price. This equilibrium price is simply the price at which it is possible to supply, in the long run, each commodity in a quantity that will equal "effective demand" *at that price*. This again is the price that will, in the long run, just cover costs. And these, in turn, are equal to the sum total of wages, profits, and rents that have to be paid or imputed at their *"ordinary or average rates"*. Thus, we also get a glimpse of Marshall's distinction between short-run and long-run phenomena, A. Smith's market price being essentially a short-run phenomenon, his "natural" price a long-run phenomenon – Marshall's long-run normal.'

71. Hollander, S., *The Economics of Adam Smith*, Toronto, 1973, p. 44.
72. Id., p. 13. According to Hollander, Smith was operating within the same framework as used by Walrasian equilibrium theorists:

'we adopt the position that the use of modern analytical tools, concepts and procedures may be of considerable aid in an analysis of the work of an early writer, *provided that he was operating within the general frame for which these devices are appropriate*. In particular, we believe that there is justification for'

73. See for example Hollander, S., *The Economics of Adam Smith*, Toronto, 1973, pp. 122–124.
74. Id., p. 307. Cf. O'Donnell, R., *Adam Smith's Theory of Value and Distribution*, London, 1990, pp. 172–173.

75. O'Donnell, R., *Adam Smith's Theory of Value and Distribution*, London, 1990, pp. 171–193.

76. Id., p. 196. See also pp. 6, 192–194 and 226.

77. For an example of O'Donnell's demonstration of how Hollander infuses Smith's text with his Walrasian general equilibrium frame see O'Donnell's discussion of Hollander's interpretation of Smith's use of the notions of supply and demand:

'The "market price" of a commodity is said to be "regulated by the proportion between the quantity which is actually brought to market, and the demand of those who are willing to pay the natural price" or the "effectual" demand for the commodity. Supply and demand are thus formally defined as specific quantities. But the argument which follows to substantiate the preceding proposition makes it clear that Smith had in mind the concept of a negatively-sloped demand schedule; the "effectual demand" was, in other words, understood as a quantity demanded at a particular price, namely at the long-run cost price. That a positively-sloped supply curve applicable to the market period was similarly envisaged may also be demonstrated.

The degree of any increase in price above the long-run cost level depends in part, Smith argued, upon the magnitude of excess demand at the latter level; but given the excess demand, other forces will determine the extent of price increase. In effect this argument amounts to an attempt to explain the degree of demand elasticity. ...

In the case of an excess supply at cost price, two mechanisms are said to operate. In the first place, there is competition on the part of consumers. ... In addition Smith remarks that in the case at hand market price will fall "according as the greatness of the excess increases more or less the competition of the sellers, or according as it happens to be more or less important to them to get immediately rid of the commodity. ..." Here the emphasis is upon the responsiveness of supply. In effect an attempt is made to determine supply elasticity. ...

It follows from the above account that the "quantity which is actually brought to market" was not in fact regarded as decisive by Smith, because of the necessity of allowing for possible withdrawal of supplies. That Smith did not recognize the equivalent complication in the case of an excess demand where the drawing down of inventories would be a relevant consideration, but placed the entire burden of response on demand, seems to be merely the accidental consequence of the particular formulation adopted rather than a matter of principle. Accordingly, we may say that some justification is provided both for a negatively-sloped demand curve and also for a positively-sloped supply curve – throughout their respective lengths – relating to the market period.'

(Hollander, S., *The Economics of Adam Smith*, Toronto, 1973, pp. 117–118)

O'Donnell argues that it is not clear that Smith for example had in mind a negatively-sloped demand schedule:

'the *[Hollander's]* argument ... is no more than that price will rise when "quantity brought to market" falls short of the "effectual demand" and *visa versa* (*WN*, I.vii. 8–11). This *observation* is *not* equivalent to the supply and demand *theory* of value. As Garegnani notes, in that *theory* "we are ... dealing with a much stricter notion than the immediately plausible one according to which an accidental fall in the quantity supplied below its normal level is likely to be accompanied by a rise in the price" (1983, p. 309), Nor is the *observation* that, at that accidentally high price, less is purchased than at the natural price, evidence of the "analytical reasoning" (to use Hollander's own criterion) that underlies a demand schedule...' (O'Donnell, R., *Adam Smith's Theory of Value and Distribution*, London, 1990, p. 174)

See also the following two quotes from Hollander as illustrations of how problems with interpreting Smith's text in a Walrasian general equilibrium framework are 'solved'.

'In chapter 4 Smith's theory of exchange value is discussed within a general equilib-

rium framework. Particular attention is paid to a number of restrictive assumptions regarding the properties of the production function implicit in the formal treatment of "market and natural price". But it will be made clear that the formal analysis does not represent Smith's entire contribution, since allowance is made for "substitution" relationships of various kinds in actual applications of the analysis. Similarly, the crucial role played by demand in allocation theory is illustrated within a broad context where the strict assumptions of the formal analysis are relaxed.'
(p. 22)

'while in Book I.vii Smith, as we have seen, assumed constant aggregate supplies of the factors, the theoretical question arises how, upon alterations in the relative amounts of the factors the equilibrium process would operate under the restrictive conditions in question. It is, of course, possible that the assumptions of the formal account of the general equilibrium process were introduced as a deliberate first approximation. But whether this is so or whether, as it is more likely, Smith was simply unaware of all the assumptions implicit in his analysis, the fact is that he did allow in practical applications, for certain substitution relationships. ... Thus, while it is true that he did not formally introduce the substitution relation into his analysis as a general phenomenon, certain specific aspects thereof were recognized in the treatment of particular problems within the economics of allocation.'
(p. 124)

78. Cf. O'Donnell, R., *Adam Smith's Theory of Value and Distribution*, London, 1990, pp. 2 and 6.
79. O'Donnell, R., *Adam Smith's Theory of Value and Distribution*, London, 1990, p. 229:
    'Smith was a *part* of the development of classical theory. This proposition, as re-fashioned in this study, does not require the attribution of any later theories to Smith. Nor does it require any speculation concerning what Smith may have "had in mind", as opposed to what he said. Nor does it require any explanation as to why Smith's anticipation of sophisticated theories was so completely misunderstood by his successors. Finally, the case presented here does not require that where Smith was confused, unclear or contradictory he must be said to have been moving in the direction of surplus theory. Indeed, what has emerged is that a surplus approach to value and distribution was only a small part of a work which contained many elements. These elements may, in fact, be parts of systematic lines of thought inherited from various predecessors. It has not been possible, in this study, to trace the *origin* of many of Smith's ideas. Ultimately, the case made rests on what has been cited from his work.'
80. Smith, A., *An Inquiry into the Nature and Causes of the Wealth of Nations*, Oxford, 1976, p. 13.
81. WN I.vii.1–2.
82. WN I.vii.3.
83. WN I.vii.4.
84. WN I.vii.4.
85. WN I.vii.7.
86. To avoid misunderstanding we will point out, once more, that we refer here to the conventional interpretation of Walras' and Marshall's economic analysis as represented by Schumpeter in his *History of Economic Analysis*. Present-day re-interpretations of, for example, Walras' work by Maks, Van Witteloostuyn, Jolink or Walker are not addressed in this discussion. Cf. Maks, J. and A. van Witteloostuyn, 'Walras Understood or Mis-understood', *Research Memorandum 86–014, Rijksuniversiteit Limburg, 1986*; Jolink, A., *Liberté, Egalité, Rareté. The Evolutionary Economics of Léon Walras: An Analytical Reconstruction*, Amsterdam, 1991; Jolink, A., 'Onvoltooid verleden tijd', *Economenblad*,

vol. 13, 1991, 27 November, pp. 3; and Walker, D., 'Walras' Theories of Tâtonnement', *Journal of Political Economy*, vol. 95, 1987, pp. 758–774.

87. WN I.vii.8.
88. WN I.vii.9 en 14.
89. Schumpeter, J.A., *History of Economic Analysis*, New York, 1954/1959, pp. 308–309. Here again, it is important to note that we do not discuss Schumpeter's point of view that Marshall's price theory is just a special case of the Walrasian general equilibrium theory. See for example Schumpeter, J.A., *History of Economic Analysis*, New York, 1954/1959, pp. 836–837, 996–997.
90. WN I.vii.15.
91. This means mainstream Walrasian general equilibrium analysis, illustrated in Schumpeter's *History of Economic Analysis*, New York, 1954/1959.
92. WN I.ii.2.
93. Cf. pp. 134-135.
94. WN I.ii.2.
95. TMS II.ii.3.5.
96. WN I.ii.1–2. The editors of *The Glasgow Edition* of *The Wealth of Nations* rightly remark:
   'In LJ (B) 221, ed. Cannan 171, Smith argued in referring to the division of labour that "The real foundation of it is that principle to persuade which so much prevails in human nature." The same point is made in LJ (A) vi.56.'
   (note 3)
   See also pp. 134-135
97. WN I.x.b.2.
98. Cf., for instance, p. 95.
99. Hayek, F.A., 'Economics and Knowledge', 1937, reprinted in Hayek, F.A., *Individualism and Economic Order*, London, 1949.
100. TMS I.i.4.9, I.ii.2.6 and III.3.2–4. The question
   'how comes it that our active principles should so often be so generous and so noble?'
   from III.3.2–4 is preceded by
   'Let us suppose that the great empire of China, with all its myriads of inhabitants, was suddenly swallowed up by an earthquake, and let us consider how a man of humanity in Europe, who had no sort of connexion with that part of the world, would be affected upon receiving intelligence of this dreadful calamity. He would, I imagine, first of all, express very strongly his sorrow for the misfortune of that unhappy people ... He would too, perhaps, if he was a man of speculation, enter into many reasonings concerning the effects which this disaster might produce upon the commerce of Europe, and the trade and business of the world in general. And when all this fine philosophy was over, when all these humane sentiments had been once fairly expressed, he would pursue his business or his pleasure, take his repose or his diversion, with the same ease and tranquillity, as if no such accident had happened. The most frivolous disaster which could befal himself would occasion a more real disturbance. If he was to lose his little finger to-morrow, he would not sleep to-night; but, provided he never saw them, he will snore with the most profound security over the ruin of a hundred millions of his brethren, and the destruction of that immense multitude seems plainly an object less interesting to him, than this paltry misfortune of his own. To prevent, therefore, this paltry misfortune to himself, would a man of humanity be willing to sacrifice the lives of a hundred millions of his brethren, provided he had never seen them? Human nature startles with horror at the thought, and the world, in the greatest depravity and corruption, never produced such a villain as could be

capable of entertaining it. But what makes this difference? When our passive feelings are almost always so sordid and so selfish.'

101.   Schumpeter, J.A., *History of Economic Analysis*, New York, 1954/1959, p. 1008.

V Adam Smith and the Crisis of Modern Economics

The time has come for an attempt to assess the consequences, for the direction of the economic thought of our day, of the demise of the general equilibrium paradigm we have witnessed in recent decades.

(L.M. Lachman, *The Market as an Economic Process*, Oxford, 1986, p. 1)

Introduction

Smith used the expression *invisible hand* to indicate that behaviour which is motivated by a self-interested perspective on prevailing social values and rules, not only promotes the wealth of the actor but also the wealth of other people in the economy. In nineteenth-century modern economics which focused on the analysis of the market economy the *invisible hand* became synonymous with the *price mechanism*. Along with the notion of the *price mechanism*, the idea of the *invisible hand* has periodically been the subject of fierce debate. However, in the 1970s and 1980s a fundamental change took place. Whereas in the past the debate was polarized between supporters and opponents of the free market economy and its price mechanism, today almost every school of economic thought recognizes the relevance of the market for achieving a prosperous society. Current differences focus on a new process approach of the market economy.

At first sight we might characterize today's debate on different interpretations of the *price mechanism* as a crisis of vision.[1] However, today's discussions between various schools of economic thought about the principle of (methodological) individualism, about deregulation and institutions, about the relevance of social capital to the performance of an economy, indicate that there is mounting dissatisfaction with the traditional dualistic interpretation of key concepts such as the individual and society, market coordination and government regulation, positive and normative economics, general theory and historic contextual understanding. Hence we think that it is more accurate to characterize today's crisis as a *crisis of modern economics*.

In this chapter it will be shown how a rereading of Smith cast in the form of a dialogue between reader and the text may contribute to the search for a new understanding of the market economy based on a relational interpretation of the aforementioned key concepts. The chapter comprises five sections.

In section 1 our earlier discussions of Smith's view of the market economy will be summarized within the context of the current debate on rethinking the market economy.

Sections 2, 3, and 4 focus on the question: 'What can a rereading of Smith contribute to solving the long-standing conflict between economics based on the general theory or system approach and economics conceived as an historical contextual understanding of economic processes?'

Section 2 focuses on Smith's admiration for Newton's astronomy. It will be demonstrated that Smith's admiration for Newton does not imply, as has been supposed, that Smith interpreted (general) theory or system and historical contextual understanding as polar opposites, because Smith did not regard Newton's astronomy as a theory representing pre-given causal laws.

Section 3 examines the analogical use of Newton's principle of gravitation in Smith's economics and in his moral philosophy in general. In line with the conclusions of section 2, it will be shown that this analogy is misinterpreted if it is understood as indicating that Smith anticipated the (neo)classical mechanistic approach, which for instance Jevons presented as describing economic science as the mechanics of self-interest.

Section 4 shows what Smith's relational interpretation of general theory and historical contextual understanding may contribute to the discussion about interpreting the market economy as a process. The argument will be developed in discussing Charles M.A. Clark's article: *Adam Smith and Society as an Evolutionary Process*.[2]

Section 5 concludes this chapter in summary form with a series of suggestions for rethinking the principles of economics derived from our reinterpretation.

1 Smith and the New Process Approach to the Market Economy

In previous chapters we have reread Smith against the background of present-day differences among interpretations of the market economy. Today the old disputes about the pros and cons of the market economy have been resolved in favour of the free market, yet there are hardly any schools of economic thought which continue to employ the mechanistic interpretation which has been developed by (neo)classical economists since the nineteenth century. While there is a general tendency to conceive the market economy as an evolutionary process, there are significant differences between the interpretations advanced by the various schools of economic thought.

Contemporary economists who claim that a sound explanation of the performance of an economy can do without any reference to the expectations and the motives of behaviour and action of the individual actors in that economy are few and far between. It is equally hard to find an economist who still contends that the behaviour and action of the individual actor can be explained without any reference to the social-economic context of that behaviour and action. In general, there is a growing consensus that the economy should be conceived as a process in which the behaviour and actions of individuals are mutually related to the performance of the economy as a whole. However, the elaboration of this process view differs from school to school. We may take the approaches of the New Classicals and the neo-institutionalists as illustrative of these differences.[3]

In their theory of rational expectations the New Classicals acknowledge that a self-coordinating market economy presupposes that the individual subjects act in accordance with a common understanding of the economy. This relational view of man and society, however, differs substantially from the relational view adopted by neo-institutionalists. While neo-institutionalists increasingly tend towards an hermeneutical model of interpretation, the New Classicals still adhere to the old naturalistic worldview of (neo)classical economics in that they assume that individual subjects are somehow aware of or preformed by the pre-given, objective structure of the economy.

Neo-institutionalists have now begun to recognize the relevance of market exchange to a prosperous society. Interpretations of the market economy have been developed which differ from the (neo)classical mechanistic interpretation, of which the neo-institutionalists have always been severely critical – just like the older American institutionalists before them. However, it is still natural for neo-institutionalists to reserve their most severe criticism for the use of general theories in understanding economic phenomena.

In this context of changing frames of reference, Smith's economics assumes a new relevance. The old correspondence between the supposed dichotomies in Smith's work and the differences between the schools of economic thought, suggests that a new dialogical reading will help in today's discussion of the changing conception of the market economy.

In previous chapters we have reread Smith's economics in search of an answer to this question. Our conclusions may be summarized as follows:

1 In Smith's work the market economy is understood in the context of a moral philosophy based on a reinterpretation of *sympathy*.

  For Smith *sympathy* is no longer to be understood as some particular kind of feeling, such as compassion. Nor does it denote a particular motivation of behaviour or action, such as benevolence. Instead it refers to our pre-rational experience of our relationship with others based in the communication of, competition for and concurrence in praise and praiseworthiness. The concept of *sympathy* indicates that we are individuals in relation to shared beliefs, values and rules.

  The interactions of people producing and distributing wealth are dealt with as a relatively autonomous system. They are conceived as an autonomous system insofar as they constitute a changing game inspired by the desire to be praiseworthy or praised through the acquisition and exhibition of wealth and power. The system is understood as a relatively and not an absolutely autonomous system, since the desire to be wealthy and powerful is only one aspect of man's tendency to *mutual sympathy*.

2 Smith's *sympathy*-based moral philosophy may be called a general theory of man and society in the sense that the world seen from the *sympathetic* perspective can be understood as a meaningful whole, as a well-ordered system. This

interpretation of a general theory, however, should not be confused with another interpretation more familiar to modern economists.

In modern economics talk of a general theory suggests a system of abstract statements representing general or universal causal laws. In Smith's view, (general) theories are concrete in the sense that their meaning is related to a concrete context or horizon. Smith's theory of *sympathy*, for example, is a general theory which is related to the evolving *commercial society* of his own time. It marks the contemporary recognition that the interactions of people tended increasingly towards the free exchange exemplified in the intercourse of merchants.

3 The concept of *sympathy* gives Smith's moral philosophy a teleological dimension. The 'discovery', in the context of the evolving *commercial society*, that *sympathy* should be seen as the leading principle in thought about man and society, also implies a new interpretation of history. In contrast to the cyclic view of history characteristic of medieval Europe, Smith interprets history as an evolutionary process.

The evolving *commercial society* has been understood as the final phase in the evolution of *sympathy*: free and fair exchange reflects the ultimate mode of communicating, competing and concurring in *sympathy*. Thus, the concept of the market economy has, from Smith's *sympathy* perspective, a utopian connotation.

4 Smith's theory of the market economy also differs in other respects from the theories developed by (neo)classical economists. At least three differences should be noted.

  – From Smith's perspective a theory of the market economy is supposed to present a concrete order to which it is worthwhile to adhere in the context of evolving *commercial societies*. (Neo)classical theories, however, pretend to represent a pre-given causal order.

  – Like Smith, (neo)classical economists argued in favour of the autonomy of the individual actor. However, in contrast to the (neo)classical atomistic interpretation of the individual, Smith understood the individual's autonomy as relative and not absolute: the individual expresses and experiences his autonomy in relation to the prevailing beliefs, values and rules of the society.

  – Smith would not have disagreed with later economists who have considered *utility* to be one of the key-concepts of economics. However, Smith's interpretation of *utility* differs radically from that familiar to most economists. Pointing to the importance of the aesthetic dimension of utility, Smith argues that it is a misunderstanding to think that behaviour and action may be reduced to the rationalistically interpreted motive of satisfying needs. According to Smith, people are motivated to interact in the production and distribution of wealth because they expect to be admired and praised by their fellow-men for the (beauty of the) wealth and power that they have at their disposal.

From this brief resumé of our rereading of Smith's work, it will be clear that this work has a direct bearing on the discussion of the new process approaches to economies which reflect a change towards new relational interpretations of key concepts such as the individual and society. In the following three sections we will elaborate more extensively on Smith's interpretation of general theory and historic contextual understanding. In the previous chapters' discussion of Smith's view of philosophy and science, we indicated that Smith did not anticipate the dualistic interpretation familiar to today's economists. However, there are also new readings of Smith which suggest the opposite as a result of a tendency among economists to reproduce the oppositional interpretation of these key concepts in their new process approaches. Before we discuss one such rereading of Smith, we will deal with Smith's discussion and references to Newton's astronomy in the following two sections.

2 Smith's Appraisal of Newton's Astronomy

In *The History of Astronomy* Smith praises Newton for using 'so familiar a principle of connection', which successfully represents the movements of the planets as a well-ordered whole:

> 'The superior genius and sagacity of Sir Isaac Newton, ..., made the most happy, and, we may now say, the greatest and most admirable improvement that was ever made in philosophy, when he discovered, that he could join together the movements of the Planets by so familiar a principle of connection, which completely removed all the difficulties the imagination had hitherto felt in attending to them.'[4]

Smith concludes that Newton's astronomy is 'now' considered to be superior to all the competing systems which had preceded it:

> 'His system, ..., now prevails over all opposition, and has advanced to the acquisition of the most universal empire that was ever established in philosophy. His principles, it must be acknowledged, have a degree of firmness and solidity that we should in vain look for in any other system. The most sceptical cannot avoid feeling this. They not only connect together most perfectly all the phaenomena of the Heavens, which had been observed before his time, but those also which the persevering industry and more perfect instruments of later Astronomers have made known to us; have been either easily and immediately explained by the application of his principles, or have been explained in consequence of more laborious and accurate calculations from these principles, than had been instituted before.'[5]

Newton's astronomy is so convincing, Smith suggests, that even if we believe theories to be no more than the products of the imagination, we have trouble resisting the temptation to consider it as mirroring a pre-given cosmic system, that is to say a real system existing outside and separately from our consciousness and our knowledge:

'And even we, while we have been endeavouring to represent all philosophical systems as mere inventions of the imagination, to connect together the otherwise disjointed and discordant phaenomena of nature, have insensibly been drawn in, to make use of language expressing the connecting principles of this one, as if they were the real chains which Nature makes use of to bind together her several operations.'[6]

Smith discusses Newton's astronomy in the context of a history of astronomy which is intended to illustrate 'the principles which lead and direct philosophical enquiries'.[7] The quoted excerpts, however, show that for Smith the importance of Newton's approach is more than a simple illustration of these principles. To Smith, Newton's astronomy represents the highest achievement in science to date, and as such his use of the principle of gravitation is considered to exemplify scientific research in general:

'Such is the system of Sir Isaac Newton, a system whose parts are all more strictly connected together, than those of any other philosophical hypothesis. Allow his principle, the universality of gravity, and that it decreases as the squares of the distance increase, and all appearances, which he joins together by it, necessarily follow. Neither is their connection merely a general and loose connection, as that of most other systems, in which either these appearances, or some such like appearances, might indifferently have been expected. It is every where the most precise and particular that can be imagined, and ascertains the time, the place, the quantity, the duration of each individual phaenomenon, to be exactly such as, by observation, they have been determined to be. Neither are the principles of union, which it employs, such as the imagination can find any difficulty in going along with. The gravity of matter, is of all its qualities, after its inertness, that which is most familiar to us. We never act upon it without having occasion to observe this property.'[8]

Smith's praise of Newton's astronomy is not based simply on the fact that it allows individual phenomena to be united and explained in the context of one all-encompassing system by means of the principle of gravitation. According to Smith, it is also important that the explanatory principle appeals to our imagination because we are completely familiar and at ease with it from daily experience.

Given his belief that Newton's astronomy exemplified sound scientific method, it is natural that Smith would in turn model his theory of the self-coordinating market economy by analogy with Newton's theory of gravitation. However, this debt to Newton's astronomy does not imply that Smith anticipated (neo)classical mechanistic economics and its belief that science aims at revealing the pre-given causal laws of, for instance, economic behaviour.[9]

We have already shown that the (neo)classical interpretation of Book 1, Chapter VII of *The Wealth of Nations* is incompatible with Smith's *sympathy*-based view of man and society and its related theory of philosophy and science. In this section we will return to this point and examine Smith's view philosophy and science and the positivistic orientation of (neo)classical economic science in greater detail.

In Chapter III we noted Smith's observation that Newton's astronomy is so impressive that one could almost forget that it is no more and no less than a construct, a well-ordered system, which gives sense and meaning to experiences and phenomena. We further argued that Smith would reject the positivist view of (neo)classical economic science.[10] Referring to Milton Friedman, it may, however, be argued that while some nineteenth- and early twentieth-century economists may be described as positivists, it is not evident that contemporary economic science is concerned with representing the so-called real chains of nature in economic life. In his now classic essay, *The Methodology of Positive Economics*, Friedman asserts that theories are no more than constructs which help us to make predictions.[11] In this instrumentalist view the adequacy of economic theory's description of the real world is no longer relevant.

There is, of course, a difference between Friedman's view and the old positivist claim that science has to be assessed on the correspondence between theory and reality. However, there is still a substantial difference between Smith's view of science and Friedman's contention that scientific theories are no more than constructs which help us to make correct predictions. Smith felt that a theory should be realistic. For example, from the fragments quoted above it is clear that Smith felt it was very important that the principle of gravitation was familiar from everyday experience.

This call for realism, in combination with the idea that theories are constructs, indicates that Smith's interpretation of realism differs from the objectivist interpretation current among economists. While the objectivist view presupposes an opposition between subject and object, Smith believed both to be related. In Smith's view science is primarily a professionalization of what people do in everyday life: namely, construct theories to give sense and meaning to their experiences. The images projected by the theories are felt to be real to the extent that they succeed in giving sense and meaning to experiences and observed phenomena.

Smith's observation that the firmness and solidity of Newton's system must be apparent to even the most sceptical reminds us of his argument that science is directed and led by feelings.[12] Feelings of wonder, surprise and admiration, move science to create new theories and even to develop new conceptual paradigms which take away the feelings of disquiet evoked by experiences which cannot be explained by existing theories.[13]

As mentioned before, Smith's idea of changing conceptual frameworks has led Skinner and Thompson to draw a parallel between *The History of Astronomy* and Kuhn's *The Structure of Scientific Revolutions*.[14] It is, however, important to note that in Smith's view, not only the history of a science is characterized by paradigm-shifts, but that the idea of science itself is produced by a change in conceptual frameworks. Science is related to civilized societies where people tend to understand the world as a well-ordered system, according to Smith in the section titled 'Of the Origin of Philosophy' in *The History of Astronomy*, discussed above.[15]

According to this view, a theory which explicates the structure of a market economy is understood as contributing to the process in which people in a commercial society give their experiences sense and meaning. Accordingly, a general theory of the market economy cannot be divorced from an historical contextual understanding of economic phenomena or even from normative discussions about economic order and policy. They are related in the sense that they produce their distinctive sense and meaning in relation to each other. The new order of a self-coordinating market economy becomes apparent from the perspective of the historical process of liberalization and commercialization of Western societies during the sixteenth, seventeenth and eighteenth centuries and vice versa.

3 Smith's Interpretation of Newton's Astronomy: Gravitation

In the previous section we argued that it is a mistake to view Smith's economics as anticipating (neo)classical positive economics. While Smith did point to Newton's astronomy as an example of sound science, his appraisal of Newton's astronomy is grounded in a view of science which substantially differs from that underpinning (neo)classical positive economics.

In this section we will focus on Smith's use of the idea of *gravitation* in his economics and more generally in his moral philosophy. First, we will discuss some examples that demonstrate that Smith used the principle of *gravitation* in a metaphorical-analogical sense. Then we will demonstrate that this analogical use of *gravitation* undermines rather than confirms the traditional view that Smith anticipated the (neo)classical mechanistic interpretation of the price mechanism, exemplified by Walrasian general equilibrium analysis.

As we have seen, Smith invoked the principle of gravitation in his discussion of *natural* and *market prices*:

'The natural price, ..., is, as it were, the central place, to which the prices of all commodities are continually gravitating. Different accidents may sometimes keep them suspended a good deal above it, and sometimes force them down even somewhat below it. But whatever may be the obstacles which hinder them from settling in this center of repose and continuance, they are constantly tending towards it.'[16]

In this excerpt Smith draws a parallel between the self-coordination of market economies and the coordination of planets by the principle of gravitation. Close reading reveals nothing to suggest that Smith's economics should be interpreted as applied mechanics. As the expression *as it were* indicates, Smith's analogical use of the principle of *gravitation* is metaphorical. This interpretation is confirmed by more implicit uses of the idea of *gravitation* elsewhere in both *The Wealth of Nations* and *The Theory of Moral Sentiments*. Two examples – one from each these books – may illustrate this point.

1 The first example, taken from *The Theory of Moral Sentiments*, deals with the differences between our personal concern with friends, common acquaintances and strangers:

'We expect less sympathy from a common acquaintance than from a friend: we cannot open to the former all those little circumstances which we can unfold to the latter: we assume, therefore, more tranquillity before him, and endeavour to fix our thoughts upon those general outlines of our situation which he is willing to consider. We expect still less sympathy from an assembly of strangers, and we assume, therefore, still more tranquillity before them, and always endeavour to bring down our passion to that pitch, which the particular company we are in may be expected to go along with.'[17]

Although Smith does not explicitly refer to Newtons's theory of gravitation, the parallel with the idea that the mutual attraction between planets is inversely related to distance, presses itself spontaneously on the reader.[18] Though the principle of *sympathy* differs substantially from the principle of *gravitation*, the metaphorical-analogical use of the principle of *gravitation*, may help us to conceive the experienced differences between *sympathy* with friends, common acquaintances and strangers as a pattern: personal mutual concern decreases and transmutes into more general solidarity.

2 The second example is taken from Smith's discussion in *The Wealth of Nations* about the contribution of labour, capital and land to the wealth of nations and the share of each in that wealth.[19] Instead of deducing the respective contributions and shares from functionalistic assumptions about quantity and productivity of the inputs, Smith discusses these issues in relation to the orders which the labourers, the manufacturers and the landlords are part of, when involved in the competition for wealth and power. For instance, the threat to public wealth posed by manufacturers is explained with reference to the tendency of manufacturers to create factions of inward communication and concurrence:

'as dangerous as it has now become to attempt to diminish in any respect the monopoly which our manufacturers have obtained against us. This monopoly has so much increased the number of some particular tribes of them, that, like an overgrown standing army, they have become formidable to the government, and upon many occasions intimidate the legislature.'[20]

Conflicting interests are discussed as a problem of diminishing attraction towards common national values in favour of an increasing attraction to values of a more immediate group. Thus, here again we find a discussion, framed by the metaphorical-analogical use of gravitation.

For a clear understanding of the meaning and relevance of the principle of *gravitation* to Smith's work, it is also important to deal more extensively with the discussion of this principle in *The History of Astronomy*, in particular its treatment in relation to Descartes' principle of *impulse*.

According to Smith, Descartes was the first person to really try to represent the cosmos as an order based on one single principle. In demonstrating that matter had no aversion to motion, Descartes suggested that all space was filled with matter and that God had impressed upon it a certain quantity of motion:

'Des Cartes was the first who attempted to ascertain, precisely, wherein this invisible chain consisted, and to afford the imagination a train of intermediate events, which, succeeding each other in an order that was of all others the most familiar to it, should unite those incoherent qualities, the rapid motion, and the natural inertness of the Planets. Des Cartes was the first who explained wherein consisted the real inertness of matter; that it was not in an aversion to motion, or in a propensity to rest, but in a power of continuing indifferently either at rest or in motion, and of resisting, with a certain force, whatever endeavoured to change its state from the one to the other. According to that ingenious and fanciful philosopher, the whole of infinite space was full of matter, ... Upon this infinitude of matter ... a certain quantity of motion was originally impressed by the Creator of all things, and the laws of motion were so adjusted as always to preserve the same quantity in it, without increase, and without diminution.'[21]

Descartes explained the existence and motion of planets by deduction from the collision and rubbing of

'an infinite number of very small cubes; all of which, being whirled about upon their own centers.'[22]

However, in time, Newton's *gravitation*-based astronomy came to be substituted for Descartes' *impulse*-based astronomy since the latter left ever more phenomena unexplained:

'So far, ..., from accommodating his system to all the minute irregularities, which Kepler had ascertained in the movements of the Planets; or from shewing, particularly, how these irregularities, and no other, should arise from it, he [*Descartes*] contented himself with observing, that perfect uniformity could not be expected in their motions, from the nature of the causes which produced them; that certain irregularities might take place in them, for a great number of successive revolutions, and afterwards give way to others of a different kind: a remark which, happily, relieved him from the necessity of applying his system to the observations of Kepler, and the other Astronomers.
    But when the observations of Cassini had established the authority of those laws, which Keppler had first discovered in the system, the philosophy of Des Cartes, which could afford no reason, why such particular laws should be observed, might continue to amuse the learned in other sciences, but could no longer satisfy those that were skilled in Astronomy. ... The superior genius and sagacity of Sir Isaac Newton, ..., made the most happy, and, we may now say, the greatest and most admirable improvement that was ever made in philosophy, when he discovered, that he could join together the movements of the Planets by so familiar a principle of connection, which completely removed all the difficulties the imagination had hitherto felt in attending to them.'[23]

By analogy with Smith's contention that the philosophy of Descartes

'might continue to amuse the learned in other sciences, but could no longer satisfy those that were skilled in Astronomy,' it could be argued that Smith himself was no longer satisfied with the moral philosophy of such scholars as Hobbes, Pufendorf and Mandeville. Just as the astronomers were no longer satisfied by Descartes' deductions from

'an infinite number of very small cubes; all of which, being whirled about upon their own centers,'

so Smith's moral philosophy rejects the idea that order has to be explained by deductions from atomistic, egocentric individuals.[24] Smith, in the field of moral philosophy, argued in favour of a change to a principle of mutual attraction, as Newton did in the field of astronomy. However, his principle of *(mutual) sympathy* proved to be misunderstood by later (neo)classical economists. Interpreting *sympathy* as benevolence – i.e. the opposite of self-interest – they did not follow Smith in his *sympathy*-related reinterpretation of self-interest. They upheld the interpretation of Hobbes, Mandeville and Pufendorf, which was modelled according to the paradigm of rationalistic atomistic individuals.

4 Rethinking Economics and Changing Paradigms

The various new process approaches in economics reflected in today's Adam Smith renaissance mark the transition to a new style of economics which, following a more general cultural logic, might be called *post-modern*. Economics shares a more general philosophical unease with the habit of describing the world in terms of opposed binary pairs such as the individual versus society, science versus normative beliefs, universal causal laws versus history.

Reviewing the new process approaches and the new Smith literature reveals that despite the changing paradigms various traditional dichotomies are reproduced. We will consider Charles M.A. Clark's *Adam Smith and Society as an Evolutionary Process*, not just to illustrate this situation, but also to underline the importance of conceiving the re-reading of Smith as a dialogue when breaking ground for new relational interpretations.[25]

Clark's article is of interest to the discussion about new relational interpretations of the individual and society in economics. However, with reference to the reinterpretation of Smith's understanding and use of Newton's astronomy in the previous sections, we will demonstrate how old dichotomies are reproduced when the rereading of Smith is not modelled as a dialogue.

Following Werner Stark, Clark describes the proposed evolutionary process view of society as the third basic form of social thought after the oppositional *unity* and *multiplicity* views.[26] In the *unity* view individuals are considered simply as parts of the whole, i.e. society; in the *multiplicity* view society is seen as a collection of individual actors. Both views are reductionist: the first denies the individual's autonomy of action, thought and feeling; the second leaves no room for the human experience of community and its accompanying feeling that society is a (virtual) real entity.[27]

The *third view* which is according to Clark implicitly endorsed by Smith, has been described as follows,

'The society-as-an-evolutionary-process approach ... defines society as the creation
of the interaction between the individual and social institutions, both of which adjust
to the influence of the other.'[28]

This description may, at first sight, suggest a correspondence to our relational
sympathy-based perspective of man and society. However, the resemblance
becomes strained when Clark calls for a break with the tradition of analysing
economic phenomena in accordance with Smith's natural law approach and argues
that economists should rethink economics in accordance with the *third view*
implicit in Smith's work:

'Smith's contributions, not only to economics, but to social science in general, come
from his analysis of social processes, and it is here that we look to Smith for inspiration. Unfortunately, Smith's lasting impact in economics has been from the natural
law aspects of his works. A more realistic and useful economic theory would start
with Smith's historical and institutional analysis, method and outlook. This implies
a view of society as an evolutionary process, taking into account the change and
development of social institutions and habits. This is the legacy of Smith that must
be carried on.'[29]

Here we see that Clark does not really succeed in breaking away from the old
conflict between paradigms framed around an oppositional interpretation of key
concepts. While Stark's discussion of the *third view* could have helped to break
new ground, Clark upholds the old dichotomous interpretation of Smith and
reproduces the old conflict in arguing for a change from a general theory
approach towards a historical approach:

'The existence of a dual nature in Smith's work is not a recent observation. The most
famous example is "Das Adam Smith Problem" of the late nineteenth and early
twentieth centuries. Here the dichotomy was between Smith's two great works, *The
Wealth of Nations (WN)* and *The Theory of Moral Sentiments (TMS)* – specifically,
between the importance of sympathy in the latter book and of self-interest in the
former.
    A second dichotomy can be seen in Smith's research program and in his exposi-
tion and method of investigation of this program. Smith's research program was the
search for natural laws, while his method of discovering these laws included the use
of history and institutional observations. This dichotomy was the result of Smith's
belief in the providential order of the social universe and the influence of Natural
Theology on the Scottish school of moral philosophy.'[30]

Apparently, Clark is unaware that the traditional Smith interpretation is based on
the same dichotomous perspective with which he aims to break in his discussion
of the *third view*. It is important that Clark points to the interaction between the
individual and social institutions. But it is equally important to understand that
Smith did not address these interactions from an objectivistic perspective on the
world which raises the conflict between general theory and history in the sense
of an opposition between discovering general causal laws and historical understanding of behaviour as the cause and effect of social processes.[31] For Smith a

theory is not a representation of objectivistically conceived causal chains, but a belief system people share in order to give sense and meaning to experience and phenomena. From this perspective, general theory and history are not antithetical but complementary. It is in relation to a general theory of society that an actual evolutionary historic process derives its sense and meaning and vice versa.

Two examples may help illustrate the fact that while Clark rightly draws attention to Smith's evolutionary process view of society, he misses the full implications of this view for contemporary differences about the principles of economic science.

1 The first example concerns Clark's discussion of the theory of *sympathy*. Clark quotes G.R. Morrow, who noted that,

> 'sympathy was used by Smith as a "principle of communication by means of which the sentiments of one individual influence and are influenced by the sentiments of his fellow men".'[32]

Because of Smith's interest in the interaction between the individual and society, Clark concludes that

> 'at least, at this general level, Smith's moral theory has a lot in common with the society-as-an-evolutionary-process approach.'[33]

However, this is not Clark's final position: instead he cites Smith's argument that people desire praiseworthiness rather than praise as evidence that the theory is ultimately concerned with pre-given laws, i.e. 'the moral rules of the design'.[34] As such Clark fails to recognize that because Smith does not subscribe to an objectivist worldview it is inappropriate to assume that his notion of praiseworthiness refers to some pre-given universal law. By distinguishing between praise and praiseworthiness, and demonstrating that people actually want to be praiseworthy and not simply praised, Smith stresses that action is ruled by social values produced in the communication of, competition for and concurrence in *mutual sympathy*.

2 The second example concerns Smith's distinction between *natural* and *market prices*. Referring to Jeffrey T. Young, Clark notes that Smith's notion of *natural price* is related to the notion of *praiseworthiness* as employed in the theory of *sympathy*.[35] However, here again Clark's implicit assumption that Smith subscribes to an objectivist worldview leads his analysis astray. *Natural price* and *market price* do not belong to two different explanations of the market economy. The two types of price are related to each other in Smith's model of the market economy. Like his concept of *praiseworthiness*, Smith's concept of *natural price* reflects the horizon of social values people share in the social processes of producing and distributing wealth. Similarly, *market price* resembles *praise* in that it describes the contingent value judgements produced in the actual interaction of

daily life. Smith refers to a relational understanding of the *individual* and *society* according to which the autonomy of the individual is understood as the autonomy which the individual shows in his relation to society, and society is understood as a (virtual) real entity manifesting itself in the sense and meaning people derive from social intercourse.

With reference to the ongoing debate on the subject of general theory versus history, it is finally important to note that Smith provides no grounds for criticizing the (neo)classical attempt to describe the production and distribution of wealth in a commercial society in terms of a system, namely a market economy. On the contrary, attempts to conceive the economy as a system would have been applauded by Smith. However, Smith did not regard such systems as representations of pre-given causal laws.

Smith felt that people in societies such as his own had an existential need to understand their own society as an admirable well-ordered system.[36] Since people use such systems as a point of reference in their behaviour, the system is important both for maintaining order and stimulating the wealth of the nation, especially in a commercial society characterized by ever increasing freedom of belief, thought and action.[37] This desire also explains the today's general tendency to dismiss, in particular, neoclassical economic theories as unrealistic. People want theories which help them to give sense and meaning to the processes of producing and distributing wealth in which they are involved.

5 Adam Smith and the Principles of Economic Science

After rereading Smith in his historical context we concluded that his view of the evolving commercial society differed substantially from that of other philosophers similarly positioned at the threshold of modern philosophy and science. While Smith's work mirrors the new tendency to explain the emerging order through an appeal to the human faculties of reason and experience, unlike many of his contemporaries, Smith did not explain individual behaviour or social processes through reference to pre-given causal laws or universalized characteristics of man.

According to Smith, our understanding of the world and of who we are, is based in our communication, competition and concurrence with our fellow-men. This implicit rejection of the emerging objectivistic or positivistic view of science has, however, not been generally remarked with the result that Smith's work has appeared to comprise a collection of separate discourses which when read through modern eyes often seem to contain dichotomies which render his text self-contradictory.

In economics, the widespread uneasiness with the tenets of modernism, has shown itself in a desire to rethink the principles of economic science and to reread the founding fathers of the discipline – especially Adam Smith. Our own hermeneutically based rereading of Smith has led us to the following conclusions:

1 In *The History of Astronomy* Smith praises Newton's astronomy for its exemplary scientific method. In *The Wealth of Nations* he used the principle of *gravita-*

tion to elucidate his theory of the market economy. This enthusiasm for Newton does not, however, entail that Smith would have endorsed the (neo)classical conception of economics as a mechanics of self-interest. Smith did not think of economics as a science which explained the production and distribution of wealth according to pre-given causal laws about the behaviour of atomistic individuals. The important analogy between Newton's and Smith's theories lies in their relationship to their predecessors. According to Smith, Newton was the first to succeed in presenting the phenomena of the skies as parts of an admirable system by means of a principle of mutual attraction with which everyone was familiar. Smith, we believe, would have viewed the relationship between his economics and older theories in the same light.

The analogical relationship can be seen in Newton's account of the motion of the planets around the sun and Smith's account of the fluctuation of *market prices* around *natural prices*. The analogy with the motion of planets explained in relation to the principle of *gravitation* is meant simply to help the reader to conceive order in the fluctuations of market prices in relation to the idea of *sympathy*-based self-interest. Thus the analogy describes, metaphorically, a similarity between two relationships – it is in effect an *analogia proportionalitatis* and is not to be understood as an *analogia proportionis*: i.e. as suggesting that the market mechanism is susceptible to the same mechanistic explanation as Newton's principle of *gravitation*.

2 Rereading *The Wealth of Nations* alongside Smith's other texts, we concluded that Smith understood the market economy as a play between independent individual subjects. However, it has also become clear that the notion of *play* has to be interpreted within a different framework than that of (neo)classical functionalism. In mainstream (neo)classical economics, interaction or exchange is understood as the effect of the ends-means rationality of atomistic individuals. Smith's *sympathy*-based view of man and society avoids this functionalistic reduction of interaction and exchange.

According to Smith's interpretation of *mutual sympathy*, man gives shape and substance to himself and society in communicating, competing and concurring with fellow-men in pursuit of praiseworthiness. In their urge for praiseworthiness people are induced to enter into systems of shared values, beliefs and rules. From the *sympathy*-perspective, *market prices* stand in the same relationship to *natural prices* as *praise* to *praiseworthiness*.[38] *Natural prices* express what is felt to be praiseworthy within the field of wealth production and distribution. Because they reflect shared values they also serve to guide and coordinate behaviour and action.

In an abstract and philosophical light, the market economy looks like a regular and harmonious system which produces numerous agreeable effects.[39] From Smith's *sympathy* perspective, however, this so-called regular and harmonious system lacks the functionalistic connotations reflected by, for example, the Walrasian general equilibrium approach. Well-orderedness – the 'utilitarian' or 'functional' aspect of, for example, the social processes of producing and distributing wealth through free exchange – is in Smith's view one part of the value and belief system which people in ordered and prosperous societies employ to give sense and meaning to their experiences.

3 According to Smith, scientific research is a professionalized expression of the everyday urge to understand and explain experiences through reference to a familiar and well-ordered framework. Science is depicted as a professional discourse which is ultimately related to the social processes through which people give sense and meaning to their experiences. In contrast to the traditional objectivistic or positivistic interpretation of science, Smith did not consider scientific theory to be a representation of pre-given causal laws. Instead he viewed theories as constructs: the reality of the order presented by a theory is a virtual reality, in the sense that people perceive the order as real when it 'really' gives sense and meaning to experiences and phenomena.

This account of scientific theory sheds a different light on Smith's market economy-based criticism of specific contemporaneous economic situations. In the (neo)classical framework, this criticism has traditionally been interpreted as an appeal to remove all conventions, agreements or government-policies which obstruct the pre-given, universal laws of the market economy. Smith, however, does not interpret the idea of the market economy as a representation of pre-given economic laws. Instead he regards the system of market economy as a construct aimed at giving sense and meaning to contemporaneous processes of liberalization and commercialization in the production and distribution of wealth. While the system of *sympathy* addresses the evolving commercial society as a whole, the related system of the market economy focuses on the production and distribution of wealth, which was at the time differentiating itself into a (relative) autonomous field of social exchange.

Considering the theory of the market economy as a construct intended to give sense and meaning to the evolving liberal and commercial economy, it becomes clear that Smith's theory is both explanatory and normative. Considered also as the *natural system of perfect liberty and justice*, the theory even assumes a utopian dimension insofar as it presents an horizon for socio-economic change. To read Smith's discourse on the market economy today is to enter into a dialogue with Smith which helps us understand and evaluate contemporaneous market economies from the perspective of commercial societies still evolving towards the utopia of *natural liberty and justice*.

4 Economists from (neo)classical schools – including contemporaneous related schools such as the New Classicals – have rightly used the market economy as a model for addressing the economies of our commercial societies. With regard to Smith, however, they have committed a fundamental mistake in interpreting the market economy within a modernist framework. Unlike Smith, (neo)classical and related economists tend to understand the world in terms of opposed or dualistic concepts. Until very recently mainstream economic science has been structured by a number of unquestioned binary pairs such as the individual versus society,

the market versus government, positive versus normative economics and general theory versus history.

Economists critical of the lack of realism in (neo)classical and related economic theory will find an ally in Smith. However, it is important to note that according to Smith, a lack of realism does not denote some inadequacy in the representation of a pre-given causal order. For Smith it is the alienation implicit in (neo)classical and related economics that deserves critical censure. People have an intuitive feeling that the sense and meaning of human life is grounded in their commitment to their fellow-men, he argues. However, (neo)classical and related economics attempt to represent fundamental laws by reducing social life to functionalistic interactions between atomistic individuals driven by the ends-means calculus.

In Smith's perspective, economic science is a discourse whose autonomy in relation to other discourses addressed to ordering our social experience consists in demonstrating the admirable order of a free and commercial economy. Interpreting the contemporaneous market economy in the context of the evolving commercial society, economics has to explain the real processes of producing and distributing wealth against the background of the idea of the self-coordinating market economy, conceived as the utopian *system of perfect liberty and perfect justice*. To fulfil this role, economic science also has to be independent, and should thus be impartial to the special interests of the various orders of society, whether politicians, legislators, labourers or entrepreneurs.

In rethinking the principles of economics in dialogue with Smith it is important to note that Smith's discourse on the market economy was not abstract and certainly not naive. In line with his concrete understanding of *sympathy*, Smith criticized the man of system, acknowledged the continuous threat of factions, and was worried about the competence and the commitment of people when discussing institutional change in the evolving free market economy. According to Smith's interpretation of *sympathy*, economic science is a critical science. It gives sense and meaning to contemporary economic processes in the light of the utopia of the *free market economy*:

– It interprets and explains contemporary social processes of producing and distributing wealth in relation to the idea of the *free market economy* and vice versa.

– It holds up the mirror of the *free market economy* to the public discourse on the production and distribution of wealth.

– It points out, especially to the government, how to support the evolution of an economy in which the actors are free and competent to give shape and substance to the economic aspects of their lives in the context of the communication of, competition for and concurrence in *sympathy*.

Notes

1. Cf. Heilbroner, R. and W. Milberg, *The Crisis of Vision in Modern Economic Thought*, Cambridge, 1995.
2. Clark, Ch.M.A., 'Adam Smith and Society as an Evolutionary Process', *Journal of Economic Issues*, vol. 24, 1990, pp. 825–844.
3. To avoid misunderstanding, it must be emphasized that by neo-institutionalists, we mean economists standing in the old tradition of the American institutionalists of the nineteenth century and the first decades of the twentieth century. Cf. Hodgson, G.M., 'Institutionalism, "Old" and "New"', in Hodgson, G.M., W.J. Samuels and M.R. Tool (eds.), *The Elgar Companion to Institutional and Evolutionary Economics*, Aldershot, 1994, pp. 397–402.
4. EPS Astronomy, IV.67.
5. EPS Astronomy, IV.76.
6. EPS Astronomy, IV.76. This, the final paragraph of the *History of Astronomy*, continues:
   'Can we wonder then, that it should have gained the general and complete approbation of mankind, and that it should now be considered, not as an attempt to connect in the imagination the phaenomena of the Heavens, but as the greatest discovery that ever was made by man, the discovery of an immense chain of the most important and sublime truths, all closely connected together, by one capital fact, of the reality of which we have daily experience.'
7. Cf. the full title of *The History of Astronomy*:
   The Principles which lead and direct Philosophical Enquiries: illustrated by the History of Astronomy.
8. EPS Astronomy, IV.76.
9. Ricardo might be cited as an example of a scholar who was so impressed by Smith's system of the market economy, that he mistakenly interpreted it as a representation or imitation of the pre-given causal laws of the production and distribution of wealth. See, for instance, The 'Preface' of *The Principles of Political Economy and Taxation* or the following quote from the chapter 'On Natural and Market Price':
   'In the 7th chap. of the Wealth of Nations, all that concerns this question is most ably treated. Having fully acknowledged the temporary effects which, in particular employments of capital, may be produced on the prices of commodities, as well as on the wages of labour, and the profits of stock, by accidental causes, without influencing the general price of commodities, wages, or profits, since these effects are equally operative in all stages of society, we will leave them entirely out of our consideration, whilst we are treating of the laws which regulate natural prices, natural wages and natural profits, effects totally independent of these accidental causes. In speaking then of the exchangeable value of commodities, or the power of purchasing possessed by any one commodity, I mean always that power which it would possess, if not disturbed by any temporary or accidental cause, and which is its natural price.'
   (Ricardo, D., *The Principles of Political Economy and Taxation*, 1817, edited by R.M. Hartwell, Harmondsworth, 1971, p. 114);
   With regard to the mechanistic approach of Jevons and Walras, see the following quotes from their work:
   'But as all the physical sciences have their basis more or less obviously in the general principles of mechanics, so all branches and divisions of economic science must be pervaded by certain general principles. This is to the investigation of such principles – to the tracing out of the mechanics of self-interest and utility, that this essay has been devoted. The establishment of such a theory is necessary preliminary to any definite drafting of the superstructure of the aggregate science.'

(Jevons, W.S., *The Theory of Political Economy*, 1871, edited with an introduction by R.D.C. Black, Harmondsworth, 1970, p. 50; see also 'Letter 128' in Black, R.D.C. (ed.) *Papers and Correspondence of William Stanley Jevons*, part II, London, 1973, pp. 361–362)

'We are dealing here with the determination of prices in perfect competition and which depend upon our preferences, justified or unjustified. This question alone is the object of *pure economics*. Pure economics will not be a physico-mathematical science, but one of a *psycho-mathematical* nature. By means of two conclusive examples it seems to me easy to make mathematicians see that its procedure is rigorously identical to that of two of the most advanced and uncontested physico-mathematical sciences, *rational mechanics* and *celestial mechanics*.'

(Mirowski, Ph.E. and P. Cook, 'Walras' "Economics and Mechanics": Translation, Commentary, Context', in Samuels, W.J. (ed.), *Economics as Discourse: An Analysis of the Language of Economists*, Boston, 1990, p. 208)

(Walras, L., *Economique et Méchanique*, 1909, translated and republished in Samuels, W.J. (ed.), *Economics as Discourse: An Analysis of the Language of Economists*, Boston, 1990, p. 208.)

See also Thoben, H., 'Mechanistic and Organistic Analogies in Economics Reconsidered', *Kyklos*, 1982(35), pp. 292–305, in particular pp. 294–295.

10. Cf., for instance, pp. 87–88.
11. Friedman, M., The Methodology of Positive Economics, in: Friedman, M., *Essays in Positive Economics*, Chicago, 1953, pp. 3–43.
12. EPS Astronomy, IV.76.
13. EPS Astronomy, I–II.
14. Thompson, H.F., 'Adam Smith's Philosophy of Science', *Quarterly Journal of Economics*, vol. 79, 1965, pp. 212–233, Skinner, A.S., 'Adam Smith: An Aspect of Modern Economics', *Scottish Journal of Political Economy*, vol. 26, 1979, pp. 109–125 and Kuhn, Th.S., *The Structure of Scientific Revolutions*, Chicago, 1970.
15. EPS Astronomy, III.
16. WN I.vii.15. See also WN I.vii.21.
17. TMS I.i.4.9.
18. As is generally known, the formula for gravitation is:

$$F = f \frac{m_1 m_2}{r^2}$$

m_1: body (mass) 1
m_2: body (mass) 2
r: the distance between bodies 1 and 2.

Otherwise, Hutcheson, Smith's teacher, explicitly compares the *universal benevolence* toward all men with the principle of *gravitation*:

'We have already endeavoured to prove, "that there is a *universal determination* to *benevolence* in mankind, even toward the most distant parts of the species;" but we are not to imagine, that all benevolent affections are of one kind, or alike strong. There are nearer and stronger kinds of benevolence, when the objects stand in some nearer relations to ourselves, which have obtained distinct names; such as *natural affection, gratitude, esteem.*

... The universal *benevolence* toward all men, we may compare to that principle of *gravitation*, which perhaps extends to all bodies in the universe; but increases as the distance is diminished, and is strongest when bodies come to touch each other.'

(Hutcheson, F., *Concerning Moral Good And Evil*, V.I–II, in Raphael, D.D. (ed.), *British Moralists. 1650–1800*, Oxford, 1969, pp. 289–290)

19. WN I.xi.p. 7–10.
20. WN IV.ii.43. See also, for example, WN I.xi.p. 10.
21. EPS Astronomy, IV.61. See also WN V.i.f.25 and LRBL ii.133–134, ed. Lothian 140 (mentioned in the editors' note 17 of WN V.i.f.25).
22. EPS Astronomy, IV.61. See also EPS Astronomy, IV.62–66.
23. EPS Astronomy, IV.66–67.
24. EPS Astronomy, IV.61. See also EPS Astronomy, IV.62–66.
25. Clark, Ch.M.A., Adam Smith and Society as an Evolutionary Process, *Journal of Economic Issues*, vol. 24, 1990, pp. 825–844.
26. Ibidem, p. 826.
27. Cf. Clark, Ch.M.A., 'Adam Smith and Society as an Evolutionary Process', *Journal of Economic Issues*, 1990 (24), 3, p. 826 with regard to successively the 'unity' view and the 'multiplicity' view:
    'Individual actors are like parts of the body, diligently performing their functions to promote the health and survival of the social body.'

    '... the individual is real, but ... society is merely a fiction, having no existence beyond a collection of individuals.'
28. Ibidem, p. 828.
29. Ibidem, p. 842.
30. Ibidem, p. 829.
31. Cf. ibid., pp. 832–833, 839 and 842, for example:
    'Smith's natural law conceptions and his concern for the final causes of the design limit his analysis. In his consideration of efficient causes, of the mechanisms of social forces, Smith adopts the view of society as an evolutionary process. However, when he considers final causes, he must abandon this view for a natural law outlook.' (p. 842)

    'The inconsistencies in Smith's theory of value are the necessary result of attempting to discover the invariant natural laws (final causes) of a social system or phenomena by investigating its history and social setting (efficient causes).' (p. 839)
32. Ibidem, p. 835.
33. Quoting another pioneer of today's Smith renaissance – A.L. Macfie – Clark argues:
    'Moral rules "develop only through the slow and imperfect process of individual judgment, based on sympathy, but guided by social education and socially established rules of behaviour" ... Thus, at least, at this general level, Smith's moral theory has a lot in common with the society-as-an-evolutionary-process approach. The central concern and mechanism is the interaction between individuals and society, and the resulting social institution – moral rules – developing out of this interaction.' (Ibidem, p. 835)
34. Ibidem, p. 836.
35. Ibidem, p. 833.
36. TMS IV.1.11:
    'The perfection of police, the extension of trade and manufactures, are noble and magnificent objects. The contemplation of them pleases us, and we are interested in whatever can tend to advance them. They make part of the great system of government, and the wheels of the political machine seem to move with more harmony and ease by means of them. We take pleasure in beholding the perfection of so beautiful

and grand a system, and we are uneasy till we remove any obstruction that can in the least disturb or encumber the regularity of its motions. ... From a certain spirit of system, ..., from a certain love of art and contrivance, we sometimes seem to value the means more than the end, and to be eager to promote the happiness of our fellow-creatures, rather from a view to perfect and improve a certain beautiful and orderly system, than from any immediate sense or feeling of what they either suffer or enjoy. ... Nothing tends so much to promote public spirit as the study of politics, of several systems of civil government, their advantages and disadvantages, of the constitution of our own country, its situation, and interest with regard to foreign nations, its commerce, its defence, the disadvantages it labours under, the dangers to which it may be exposed, how to remove the one, and how to guard against the other. Upon this account political disquisitions, if just, and reasonable, and practicable, are of all the works of speculation the most useful. Even the weakest and the worst of them are not altogether without their utility. They serve at least to animate the public passions of men, and rouse them to seek out the means of promoting the happiness of the society.'

See also TMS II.ii.3.5 and IV.1.9.

37. In WN IV.Intro.1, Smith gives the following description of political economy:

'Political oeconomy, considered as a branch of the science of a statesman or legislator, proposes two distinct objects; first, to provide a plentiful revenue or subsistence for the people, or more properly to enable them to provide such a revenue or subsistence for themselves; and secondly, to supply the state or commonwealth with a revenue sufficient for the publick services. It proposes to enrich both the people and the sovereign.'

See also TMS II.ii.1.8. Regarding the importance of maintaining justice for man and society, see TMS II.ii.3.2 and 4.

38. See for example TMS III.2.32.

39. TMS VII.iii.1.2:

'Human society, when we contemplate it in a certain abstract and philosophical light, appears like a great, an immense machine, whose regular and harmonious movements produce a thousand agreeable effects.'

Bibliography

Works by Adam Smith
(Works by Smith are cited and referred to by the initials that follow the titles listed below)

Raphael, D.D. and A.L. Macfie (eds.), *The Theory of Moral Sentiments* [TMS], Oxford, 1976/1991

Campbell, R.H., Skinner, A.S. and W.B. Todd (eds.), *An Inquiry into the Nature and Causes of the Wealth of Nations* [WN], Oxford, 1976/1979

Wightman, P.D., Bryce, J.C. and I.S. Ross (eds.), *Essays on Philosophical Subjects* [EPS], Oxford, 1980

Bryce, J.C. (ed.), *Lectures on Rhetoric and Belles Lettres* [LRBL], Oxford, 1983

Meek, R.L., Raphael, D.D. and P.G. Stein (eds.), *Lectures on Jurisprudence* [LJ(A), LJ(B), Oxford, 1978/1987

Mossner, E.C. and I.S. Ross (eds.), *Correspondence of Adam Smith* [Corr.], Oxford, 1987

Other Authors

Addleson, M., '"Radical Subjectivism" and the Language of Austrian Economics' in Kirzner, I.M. (ed.), *Subjectivism, Intelligibility and Economic Understanding*, London, 1986, pp. 1–15

Ahmad, S., 'Adam Smith's Four Invisible Hands', *History of Political Economy*, vol. 22, 1990, pp. 137–144

Albeda, W., 'Smith: vrijheid en gelijkheid' in Kastelein, T. (ed.), *Adam Smith, 1776–1976, 200 jaar sedert de 'Wealth of Nations'*, Leiden, 1976, pp. 117–132

Applebaum, E., 'Radical Economics', in Weintraub, S. (ed.), *Modern Economic Thought*, Philadelphia, 1977, pp. 559–574

Backhouse, R.E., *A History of Modern Economic Analysis*, Oxford, 1985,

Backhouse, R.E., *Economists and the Economy. The Evolution of Economic Ideas. 1600 to the Present Day*, Oxford, 1988

Bagehot, W., 'Adam Smith as a Person', *The Fortnightly Review*, 1876; in St John-Stevas, N. (ed.), *The Collected Works of Walter Bagehot*, London, 1968, part 3, pp. 84–112

Bagehot, W., 'The Centenary of *The Wealth of Nations*, *The Economist*, 1876; in St John-Stevas, N. (ed.), *The Collected Works of Walter Bagehot*, London, 1968, part 3, pp. 113–119

Bagehot, W., 'Adam Smith and Our Modern Economy' in *Economic Studies*, 1880; in St John-Stevas, N. (ed.), *The Collected Works of Walter Bagehot*, London, 1978, part 11, pp. 298–328

Bailey, S., *A Critical Dissertation on the Nature, Measure and Causes of Value*, 1825, reprint New York 1967

Barry, N.P., 'Varieties of Liberalism', *Government and Opposition*, vol. 24, 1989, pp. 357–362 (Review of Haakonssen (ed.), K., *Traditions of Liberalism: Essays on John Locke, Adam Smith and John Stuart Mill*, St Leonards, 1988)

Barry, N.P., *Hayek's Social and Economic Philosophy*, London, 1979/1982

Bassiry, G.R. and M. Jones, 'Adam Smith and the Ethics of Contemporary Capitalism', *Journal of Business Ethics*, vol. 12, 1993, pp. 621–627

Baumol, W.J., *Jean-Baptiste Say und der »Traité«*, Düsseldorf, 1986

Beer M. , *Early British Economics from XIIIth. to the Middle of the XVIIIth. Century*, London, 1938

Bell, D. and I. Kristoll (eds.), *The Crisis in Economic Theory*, New York, 1981

Bell, D., 'Models and Reality in Economic Discourse' in Bell, D. and I. Kristoll (eds.), *The Crisis in Economic Theory*, New York, 1981, pp. 46–80

Benassy, J.-P., *Macroeconomics: An Introduction to the Non-Walrasian Approach*, Orlando, 1986

Begg, D.K.H., *The Rational Expectations Revolution in Macroeconomics. Theory & Evidence*, Oxford, 1982

Berger, L.A., 'Self-Interpretattion, Attention, and Language: Implications for Economics of Charles Taylor's Hermeneutics', in Lavoie, D. (ed.), *Economics and Hermeneutics*, London, 1990, pp. 262–284

Berns, E. (ed.), *Adam Smith. Ethiek, politiek, economie*, Tilburg, 1986

Berns, E. and R. van Stratum, 'De plaats van de economie in Adam Smith's "Moral Philosophy"' in Berns, E. (ed.), *Adam Smith. Ethiek, politiek, economie*, Tilburg, 1986

Billet, L., 'The Just Economy: the Moral Basis of the Wealth of Nations', *Review of Social Economy*, vol. 34, 1976, pp. 295–316

Bitterman, H.J., 'Adam Smith's Empiricism and the Law of Nature', *Journal of Political Economy*, vol. 48, 1940, pp. 487–520 and 703–734

Black, R.D.C., 'Introduction' in Black, R.D.C. (ed.), Jevons, W.S., *The Theory of Political Economy*, 1871, Harmondsworth, 1970, pp. 7–40

Black, R.D.C., 'Smith's Contribution in Historical Perspective' in Wilson, T. and A.S. Skinner (eds.), *The Market and The State, Essays in Honour of Adam Smith*, Oxford, 1976, pp. 42–72

Black, R.D.C. (ed.) *Papers and Correspondence of William Stanley Jevons*, parts I and II, London, 1972 and 1973, part VI, London, 1977

Blaug, M., 'Kuhn versus Lakatos or Paradigms versus Research Programmes in the History of Economics' in Latsis, S. (ed.), *Method and Appraisal in Economics*, Cambridge, 1976

Blaug, M., *The Methodology of Economics*, Cambridge, 1980

Blaug, M., *Economic Theory in Retrospect,* Cambridge, 1978/1985

Blaug, M. (ed.), Adam Smith (1723–1790), *Pioneers in Economics*, part I en II, Aldershot, 1991

Bloomfield, A.I., 'Adam Smith on the Theory of International Trade' in Skinner, A.S. and T. Wilson (eds.), *Essays on Adam Smith*, Oxford, 1975, pp. 445–481

Bloor, D., *Wittgenstein. A Social Theory of Knowledge*, London, 1983

Boer, Th. de, *Grondslagen van een kritische psychologie*, Baarn, 1980

Böhme, G. (ed.), *Isaac Newton. 'Über die Gravitation ...', Texte zu den philosophischen Grundlagen der klassischen Mechanik; Text lateinisch-deutsch Übetsetzt und erläutert von Gernot Böhme*, Frankfurt am Main, 1988

Boland, L.A., 'A Critique of Friedman's Critics', *Journal of Economic Literature*, vol. 17, 1979, pp. 503–522

Boland, L.A., *Methodology for a New Microeconomics. The Critical Foundations*, Boston, 1986

Bonar, J., *Philosophy* and *Political Economy*, London, 1922

Bouckaert, L. and G. Bouckaert (eds.), *Metafysiek en engagement. Een personalistische visie op gemeenschap en economie*, Leuven, 1992

Boulding, K.E., 'Economics as a Moral Science', *The American Economic Review*, vol. 59, 1969, pp. 1–12

Bradley, I, and M. Howard (eds.), *Classical and Marxian Political Economy: Essays in Honour of Ronald L. Meek,* New York, 1982

Brown, K.L., (Review in *Contemporary Sociology,* vol. 22, 1993, pp. 751–752 of Muller, J., *Adam Smith in His Time and Ours: Designing the Decent Society,* New York, 1993)

Brown, M., *Adam Smith's Economics: Its Place in the Development of Economic Thought,* London, 1988

Brown, V., The System of Natural Liberty and "The Wealth of Nations", paper presented at the *History of Economic Thought Conference,* Groningen, 1989

Brown, V., (Review in *The Economic Journal,* vol. 103, 1993, pp. 230–232 of Pack, S., *Capitalism as a Moral System: Adam Smith's Critique of the Free Market Economy,* Aldershot, 1991 and Werhane, P., *Adam Smith and His Legacy for Modern Capitalism,* Oxford, 1991)

Brown, V., 'Signifying Voices: Reading the "Adam Smith Problem"', *Economics and Philosophy,* vol. 7, 1991, pp. 187–220

Brugmans, E., *Morele sensibiliteit. Over de moraalfilosofie van Adam Smith,* Tilburg, 1989

Brunner, K., 'Mensbeeld en "Maatschappij"-opvatting', *Rotterdamse Monetaire Studies,* no. 26, 1987

Bryce, J.C., see Wightman, W.D., Bryce, J.C. and I.S. Ross

Bryce, J.C. (ed.), *Adam Smith. Lectures on Rhetoric and Belles Lettres,* Oxford, 1983

Bryce, J.C., 'Introduction' in Bryce, J.C. (ed.), *Adam Smith. Lectures on Rhetoric and Belles Lettres,* Oxford, 1983, pp. 1–37

Bryson, G., *Man and Society. The Scottish Inquiry of the Eighteenth Century,* Oxford, 1945

Buchanan, J., 'Public Goods and Natural Liberty' in Wilson, T., and A.S. Skinner (eds.), *The Market and the State, Essays in Honour of Adam Smith,* Oxford, 1976, pp. 271–286

Buuren, M.B. van, *Filosofie van de algemene literatuurwetenschap,* Leiden, 1988

Cairncross, A., 'The Market and the State' in Wilson, T. and A.S. Skinner (eds.), *The Market and the State. Essays in Honour of Adam Smith,* Oxford, 1976, pp. 113–134

Caldwell, B., *Beyond Positivism. Economic Methodology in the Twentieth Century,* London, 1982

Caldwell, B. and A.W. Coats, 'Communications. The Rhetoric of Economists: A Comment on McCloskey', *Journal of Economic Literature,* vol. 22, 1984, pp. 579–580

Campbell, R.H., Skinner A.S. and W. Todd (eds.), *Adam Smith. An Inquiry into the Nature and Causes of the Wealth of Nations,* Oxford, 1976/1979

Campbell, R.H. and A.S. Skinner, 'General Introduction' in Campbell, R.H., Skinner A.S. and W.B. Todd (eds.), *Adam Smith. An Inquiry into the Nature and Causes of the Wealth of Nations,* Oxford, 1976/1979, pp. 1–60

Campbell, R.H. and A.S. Skinner (eds.), *The Origins and Nature of the Scottish Enlightenment,* Edinburgh, 1982

Campbell, R.H., 'The Enlightenment and the Economy', in Campbell, R.H. and A.S. Skinner (eds.), *The Origins and Nature of the Scottish Enlightenment,* Edinburgh, 1982

Campbell, T.D., *Adam Smith's Science of Morals,* London, 1971

Campbell, T.D., 'Francis Hutcheson: Father of the Scottish Enlightenment' in Campbell, R.H. and A.S. Skinner (eds.), *The Origins and Nature of the Scottish Enlightenment,* Edinburgh, 1982, pp. 167–185

Cannan, E.G. (ed.), *The Wealth of Nations,* New York, 1937

Cannan, E.G., 'Alfred Marshall, 1842–1924', *Economica,* vol. 4, 1924, pp. 257–261; in Wood, J.C. (ed.), *Alfred Marshall: Critical Assessments,* part I, pp. 66–70

Cannan, E.G., 'Adam Smith as an Economist' in Wood, J.C. (ed.), *Adam Smith. Critical Assessments,* part I, London, 1984, pp. 20–28

Cant, R.G., 'Origins of the Enlightenment in Scotland: the Universities', in Campbell, R.H. and A.S. Skinner (eds.), *The Origins and Nature of the Scottish Enlightenment,* Edinburgh, 1982

Carabelli, A., 'Keynes on Cause, Change and Possibility' in Lawson, T. and H. Pesaran (eds.), *Keynes' Economics. Methodological Issues*, London, 1985, pp. 151–180

Chalk, A.F., 'Natural Law and the Rise of Economic Individualism', *Journal of Political Economy*, vol. 59, 1951, pp. 232–347

Clark, Ch.M.A., 'Equilibrium, Market Process and Historical Time', *Journal of Post Keynesian Economics*, vol. 10, 1987, pp. 27–281

Clark, Ch.M.A., 'Natural Law Influences on Adam Smith', *Quaderni di Storia dell' Economica Politica*, vol. 6, no. 3, 1988, pp. 59–86

Clark, Ch.M.A., 'Equilibrium for What?: Reflections on Social Order in Economics', *Journal of Economic Issues*, vol. 23, 1989, pp. 597–606

Clark, Ch.M.A., 'Adam Smith and Society as an Evolutionary Process', *Journal of Economic Issues*, vol. 24, 1990, pp. 825–844

Clark, Ch.M.A., *Economic Theory and Natural Philosophy: The Search for the Natural Laws of the Economy*, Aldershot, 1992

Clark, J.M. (ed.), *Adam Smith 1776–1926*, Chicago, 1928/New York, 1966

Clark, J.M., 'Adam Smith and the Currents of History' in Clark, J.M. (ed.), *Adam Smith 1776–1926*, Chicago, 1928/New York, 1966

Cleaver, K.C., 'Adam Smith on Astronomy', *History of Science*, vol. 27, 1989, pp. 211–218

Clower, R.W., 'The Keynesian Counterrevolution: A Theoretical Appraisal' in Hahn, F. and R. Brechling (eds.), *The Theory of Interest Rates*, London, 1965, pp. 103–125

Clower, R.W., 'Reflections on the Keynesian Perplex', *Zeitschrift für Nationalökonomie*, 1975, vol. 35, 1975, pp. 1–24

Coats, A.W., 'Adam Smith: The Modern Re-Appraisal', *Renaissance and Modern Studies*, vol. 6, 1962, pp. 25–48

Coddington, A., 'Keynesian Economics: The Search for First Principles', *Journal of Economic Literature*, vol. 14, 1966, pp. 1258–1273

Coddington, A., 'Hicks's Contribution to Keynesian Economics', *Journal of Economic Literature*, vol. 17, 1979, pp. 970–988

Cohen, E.S., 'Justice and Political Economy in Commercial Society: Adam Smith's "Science of a Legislator"', *Journal of Politics*, vol. 51, 1989, pp. 50–72

Coker, E.W., 'Adam Smith's Concept of the Social System', *Journal of Business Ethics*, vol. 9, 1990, pp. 139–142

Cook, P., see Mirowski, Ph. and P. Cook

Coreth, E., *Einführung in die Philosophie der Neuzeit, Band I: Rationalismus – Empirismus – Aufklärung*, Freiburg, 1972

Cropsey, J., 'The Invisible Hand: Moral and Political Considerations' in O'Driscoll Jr., G.P. (ed.), *Adam Smith and Modern Political Economy Bicentennial Essays on 'The Wealth of Nations'*, Ames Iowa, 1979, pp. 165–176

Currie, L.B., see Keyserling, L.H., Nathan, R.R. and L.B. Curry

Danner, P.L., 'Sympathy and Exchangeable Value: Keys to Adam Smith's Social Philosophy', *Review of Social Economy*, vol. 34, 1976, pp. 317–332

Darnton, R., 'The Social History of Ideas' in Darnton, R., *The Kiss of Lamourette: Reflections in Cultural History*, London, 1990, pp. 219–252

Davidson, P., *Money and the real World*, London, 1978

Davidson, P., 'Post Keynesian Economics' in Bell, D. and I. Kristol (eds.), *The Crisis in Economic Theory*, New York, 1981, pp. 151–173

Davidson, P., 'Rational Expectations: a Fallacious Foundation for Studying Crucial Decision-Making Processes', *Journal of Post Keynesian Economics*, vol. 5/6, 1982/1983, pp. 182–48

Davidson, P., *Controversies in Post Keynesian Economics*, Aldershot, 1991

De Gaay Fortman, B. (ed.), *Economie en waarde*, Alphen aan de Rijn, 1982

De Roos, W.A.A.M., 'Post-Keynesiaanse economie als gemeenschappelijke noemer voor een progressief researchprogramma', *Maandschrift Economie*, vol. 44 (1), 1980, pp. 1–18

Dean, J.W., 'The Dissolution of the Keynesian Consensus' in Bell, D. and I. Kristol (eds.), *The Crisis in Economic Theory*, New York, 1981, pp. 19–34

Dellian, E. (ed.), *Isaac Newton, 'Mathematische Grundlagen der Naturphilosophie', Ausgewählt, übersetzt, eingeleitet und herausgegeben von Ed Dellian*, Hamburg, 1988

Derksen, A.A., *Rationaliteit en wetenschap*, Assen, 1981

Devine, T.M., 'The Scottish Merchant Community, 1680–1740', in Campbell, R.H. and A.S. Skinner (eds.), *The Origins and Nature of the Scottish Enlightenment*, Edinburgh, 1982

Dijksterhuis, E.J., *Mechanisering van het wereldbeeld*, Amsterdam, 1950/1977

Donovan, A.L., *Philosophic Chemistry in the Scottish Enlightenment. The Doctrines and Discoveries of William Cullen and Joseph Black*, Edinburgh, 1975

Douglas, P.H., 'Smith's Theory of Value and Distribution' in Clark, J.M. (ed.), *Adam Smith, 1776–1928*, New York, 1928/1966

Dow, A., 'The Hauteur of Adam Smith: An Unpublished Letter from James Anderson of Monkshill', *Scottish Journal of Political Economy*, vol. 31, 1984, pp. 284–285

Dow, A., (Review in *The Economic Journal*, vol. 102, 1992, pp. 673–674 of O'Donnell, R., *Adam Smith's Theory of Value and Distribution; A Reappraisal*, London, 1990 and West, E.G., *Adam Smith and Modern Economics: From Market Behavior to Public Choice*, Aldershot, 1990)

Downie, R.S., 'Thinkers in Relationship', *Times Literary Supplement*, May 11, 1990, p. 507

Drazen, A., 'Recent Developments in Macroeconomic Disequilibrium Theory', *Econometrica*, vol. 48, 1980, pp. 283–306

Drucker, P.F., 'Towards the Next Economics' in Bell, D. and I. Kristol (eds.), *The Crisis in Economic Theory*, New York, 1981, pp. 4–18

Drukker, J., 'Adam Smith, de welvaartseconomie en het spook van Jeremy Bentham' in Kastelein, T.J. (ed.), *Adam Smith, 1776–1976, 200 jaar sedert de 'Wealth of Nations'*, Leiden, 1976, pp. 132–148

Dunn, J., *Locke*, Oxford, 1984

Dunn, J., 'From Applied Theology to Social Analysis: the Break between John Locke and the Scottish Enlightenment' in Hont, I. and M. Ignatieff (eds.), *Wealth & Virtue. The Shaping of Political Economy in the Scottish Enlightenment*, Cambridge, 1983

Dupuy, J.P., 'A Reconsideration of *Das Adam Smith Problem*, *Stanford French Review*, vol. 17, 1993, pp. 45–57

Dwyer, J., 'Adam Smith in the Scottish Enlightenment', in Mizuta, H. and C. Sugiyama (eds.), *Adam Smith: International Perspectives*, London, 1993

Eatwell, J., Milgate, M. and P. Newman (eds.), *The Invisible Hand – The New Palgrave*, London, 1987/1989

Ebeling, R.M., 'Towards a Hermeneutical Economics: Expectations, Prices, and the Role of Interpretations in a Theory of the Market Process' in Kirzner, I.M. (ed.), *Subjectivism, Intelligibility and Economic Understanding*, London, 1986, pp. 39–55

Ebeling, R.M., 'What is a Price? Explanation and Understanding (with Apologies to Paul Ricoeur)' in Lavoie, D. (ed.), *Economics and Hermeneutics*, London, 1990, pp. 177–194

Eijffinger, A.C., 'De ontwikkelingsgang van een humanist', *Wijsgerig perspectief*, vol. 23, 1982, pp. 46–54

Eijffinger, A.C. and B.P. Vermeulen (eds.), *Hugo de Groot. Denken over oorlog en vrede*, Baarn, 1991

Ekelund Jr., R.B. and R.F. Hébert, *A History of Economic Theory and Method*, New York, 1990

El-Hodiri, M.A., (Review in the *Journal of Economic History*, vol. 51, 1991, pp. 997–998 of Hutchison, T.W., *Before Adam Smith: The Emergence of Political Economy, 1662–1776*, New York, 1988)

Elsner, W., 'Adam Smith's Model of the Origins and Emergence of Institutions: The Modern Findings of the Classical Approach', *Journal of Economic Issues*, vol. 23, 1989, pp. 189–213

Eltis, W., (Review in *The Economic Journal*, vol. 99, 1989, pp. 232–234 of Hutchison, T.W., *Before Adam Smith – The Emergence of Political Economy 1662–1776*, Oxford, 1988)

Eltis, W., (Review in *Economic History Review*, vol. 47, 1994, pp. 196–197 of Pack, S.J., *Capitalism as a Moral System: Adam Smith's Critique of the Free Market Economy*, Aldershot, 1991 and Werhane, P.H., *Adam Smith and his Legacy to Modern Capitalism*, New York, 1991)

Elzas, B., (Review in *De Economist*, vol. 135, 1987, pp. 547–549 of Berns, E. (ed.), *Adam Smith: ethiek, politiek, economie*, Tilburg, 1986)

Erreygers, G., Economen ontdekken retoriek, *Streven*, 1992, pp. 1208–1214

Euchner, W., *Naturrecht und Politik bei Jon Locke*, Frankfurt am Main, 1969/1979

Euchner, W., 'Versuch über Mandevilles Bienenfabel' in Euchner, W. (ed.), 'Mandeville, B., *Die Bienenfabel oder Private Laster, öffentliche Vorteile', Frankfurt am Main, 1980*

Evensky, J., 'The Two Voices of Adam Smith: Moral Philosopher and Social Critic', *History of Political Economy*, vol. 19, 1987, pp. 447–468

Evensky, J., 'Ethics and the Classical Liberal Thought', *History of Political Economy*, vol. 24, 1992, pp. 61–77

Evensky, J., 'Adam Smith on the Human Foundation of a Successful Liberal Society', *History of Political Economy*, vol. 25, 1993, pp. 395–412

Feiwel, G.R., 'Quo Vadis Macroeconomics' in Feiwel, G.R. (ed.), *Issues in Contemporary Macroeconomics and Distribution*, London, 1985, pp. 1–100

Feiwel, G.R. (ed.), *Issues in Contemporary Macroeconomics and Distribution*, London, 1985

Feiwel, G., 'Samuelson and the Age after Keynes' in Feiwel, G. (ed.), *Samuelson and Neoclassical Economics*, Boston, 1982, pp. 202–243

Feldstein, M., 'Supply Side Economics: Old Truths and New Claims', *American Economic Review*, vol. 76, 1988, pp. 26–30

Fellmeth, R., *Staatsaufgaben im Spiegel politischer Ökonomie. Zum Verhältnis von Wirtschaft und Staatstätigkeiten in Werken von Adam Smith und Adolph Wagner*, München, 1981

Fink, H., *Social Philosophy*, London, 1981

Foley, V., *The Social Physics of Adam Smith*, West Lafayette, Indiana, 1976

Forbes, D., 'Natural Law and the Scottish Enlightenment' in Campbell, R.H. and A.S. Skinner (eds.), *The Origins and Nature of the Scottish Enlightenment*, Edinburgh, 1982, pp. 186–204

Fortuin, H., *De natuurlijke grondslagen van De Groot's volkenrecht*, The Hague, 1946

Foster, J., *Evolutionary Macroeconomics*, Boston, 1987

Franklin, B. and F. Cordasco, *Adam Smith, a Bibliographical Checklist: An International Record of Critical Writings and Scholarship Relating to Smith and Smithian Theory, 1876–1950*, New York, 1950

Franklin, R.S., 'Smithian Economics and its Pernicious Legacy', *Review of Social Economy*, vol. 34, 1976, pp. 379–389

Frantzen, P., *Overzicht van het economisch denken van de oudheid tot heden*, part 1 en 2, Antwerpen, 1973

Friedman, M., 'The Methodology of Positive Economics' in Friedman, M., *Essays in Positive Economics*, Chicago, 1953, pp. 3–43

Friedman, M., 'The Role of the Monetary Policy', *The American Economic Review*, vol. 58, March 1968, pp. 1–17

Friedman, M., and R., *Free to Choose: A Personal Statement*, New York, 1980

Friedman, M. and R. Friedman, 'The "Tide in the Affairs of Men"', *Economic Impact*, 1989/1, no. 66, pp. 74–79

Fritz, R. and J. Fritz, 'Linguistic Structure and Economic Method', *Journal of Economic Issues*, vol. 19, 1985

Frowen, S.F. (ed.), *Unknowledge and Choice in Economics: Proceedings of a Conference in Honour of G.L.S. Schackle*, London, 1990

Fry, M., *Adam Smith's Legacy. His Place in the Development of Modern Economics*, London, 1992

Fusfeld, D., *The Age of the Economist*, Glenview Illinois, 1977

Gadamer, H.-G., *Wahrheit und Methode*, Tübingen, 1960

Gadamer, H.-G. and G. Boehm (eds.), *Seminar: Die Hermeneutik und die Wissenschaften*, Frankfurt am Main, 1978

Galbraith, J.K., 'Power and the Useful Economist', *The American Economic Review*, vol. 63, 1973, pp. 1–11

Garretsen, H., *Keynes, Coordination and Beyond. The Development of Macroeconomics and Monetary Theory since 1945*, Aldershot, 1992

Garretsen, H., 'The Relevance of Hayek for Mainstream Economics', in Birner, J. and R. van Zijp (eds.), *Hayek, Co-ordination and Evolution: His Legacy in Philosophy, Politics, Economics and the History of Ideas*, London, 1994, pp. 94-108

Gay, P., *The Enlightenment: An Interpretation / The Rise of Modern Paganism*, New York, 1966/1977

Gay, P., *The Enlightenment: An Interpretation / The Science of Freedom*, New York, 1967/1977

Gill, E.R., 'Justice in Smith: the Right and the Good', *Review of Social Economy*, vol. 32, 1976, pp. 275–294

Goudzwaard, B., *Kapitalisme en vooruitgang*, Assen, 1978

Gramm, W.S., 'The Selective Interpretation of Adam Smith', *Journal of Economic Issues*, vol. 14, 1980, pp. 119–142

Gray, J., 'Free at Last', *National Review*, vol. 45, 1993, pp. 56–58; review of Muller, J., *Adam Smith in His Time and Ours: Designing the Decent Society*, New York, 1993

Griswold, Ch.L., 'Adam Smith of Virtue and Self-Interest', *The Journal of Philosophy*, vol. 86, 1989, pp. 669–682

Groot, H. de, see Eijffinger, A.C. and B.P. Vermeulen

Grossman, H.I., 'Was Keynes a "Keynesian"? A Review Article', *Journal of Economic Literature*, vol. 10, 1972, pp. 26–30

Grüske, K.D. (ed.), *Markt und Staat. Fundamente einer freiheitlichen Ordnung in Wirtschaft und Politik. Ausgewählte Beitrage*, Göttingen, 1980

Haakonssen, K., 'What Might properly be called Natural Jurisprudence' in Campbell, R.H. and A.S. Skinner (eds.), *The Origins and Nature of the Scottish Enlightenment*, Edinburgh, 1982, pp. 205–225

Haakonssen, K., *The Science of a Legislator: The Natural Jurisprudence of David Hume and Adam Smith*, Cambridge, 1981

Hacking, I., *Representing and Intervening: Introductory Topics in the Philosophy of Natural Science*, Cambridge, 1983

Hahn, F.H., *On the Notion of Equilibrium in Economics*, Cambridge, 1973

Hahn, F.H., 'General Equilibrium Theory' in Bell, D. and I. Kristol (eds.), *The Crisis in Economic Theory*, New York, 1981, p. 123–138

Hahn, F.H., 'Reflections on the Invisible Hand', *Lloyds Bank Review*, April 1982, pp. 1–21

Hahn, F.H., 'Auctioneer' in *The New Palgrave, General Equilibrium*, 1991, London, pp. 62–67

Hamonda, O.F. and R. Rowley, *Expectations, Equilibrium and Dynamics. A History of Recent Economic Ideas and Practices*, 1988

Hamouda, O. and J.N. Smithin, 'Some Remarks on "Uncertainty and Economic Analysis"', *The Economic Journal*, vol. 98, 1988, pp. 159–164

Hansen, A.H., *A Guide to Keynes*, New York, 1953

Harris, S. (ed.), *The New Economics. Keynes' Influence on Theory and Public Policy*, London, 1947/1960

Harris, S., 'The Appraisal of the General Theory' in Harris, S. (ed.), *The New Economics. Keynes' Influence on Theory and Public Policy*, London, pp. 26–38

Hartog, F., *Zicht op de economie*, Amsterdam, 1980

Hartwell, R.M. (ed.), see Ricardo, D.

Häufle, H., *Aufklärung und Ökonomie*, München, 1978

Hayek, F.A., 'The Trend of Economic Thinking', *Economica*, 1933, pp. 121–137

Hayek, F.A., 'Economics and Knowledge', 1937, reprinted in Hayek, F.A., *Individualism and Economic Order*, London, 1949/1976

Hayek, F.A., *Profits, Interest and Investment and other Essays on the Theory of Industrial Fluctuations*, London, 1939

Hayek, F.A., *Het ware en het valse individualisme. Vraagstukken van heden en morgen*, no. 3 (*Individualism: True and False*, Dublin, 1946)

Hayek, F.A., *Individualism and Economic Order*, London, 1949/1976

Hayek, F.A., *The Counter-Revolution of Science. Studies on the Abuse of Reason*, London, 1955

Hayek, F.A., *Unemployment and Monetary Policy. Government as Generator of the "Business Cycle"*, CATO Paper no. 3, CATO Institute, Washington, 1979

Hayek, F.A., *New Studies in Philosophy, Politics, Economics and the History of Ideas*, London, 1978

Hébert, R.F., see Ekelund Jr., R.B. and R.F. Hébert

Heilbroner, R.L., 'The Paradox of Progress: Decline and Decay in "The Wealth of Nations"' in Skinner, A.S. and T. Wilson (eds.), *Essays on Adam Smith*, Oxford, 1975, pp. 524–539

Heilbroner, R.L., 'The Socialization of the Individual in Adam Smith', *History of Political Economy*, vol. 14, 1982, pp. 427–439

Heilbroner, R.L., *The Essential Adam Smith*, New York, 1986

Heilbroner, R.L. and W. Milberg, *The Crisis of Vision in Modern Economic Thought*, Cambridge, 1995

Heimann, E., *History of Economic Doctrines*, Oxford, 1945

Heimann, E., *History of Economic Doctrines*, Oxford, 1945

Hennings, K. and W.J. Samuels (ed.), *Neoclassical Economic Theory, 1870–1930*, Boston, 1990

Hewett, R., (Review in *Choice*, vol. 29, 1992, p. 1275 of Werhane, P.H., *Capitalism as a Moral System: Adam Smith's Critique of the Free Market Economy*, Oxford, 1991)

Hewett, R., (Review in *Choice*, vol. 29, 1992, p. 1130 of Pack, S.J., *Capitalism as a Moral System: Adam Smith's Critique of the Free Market Economy*, Aldershot, 1991)

Hicks, J.R., 'Mr. Keynes and the "Classics"', *Econometrica*, vol. 5, 1937, pp. 147–159

Hicks, J.R., *Value and Capital*, Oxford, 1946/1974

Hicks, J.R., 'Rehabilitation of "Classical" Economics?', *Economic Journal*, vol. 67, 1957, pp. 278–289

Hicks, J.R., 'Recollections and Documents', *Economica*, vol. 40, 1973, pp. 1–11

Hicks, J.R., *The Crisis in Keynesian Economics*, Oxford, 1974

Hicks, J.R., 'On Coddington's Interpretation: A Reply', *Journal of Economic Literature*, vol. 17, 1979, pp. 989–995

Hinterberger, F. and M. Hüther, 'Von Smith bis Hayek und zurück. Eine kleine Geschichte der Selbstorganisation in der Nationalökonomie', *Jahrbücher für Nationalökonomie und Statistik*, vol. 211, 1993, pp. 211–238

Hirsch, E.D.jr., *Validity in Interpretation*, New Haven, 1967

Hla Myint, U., 'Adam Smith's Theory on International Trade in the Perspective of Economic Development' *Economica*, vol. 44, 1977, pp. 231-248

Hodgson, G.M., *Economics and Institutions. A Manifesto for a Modern Institutional Economics*, Oxford, 1988

Hodgson, G.M., 'Persuasion, Expectations and the Limits to Keynes' in Lawson, T. and H. Pesaran (eds.), *Keynes' Economics. Methodological Issues*, London, 1985,

Hodgson, G.M., 'Institutionalism, "Old" and "New"', in Hodgson, G.M., Samuels, W.J. and M.R. Tool (eds.), *The Elgar Companion to Institutionalism and Evolutionary Economics*, Aldershot, 1994, pp. 397–402

Hodgson, G.M., Samuels, W.J. and M.R. Tool (eds.), *The Elgar Companion to Institutionalism and Evolutionary Economics*, Aldershot, 1994

Hollander, J.H., 'The Dawn of a Science' in Clark, J.M. (ed.), *Adam Smith 1776–1926*, Chicago, 1928/New York, 1966

Hollander, J.H., 'The Founder of a School' in Clark, J.M. (ed.), *Adam Smith 1776–1926*, Chicago, 1928/New York, 1966

Hollander, S., *The Economics of Adam Smith*, Toronto, 1973

Hollander, S., 'The Historical Dimensions of The Wealth of Nations', *Transactions of the Royal Society of Canada*, Series IV, 14, 1976, pp. 277–292

Hollander, S., 'Smith and Ricardo: Aspects of the Nineteenth-Century Legacy', *The American Economic Review*, vol. 67, May 1977, pp. 37–41

Hollander, S., 'On Professor Samuelson's Canonical Classical Model of Political Economy', *Journal of Economic Literature*, vol. 18, 1980, pp. 559–574

Hont, I. and M. Ignatieff, 'Needs and justice in the *Wealth of Nations*: an introductory essay' in Hont, I. and M. Ignatieff (eds.), *Wealth & Virtue. The Shaping of Political Economy in the Scottish Enlightenment*, Cambridge, 1983, pp. 1–44

Hont, I. and M. Ignatieff (eds.), *Wealth and Virtue. The Shaping of Political Economy in the Scottish Enlightenment*, Cambridge, 1983

Hoogduin, L., 'On the Difference between the Keynesian, Knightian and the 'Classical' Analysis of Uncertainty and the Development of a More General Monetary Theory', *De Economist*, vol. 135, 1987, pp. 52–65

Hoover, K.D., *The New Classical Macroeconomics. A Sceptical Inquiry*, Oxford, 1988

Hoover, K.D. (ed.), *The New Classical Macroeconomics*, part III, Aldershot, 1992

Hope, V.M., *Virtue by Consensus. The Moral Philosophy of Hutcheson, Hume, and Adam Smith*, Oxford, 1989

Howard, M., see Bradley, L. and M. Howard

Hunt, E.K., 'Economic Scholasticism and Capitalist Ideology' in Hunt. E.K. and J.G. Schwartz (eds.), *A Critique of Economic Theory*, Middlesex, 1972, pp. 186–193

Hutcheson, F., '*An Inquiry concerning Moral Good and Evil*' in Raphael, D.D., *British Moralists, 1650–1800*, Oxford, 1969, pp. 261–299

Hutchison, T.W., 'Theoretische Oekonomie als Sprachsystem', *Zeitschrift für Nationalökonomie*, vol. 8, 1937; in: Albert, H. (ed.), *Theorie und Realität*, Tübingen, 1964, pp. 191–202

Hutchison, T.W., *The Significance and Basic Postulates of Economic Theory*, London, 1937/New York, 1960

Hutchison, T.W., *Before Adam Smith: The Emergence of Political Economy, 1662–1776*, Oxford, 1988

Hutchison, T.W., *A Review of Economic Doctrines. 1870–1929*, Oxford, 1953/1966

Hutchison, T.W., *On Revolutions and Progress in Economic Knowledge*, Cambridge, 1978

Hutchison, T.W., *'Positive' Economics and Policy Objectives*, London, 1964

Hutchison, T.W., 'The Bicentenary of Adam Smith', *The Economic Journal*, vol. 86, 1976, pp. 481–492

Hutchison, T.W., *The Politics and Philosophy of Economics. Marxians, Keynesians and Austrians*, Oxford, 1981

Hüther, M., see Hinterberger, F. and M. Hüther

Ignatieff, M., see Hont, I. and M. Ignatieff

Jaffé, W., 'A Centenarian on a Bicentenarian: Léon Walras's Eléments on Adam Smith's Wealth of Nations', *Canadian Journal of Economics*, vol. 10, 1977, pp. 19–31

Jensen, H.E., 'Sources and Contours of Adam Smith's Conceptualized Reality in the "Wealth of Nations"', *Review of Social Economy*, vol. 34, 1976, pp. 259–274

Jevons, W.S., *The Theory of Political Economy*, 1871, ed. by R. Collison Black, Harmondsworth, 1970

Johansen, L., 'Mechanistic and Organistic Analogies in Economics: The Place of Game Theory. Some notes on H. Thoben's article, *Kyklos*, vol. 36, 1983, pp. 304–307

Johnson, H., 'The Keynesian Revolution and the Monetarist Counterrevolution', *The American Economic Review*, vol. 61, 1971, pp. 1–14

Johnson, R.D., 'Adam Smith's Radical Views on Property, Distributive Justice and the Market', *Review of Social Economy*, vol. 48, 1990, pp. 263–287

Jolink, A., *Liberté, Egalité, Rareté. The Evolutionary Economics of Léon Walras: An Analytical Reconstruction*, Amsterdam, 1991

Jolink, A., 'Onvoltooid verleden tijd', *Economenblad*, vol. 13, 1991, November 27, p. 3

Jolink, A., 'Economic Equilibrium in the History of Science: Reviewing "The Invisible Hand"', *The Economic Journal*, vol. 103, 1993, pp. 1303–1311

Jones, J., *Morals, Motives & Markets. Adam Smith 1723–90*, Edinburgh, 1990

Jones, M., see Bassiry, G.R. and M. Jones

Kalshoven, F., 'Een kwestie van klepjes, schuifjes en draaien aan kranen', *de Volkskrant*, March 19th, 1994, p. 45

Kastelein, T.J., 'Sympathie, eigen-belang, rijkdom en geluk', in Kastelein, T. (ed.), *Adam Smith, 1776–1976, 200 jaar sedert de 'Wealth of Nations'*, leiden, 1976, pp. 40–71

Kastelein, T.J. (ed.), *Adam Smith, 1776–1976, 200 jaar sedert de 'Wealth of Nations'*, Leiden, 1976

Kauder, E., *A History of Marginal Utility Theory*, New York, 1965

Kaufmann, F.-X. and H.G. Krüsselberg (eds.), *Markt, Staat und Solidarität bei Adam Smith*, Frankfurt am Main, 1981

Kerkhof, A.J., *De mens is een angstig dier: Adam Smith' theorie van de morele gevoelens*, Meppel, 1992

Keynes J.M., 'The General Theory of Employment', *The Quarterly Journal of Economics*, February 1937, pp. 209–223

Keynes, J.M., 'Alternative Theories of the Rate of Interest', *The Economic Journal*, vol. 47, 1937, pp. 241–252

Keynes, J.M., 'The General Theory of Employment, Interest, and Money' in *The Collected Writings of John Maynard Keynes*, Cambridge, 1973

Keyserling, L.H., R.R. Nathan and L.B. Currie, 'Discussion' bij Sweezy, A., 'The Keynesians and Government Policy, 1933–1939' and Jones, B., 'The Role of Keynesians in Wartime Policy and Postwar Planning, 1940–1946', *The American Review*, vol. 62, May 1972, pp. 116–124 and 125–133, pp. 134–141

Khalil, E.L., 'Beyond Self-Interest and Altruism. A Reconstruction of Adam Smith's Theory of Human Conduct', *Economics and Philosophy*, vol. 6, 1990, pp. 255–273

Kinneging, A.A.M., Liberalisme. Een speurtocht naar de filosofische grondslagen, *Geschrift 65*, Prof. Mr. B.M. Teldersstichting, The Hague, 1988

Kirzner, I.M. (ed.), *Subjectivism, Intelligibility and Economic Understanding. Essays in Honor of Ludwig M. Lachmann on his Eightieth Birthday*, London, 1986

Kittsteiner, H.-D., *Naturabsicht und Unsichtbare Hand: Zur Kritik des geschichtphilosophischen Denkens*, Frankfurt am Main, 1980

Klamer, A., *The New Classical Macroeconomics: Conversations with New Classical Economists and their Opponents*, Brighton, 1984

Klamer, A., 'The Textbook Presentation of Economic Discourse', in Samuels, W.J. (ed.), *Economics as Discourse. An Analysis of the Language of Economics*, London, 1990

Klamer, A., 'Towards the Native's Point of View. The Difficulty of Changing the Conversation', *Economics and Hermeneutics*, London, 1990, pp. 19-33

Klant, J.J., *Het ontstaan van de staathuishoudkunde*, Leiden, 1988

Klant, J.J., *Spelregels voor economen*, Leiden, 1979

Kleer, R.A., 'Adam Smith on the Morality of the Pursuit of Fortune', *Economics and Philosophy*, vol. 9, 1993, pp. 289–295

Knoester, A. (ed.), *Lessen uit het verleden*, Leiden, 1987

Knoester, A., 'Stagnation and the Inverted Haavelmo Effect: some International Evidence', *De Economist*, vol. 131, 1983, pp. 548–584

Kornai, J., *Anti-equilibrium: Economic Systems Theory and the Tasks of Research*, Amsterdam, 1971

Krabbe, J.J., *Historisme in economisch denken*, Assen, 1983

Kregel, J.A., *The Reconstruction of Political Economy. An Introduction to Post-Keynesian Economics*, London, 1973

Kregel, J.A., 'Markets and Institutions as Features of a Capitalistic Production System', *Journal of Post Keynesian Economics*, vol. 3/4, 1980/1981, pp. 32–48

Kregel, J.A., 'Imagination, Exchange and Business Enterprise in Smith and Shackle' in Frowen, S.F. (ed.), *Unknowledge and Choice in Economics*, London, 1990, pp. 81–95

Kristoll, I., see Bell, D. and I. Kristoll

Krüsselberg, H.G., see Kaufmann, F.-X. and H.G. Krüsselberg

Kuhn, Th.S., *The Structure of Scientific Revolutions*, Chicago, 1970

Kuipers, S. and H. van Ees, 'Macro-economische theorie en economische politiek', *Economisch Statistische Berichten*, vol. 75, 1990, pp. 32–43

Kuttner, R., 'On the State of Economics', *Dialogue*, 1986, no. 73, pp. 65–71

Lachmann, L.M., *The Market as an Economic Process*, Oxford, 1986

Lachmann, L.M., 'From Mises to Shackle: an Essay on Austrian Economics and the Kaleidic Society', *Journal of Economic Literature*, vol. 14, 1976, pp. 54–62

Lachmann, L.M., *Marktprozess und Erwartungen. Studien zur Theorie der Marktwirtschaft*, München, 1984

Lachmann, L.M., 'The Salvage of Ideas. Problems of the Revival of Austrian Economic Thought', *Zeitschrift für die gesammte Staatswissenschaft, 1982, pp. 629–645*

Lachmann, L.M., 'Austrian Economics: a Hermeneutic Approach' in Lavoie, D. (ed.), *Economics and Hermeneutics*, London, 1990, pp. 134–146

Lamb, R.B., 'Adam Smith's System: Sympathy not Self-Interest', *Journal of the History of Ideas*, vol. 35, 1974, pp. 671–682

Landreth, H. and D.C. Colander, *History of Economic Theory*, Boston, 1989

Lange, D., *Zur sozial-philosophischen Gestalt der Marktwirtschaftstheorie bei Adam Smith*, München, 1983

Lavoie, D., 'Introduction', in Lavoie, D. (ed.), *Economics and Hermeneutics*, London, 1990, pp. 1-15

Lavoie, D. (ed.), *Economics and Hermeneutics*, London, 1990

Lavoie, D. 'Euclidianism versus Hermeneutics: A Reinterpretation of Misesian Apriorism' in I. Kirzner (ed.), *Subjectivism, Intelligibility and Economic Understanding*, London, 1986, pp. 192–210

Lawson, T. and H. Pesaran (eds.), *Keynes' Economics. Methodological Issues*, London, 1985

Lawson, T., 'Uncertainty and Economic Analysis', *The Economic Journal*, vol. 95, 1985, pp. 909–927

Lawson, T., 'The Relative/Absolute Nature of Knowledge and Economic Analysis', *The Economic Journal*, vol. 97, 1987, pp. 951–970

Leeuwen, A.Th., *De nacht van het kapitaal. Door het oerwoud van de economie naar de bronnen van de burgerlijke religie*, Nijmegen, 1984

Leijonhufvud, A., *Information and Co-ordination*, New York, 1981

Leijonhufvud, A., *On Keynesian Economics and the Economics of Keynes*, New York, 1968

Leijonhufvud, A., 'Review of J.R. Hicks' Economic Perspectives: Further Essays on Money and Growth', *Journal of Economic Literature*, vol. 17, 1979, pp. 525–527

Leontief, W., 'Theoretical Assumptions and Non-observed Facts', *The American Economic Review*, vol. 61, 1971, pp. 1–9

Leslie, T.E.C., 'The Political Economy of Adam Smith', *Fortnightly Review*, November 1870, in Leslie, T.E.C., *Essays in Political and Moral Philosophy*, London, 1879, pp. 148–166

Leslie, T.E.C., 'On the Philosophical Method of Political Economy', *Hermathena*, no. 4, 1876, in Leslie, T.E.C., *Essays in Political and Moral Philosophy*, London, 1879, pp. 216–242

Letwin, W., *The Origins of Scientific Economics*, London, 1963

Letwin, W., (Review in *The Times Literary Supplement*, February 26th, 1993, p. 9 of Muller, J.Z., *Adam Smith and His Time and Ours: Designing the Decent Society*, New York, 1993)

Lightwood, M.B., *A Selected Bibliography of Significant Works about Adam Smith*, London, 1984

Lindgren, J.R., *The Social Philosophy of Adam Smith*, The Hague, 1973

Locke, J., 'An Essay on Human Understanding' in Raphael, D., *British Moralists, 1650–1800*, Oxford, 1969, pp. 137–159

Locke, J., *Two Treatises of Government*, London, 1924/1984

Lucas, R.E., 'Methods and Problems in Business Cycle Theory', *Journal of Money, Credit and Banking*, vol. 12, 1980, pp. 696–715, in Hoover, K., *The New Classical Macroeconomics*, part III, Aldershot, 1992, pp. 225–244

Lucas, R.E., 'Understanding Business Cycles', in Brunner, K. and H. Meltzer (eds.), *Stabilization of the Domestic and International Economy*, Carnegie-Rochester Conference Series on Public Policy, vol. 5, Amsterdam, pp. 7–29, in Hoover, K.D., *The New Classical Macroeconomics*, part III, Aldershot, 1992, pp. 245–267

Lukes, S., *Individualism*, Oxford, 1973

Lutz, M.A. (ed.), *Social Economics: Retrospect and Prospect*, Boston, 1990

Lydall, H.F., 'From Professor H.F. Lydall, Letters to the Editor', *Lloyds Bank Review*, July 1982, pp. 48–49

Macfie, A.L., 'The Scottish Tradition in Economic Thought', *Scottish Journal of Political Economy*, June 1955, pp. 81–103

Macfie. A.L., 'Adam Smith's Moral Sentiments as Foundations for his Wealth of nations', *Oxford Economic Papers*, vol. 11, 1959, pp. 209–228

Macfie. A.L., 'Adam Smith's Theory of Moral Sentiments', *Scottish Journal of Political Economy*, vol. 8, 1961, pp. 12–27

Macfie. A.L., 'The Moral Justification of Free Enterprise. A Lay Sermon on a Adam Smith Text', *Scottish Journal of Political Economy*, vol. 14, 1967, pp. 1–11

Macfie, A.L., *The Individual in Society: Papers on Adam Smith*, London, 1967

Macfie, A.L., 'The Invisible Hand of Jupiter', *Journal of the History of Ideas*, 1971, vol. 32, pp. 595–599

Macfie, A.L., see Raphael, D.D. and A.L. Macfie

Maddison, A., *Ontwikkelingsfasen van het kapitalisme*, Utrecht/Antwerpen, 1982

Maes, I., 'IS-LM: The Hicksian Journey', *De Economist*, 1989, vol. 137, pp. 91–104

Madison, G.B., 'Getting beyond Objectivism: the Philosophical Hermeneutics of Gadamer and Ricoeur', in Lavoie, D. (ed.), *Economics and Hermeneutics*, London, 1990, pp. 34–58

Maks, J.A.H. and A. van Witteloostuyn, 'Walras Understood or Misunderstood', *Research-memorandum 86–014, Rijksuniversiteit Limburg, 1986*

Manenschijn, G., *Moraal en eigenbelang bij Thomas Hobbes en Adam Smith*, Amsterdam, 1979

Manicas, P.T., *A History & Philosophy of the Social Sciences*, Oxford, 1987

Marcel, G., *Zijn en Hebben*, Utrecht, 1960

Marshall, A., *Principles of Economics*, London, 1920/1986

Martin, D.A., 'Economics as Ideology, On Making "The Invisible Hand" Invisible', *Review of Social Economy*, vol. 48, 1990

Martin, M., (Review in the *Journal of the History of Philosophy*, vol. 29, 1991, pp. 314–315 of Hope, V.M., *Virtue by Consensus: The Moral Philosophy of Hutcheson, Hume, and Adam Smith*, Oxford, 1989)

McCloskey, D., *The Rhetoric of Economics*, Madison, 1985

McCloskey, D., 'Communications. Reply to Caldwell and Coats', *Journal of Economic Literature*, vol. 22, 1984, pp. 579–580

McCormick, B., *Hayek and the Keynesian Avalanche*, New York, 1992

McNamara, P., 'Adam Smith: Architectonic Thinker', *The Review of Politics*, vol. 56, 1994, pp. 183–185 (Review of Muller, J.Z., *Adam Smith in his Time and Ours: Designing the Decent Society*, New York, 1993)

Medick, H., *Naturzustand und Naturgeschichte der bürgerlichen Gesellschaft. Die Ursprünge der bürgerlichen Sozialtheorie als Geschichtsphilosophie und Sozialwissenschaft bei Samuel Pufendorf, John Locke und Adam Smith*, Göttingen, 1973

Meek, R.L., 'Smith, Turgot, and the "Four Stages" Theory', *History of Political Economy*, vol. 3, 1971, pp. 9–27

Meek, R.L., D.D. Raphael and P.G. Stein (eds.), *Adam Smith. Lectures on Jurisprudence*, Oxford, 1978/1987

Meek, R.L., D.D. Raphael and P.G. Stein, 'Introduction' in Meek, R.L., Raphael, D.D and P.G. Stein (eds.), *Adam Smith. Lectures on Jurisprudence*, Oxford, 1978/1987, pp. 1–42

Meek, R.L., *Economics and Ideology and Other Essays*, London, 1967

Meek, R.L., *Social Science and the Ignoble Savage*, Cambridge, 1976

Meek, R.L., *Smith, Marx and after: Ten Essays in the Development of Economic Thought*, New York, 1977

Meikle, S., *Aristotle's Economic Thought*, Oxford, 1995

Meijdam, L., Een nieuw-klassieke synthese, in: *Economenblad*, vol. 14, 1992, pp. 5–6

Ménard, C., 'The Lausanne Tradition: Walras and Pareto', in Hennings, K. and W.J. Samuels (eds.), *Neoclassical Economic Theory, 1870 to 1930*, Boston, 1990, pp. 95–136

Meyerson, A., 'Adam Smith's Welfare State: Generous Government is Consistent with a Market Economy', *Policy Review*, vol. 50, 1989, pp. 66–67

Milgate, M., see Eatwell, J., Milgate, M. and P. Newman

Millar, J., *An Historical View of the English Government*, part II, London, 1787/1803

Miller, T.C., 'What Adam Smith and James Madison would say about the American Political Economy Today', *Public Administration Review*, vol. 52, 1992, pp. 70–76

Mirowski, Ph.E., 'Adam Smith, Empiricism, and the Rate of Profit in Eighteenth-Century England', *History of Political Economy*, vol. 14, 1982, pp. 178–198

Mirowski, Ph.E., 'Physics and the Marginalist Revolution', *Cambridge Journal of Economics*, vol. 8, 1984, pp. 361–379

Mirowski, Ph.E. and P. Cook, 'Walras "Economics and Mechanics": Translation, Commentary, Context' in Samuels, W.J. (ed.), *Economics as Discourse. An Analysis of the Language of Economics*, Boston, 1990

Mizuta, H. and C. Sugiyama (eds.), *Adam Smith: International Perspectives*, London, 1993

Moos S., 'Is Smith out of Date?', *Oxford Economic Papers*, vol. 3, 1951, pp. 187–201

Morgenstern, O., 'Thirteen Critical Points and Contemporary Economic Theory. An Interpretation', *Journal of Economic Literature*, vol. 10, 1972, pp. 1163–1189

Morrow, G.R., 'The Significance of the Doctrine of Sympathy in Hume and Adam Smith', *The Philosophical Review*, vol. 32, 1923, pp. 60–78

Morrow, G.R., 'Adam Smith: Moralist and Philosopher' in Clark, J.M. (ed.), *Adam Smith, 1776–1926*, Chicago, 1928/New York, 1966, pp. 156–179

Morrow, G.R., *The Ethical and Economic Theories of Adam Smith. A Study in the Social Philosophy of the 18Th Century*, New York, 1923/1969/1973

Mossner, E.C.S. and I. Ross (eds.), *The Correspondence of Adam Smith*, Oxford, 1987

Muldrew, C., 'Interpreting the Market: The Ethics of Credit and Community Relations in Early Modern England', *Social History*, vol. 18, 1993, pp. 163–183

Muller, J.Z., *Adam Smith in His Time and Ours: Designing the Decent Society*, New York, 1993

Musgrave, R.A., 'Adam Smith on Public Finance and Distribution' in Wilson, T. and A.S. Skinner (eds.), *The Market and the State. Essays in Honour of Adam Smith*, Oxford, 1976, pp. 296–319

Myers, M.L., *The Soul of Modern Economic Man. Ideas of Self-Interest. Thomas Hobbes to Adam Smith*, Chicago, 1983

Nathan, R.R., see Keyserling, L.H., R. Nathan and L.B. Curry

Negishi, T., *History of Economic Theory*, Amsterdam, 1989

Negishi, T., *Economic Theories in a Non-Walrasian Tradition*, Cambridge, 1986

Nell, E., 'Economics: The Revival of Political Economy' in Blackburn R. (ed.), *Ideology in Social Science*, New York, 1972, pp. 76–95

Newman, P., see Eatwell, J., Milgate, M. and P. Newman

Nentjes, A. (ed.), *Keynesianisme vandaag. Jaarboek studiekring Post-Keynesiaanse economie 1987*, Alphen aan de Rijn, 1988

Newton, I., see Böhme, G. (ed.)

Newton, I., see Dellian, E. (ed.)

North, D.C., *Institutions, Institutional Change and Economic Performance*, Cambridge, 1990

North, D.C., 'Shared Mental Models: Ideologies and Institutions', *Kyklos*, vol. 47, 1994, pp. 3–31

North, D.C., 'Economic Performance Through Time', *The American Economic Review*, vol. 84, 1994, pp. 359–368

O'Brien, D.P., 'The Longevity of Adam Smith's Vision: Paradigms, Research Programmes and Falsifiability in the History of Economic Thought', *Scottish Journal of Political Economy*, vol. 23, 1976, pp. 133–151

O'Brien, D.P., *The Classical Economists*, Oxford, 1975

O'Brien, J., 'The Role of Economics and Ethics in Civilisation and Progress', *International Journal of Social Economics*, vol. 8, 1981, no. 4, pp. 1–21

O'Donnell, R., *Keynes: Philosophy, Economics & Politics*, London, 1989

O'Donnell, R., *Adam Smith's Theory of Value and Distribution*, London, 1990

O'Driscoll Jr., G.P. (ed.), *Adam Smith and Modern Political Economy. Bicentennial Essays on 'The Wealth of Nations'*, Ames Iowa, 1979

O'Driscoll Jr., G.P. and M.J. Rizzo, *The Economics of Time & Ignorance*, Oxford, 1985

Pack, S.J., *Capitalism as a Moral System: Adam Smith's Critique of the Free Market Economy*, Aldershot, 1991

Patinkin, D., *Money, Interest, and Prices. An Integration of Monetary and Value Theory*, New York, 1965

Patinkin, D., 'Keynes and Economics Today', *The American Economic Review*, vol. 74, 1984, pp. 97–102

Paul, J., (Review in *Ethics*, vol. 103, 1993, p. 414 of Pack, S.J., *Capitalism as a Moral System: Adam Smith's Critique of the Free Market Economy*, Aldershot, 1991

Peer, W. van and K. Dijkstra (eds.), *Sleutelwoorden. Kernbegrippen uit de hedendaagse literatuurwetenschappen*, Leuven, 1991

Peil, J., zie Plattel, M.A.D. en J. Peil

Peil, J., 'Adam Smith en economische wetenschap', *Research Memorandum 8602*, Economisch Instituut KUN, Nijmegen, 1986

Peil, J., 'Adam Smith en de economische wetenschap' in Berns, E. (ed.), *Adam Smith. Ethiek, politiek, economie*, Tilburg, 1986, pp. 268–309

Peil, J., 'Is it all in Adam Smith?', *Working Paper 8701*, Institute of Economics, University of Nijmegen, 1987

Peil, J., 'A New Look at Adam Smith', *Research Memorandum 8704*, Institute of Economics, University of Nijmegen, 1987

Peil, J., 'Adam Smith. A Reconstruction of His Economic Thought', *Research Memorandum 8802*, Institute of Economics, University of Nijmegen, 1988

Peil, J., 'Een Adam Renaissance', *Working Paper 8809*, Institute of Economics, University of Nijmegen, 1988

Peil, J., 'A New Look at Adam Smith', *International Journal of Social Economics*, vol. 16, 1989, pp. 52–72

Peil, J., 'A New Look at Adam Smith' in Blaug, M. (ed.), Adam Smith (1723–1790), *Pioneers in Economics*, part II, Aldershot, 1991, pp. 279–299, and in Wood, J.C. (ed.), *Adam Smith. Second Series: Critical Assessments*, vol. vi, New York, 1994, pp. 276-299

Peperzak, A., 'Kan de verlichting ons verlichten', *Tijdschrift voor Filosofie*, vol. 24, 1962, pp. 243–278

Pesaran, M.H., *The Limits to Rational Expectations*, Oxford, 1987

Pesaran, H., see Lawson, T. and H. Pesaran

Peters, P.J.L.M., '(On)evenwichtigheidsregimes in Nederland 1973–1987' in Knoester, A. (ed.), *Lessen uit het verleden*, Leiden, 1987, pp. 423–437

Petrella, F., (Review in *Choice*, vol. 95, 1993, p. 1360 of Muller, J., *Adam Smith in His Time and Ours: Designing the Decent Society*, New York, 1993)

Phelps, E., *Seven Schools of Macroeconomic Thought*, Oxford, 1990

Plattel, M.A.D., *Sociale Wijsbegeerte, deel I: De mens en het medemenselijke*, Utrecht, 1960/1963

Plattel, M.A.D., *Sociale Wijsbegeerte, deel II: De mens in de maatschappij*, Utrecht, 1964/1967

Plattel, M.A.D., *Utopie en kritisch denken*, Bilthoven, 1970/1972

Plattel, M.A.D., *De rode en gouden toekomst. De avontuurlijke wijsbegeerte van Ernst Bloch*, Bilthoven, 1976

Plattel, M.A.D., 'Het vraagstuk van positieve en normatieve economie' in De Gaay Fortman, B. (ed.), *Economie en waarde*, Alphen aan de Rijn, 1982, pp. 48–67

Plattel, M.A.D. and J.J.M. Peil, 'An Ethico-Political and Theoretical Reconstruction of Economic Thought', *Research Memorandum no. 149*, Tilburg University Department of Economics, Tilburg, 1984

Plattel, M.A.D. 'Economische wetenschap en ethiek', *Tijdschrift voor Theologie*, vol. 25, 1985, no. 1, pp. 4–19

Plattel, M.A.D. and J.J.M. Peil, 'An Ethico-Political and Theoretical Reconstruction of Economic Thought', *Research Memorandum 8604* (revised edition of *Research Memorandum no. 149*, Tilburg University Department of Economics, Tilburg, 1984), Economic Institute KUN, Nijmegen, 1986

Polanyi, K., *Ökonomie und Gesellschaft*, Frankfurt am Main, 1979 .

Puro, E., 'Comment' to Rosetti, J., 'Deconstructing Robert Lucas', in Samuels, W.J. (ed.), *Economics as Discourse. An Analysis of the Language of Economics*, London, 1990, pp. 251–256

Rae, J., *Life of Adam Smith*, London, 1895/Bristol, 1990

Randall, J., *The Career of Philosophy. From the Middle Ages to the Enlightenment*, New York, 1962

Raphael, D.D., *British Moralists.1650–1800*, Oxford, 1969

Raphael, D.D. and A.L. Macfie (eds.), *Adam Smith. The Theory of Moral Sentiments*, Oxford, 1976/1991

Raphael, D.D. and A.L. Macfie, 'Introduction' in Raphael, D.D. and A.L. Macfie (eds.), *Adam Smith. The Theory of Moral Sentiments*, Oxford, 1976/1991, pp. *1–52*

Raphael, D.D., see Meek, R.L., Raphael, D.D. and P.G. Stein

Raphael, D.D. and A.S. Skinner, 'General Introduction', *Adam Smith. Essays on Philosophical Subjects*, Oxford, 1980, pp. 1–21

Rashid, S., 'Adam Smith's Rise to Fame: A Re-examination of the Evidence', *The Eighteenth Century*, vol. 23, 1982, pp. 64–85

Rashid, S., 'Political Economy as Moral Philosophy: Dugald Stewart of Edinburgh', *Australian Economic Papers*, vol. 26, 1987, pp. 145–156

Rashid, S., 'Adam Smith's Interpretation of The History of Economics and Its Influence in the 18th and 19th Centuries', *Quarterly Review of Economics and Business*, vol. 27, 1987, pp. 56–69

Rashid, S., 'Adam Smith's Acknowledgments: Neo-Plagiarism and the Wealth of Nations', *The Journal of Libertarian Studies*, vol. 9, 1990, pp. 1–24

Rashid, S., (Review in the *History of Political Economy*, vol. 22, 1990, pp. 554–556 of Teichgraeber, R.F., *Free Trade and Moral Philosophy: Rethinking the sources of Adam Smith's "Wealth of Nations"*, Durham, 1986)

Rashid, S., (Review in the *History of Political Economy*, vol. 22, 1990, pp. 573–577 of Hutchison, T.W., *Before Adam Smith: The Emergence of Political Economy, 1662–1776*, Oxford, 1988)

Rashid, S., 'Adam Smith and the Market Mechanism', *History of Political Economy*, vol. 24, 1992, pp. 129–152

Recktenwald, H.C. (ed.), *Political Economy. A Historical Perspective*, London, 1973

Recktenwald, H.C., *Adam Smith, sein Leben und sein Werk*, München, 1976

Recktenwald, H.C., 'Adam Smith heute und morgen, *Kyklos*, vol. 28, 1975, pp. 5–22

Recktenwald, H.C., 'An Adam Smith Renaissance *anno* 1976? The Bicentenary Output – A Reappraisal of His Scholarship', *Journal of Economic Literature* vol. 16, 1978, pp. 56–83

Recktenwald, H.C., 'Eine Adam Smith Renaissance anno 1976? Eine Neubeurteilung seiner Orginalität und Gelehrsamkeit', in: Grüske, K.D. (ed.), *Markt und Staat. Fundamente einer freiheitlichen Ordnung in Wirtschaft und Politik. Ausgewählte Beitrage*, Göttingen, 1980, pp. 39–69

Recktenwald, H.C., *Ethik, Wirtschaft und Staat. Adam Smiths Politische Ökonomie Heute*, Darmstadt, 1985

Recktenwald, H.C. (ed.), 'William James Baumol, Jean-Baptiste Say und der »Traité«', *Vademecum zu einem frühen Klassiker*, Düsseldorf, 1986

Recktenwald, H.C., in Trapp, M., *Adam Smith, politische Philosophie und politische Ökonomie*, Göttingen, 1987, pp. 7–11

Recktenwald, H.C., Scherer, F. and W. Stolper, *Schumpeters monumentales Werk – Wegweiser für eine dynamische Analyse*, Düsseldorf, 1988

Recktenwald, H.C. (ed.), *Adam Smith. Der Wohlstand der Nationen*, München, 1988

Reid, G.C., 'Adam Smith's Stadial Analysis as a Sequence of Societal Growth Trajectories', *Scottish Journal of Political Economy*, vol. 36, 1989, pp. 59–70

Reisman, D.A., *Adam Smith's Sociological Economics*, New York, 1976

Reisman, D.A., 'Alfred Marshall and Adam Smith', *European Economic Review*, vol. 35, 1991, pp. 323–332

Rendall, J., *The Origins of the Scottish Enlightenment*, London, 1978

Ricardo, D., *The Principles of Political Economy and Taxation*, 1817, edited by Hartwell, R.M., Harmondsworth, 1971

Richardson, G.B., 'Adam Smith on Competition and Increasing Returns' in Wilson, T., and A.S. Skinner (eds.), *The Market and The State. Essays in Honour of Adam Smith*, Oxford, 1976

Ricoeur, P., *Interpretation Theory: Discourse and the Surplus of Meaning*, Forth Worth, 1976

Ricoeur, P., *Du texte à l'action*, Paris, 1986

Rijnvos, C.J., *Monetaire Economie*, Leiden, 1988

Rizzo, M.J., see O'Driscoll Jr., G.P. and M.J. Rizzo

Robinson, J., *Further Contributions to Modern Economics*, Oxford, 1980

Robinson, J., 'What has become of the Keynesian Revolution', *Challenge*, vol. 23, 1974, pp. 6–11

Robinson, J., *Economic Heresies*, New York, 1971

Robinson, J., 'Richard T. Ely Lecture 1971: The Second Crisis of Economic Theory', *The American Economic Review*, vol. 62, May 1972, pp. 1–10

Rohrlich, G.F., 'The Role of Self-Interest in the Social Economy of Life, Liberty and the Pursuit of Happiness, anno 1976 and Beyond', *Review of Social Economy*, vol. 34, pp. 373–377

Roll, E., *History of Economic Thought*, London, 1938, 1973 (revised edition)

Roos, W.A.A.M., 'Post-Keynesiaanse economie als gemeenschappelijke noemer voor een alternatief researchprogramma', *Maandschrift Economie*, vol. 44, 1980, pp. 3–10

Rosenberg, N., 'Some Institutional Aspects of the *Wealth of Nations*', *Journal of Political Economy*, vol. 68, 1960, pp. 361–374

Rosenberg, N., 'Adam Smith and Laissez-Faire Revisited' in O'Driscoll Jr., G.P. (ed.), *Adam Smith and Modern Political Economy. Bicentennial Essays on 'The Wealth of Nations'*, Ames Iowa, 1979, pp. 19–34

Rosetti, J., 'Deconstructing Robert Lucas', in Samuels, W.J. (ed.), *Economics as Discourse. An Analysis of the Language of Economics*, London, 1990, pp. 225–250

Ross, I.S., see Wightman, W.D., Bryce, J.C. and I.S. Ross

Ross, I.S., 'Introduction' to Stewart, D., 'Account of Life and Writings of Adam Smith, LL.D' in Wightman, W.D., Bryce, J.C. and I.S. Ross (eds.), *Adam Smith. Essays on Philosophical Subjects*, Oxford, 1980, pp. 265–268

Ross, I.S., see Mossner, E.C. and I.S. Ross

Ross, I.S., *The Life of Adam Smith*, Oxford, 1995

Rothschild, E., 'Commerce and the State: Turgot, Condorcet and Smith', *The Economic Journal*, vol. 102, 1992, pp. 1197–1210

Rothschild, E., 'Adam Smith and Conservative Economics', *Economic History Review*, vol. 45, 1992, pp. 74–96

Rowe, N., *Rules and Institutions*, New York, 1989

Rowthorn, B., 'Neo-classicism, Neo-Ricardianism and Marxism', *New Left Review*, 1974, no. 86, pp. 63–87

Russell, P., (Review in *Ethics*, vol. 101, 1991, pp. 873–875 of Hope, V.M., *Virtue by Consensus: The Moral Philosophy of Hutcheson, Hume, and Adam Smith*, Oxford, 1989)

Russell, G., (Review in *Commentary*, vol. 95, 1993, pp. 60–61 of Muller, J.Z., *Adam Smith in His Time and Ours: Designing the Decent Society*, New York, 1993)

Russelman, G., 'De mechanisering van het wereldbeeld', *Intermediair*, vol. 20, 1984, pp. 7–13

Salanti, A., (Review in *Kyklos*, vol. 45, 1992, pp. 123–125 of West, E.G., *Adam Smith and Modern Economics. From Market Behaviour to Public Choice*, Aldershot, 1990)

Samuels, W.J. (ed.), *The Methodology of Economic Thought*, London, 1982

Samuels, W.J. (ed.), *Economics as Discourse. An Analysis of the Language of Economics*, Boston, 1990

Samuels, W.J., see Hodgson, G.M., Samuels, W.J. and M.R. Tool

Samuelson, P.A., *Economics. An Introductory Analysis*, New York, 1948, 1951 and 1958

Samuelson, P.A., 'The General Theory' in Harris, S. (ed.), *The New Economics*, London, 1947/1960, pp. 145–160

Samuelson, P.A., 'Liberalism at Bay', *Social Research*, vol. 39, 1972, pp. 27–28

Samuelson, P.A., 'A Modern Theorist's Vindication of Adam Smith', *The American Economic Review*, vol. 67, 1977, pp. 42–49

Samuelson, P.A., 'The Canonical Classical Model of Political Economy', *Journal of Economic Literature*, vol. 16, 1978, pp. 1415–1434

Sandkühler, H.J. (ed.), *Europäische Enzyklopädie zu Philosophy und Wissenschaften*, Hamburg, 1990

Scherer, F., see Recktenwald, H.C., Scherer, F. and W. Stolper

Schneider, L. (ed.), *The Scottish Moralists on Human Nature and Society*, 1967

Schouten, C., 'Adam Smith 1723–1790: Een kritische geest geëerd', *Osmose*, vol. 16, 1990, pp. 6–9

Schumpeter, J.A., *Das Wesen und der Hauptinhalt der Nationalökonomie*, Leipzig, 1908

Schumpeter, J.A., *History of Economic Analysis*, London, New York, 1954/1959/1972

Screpanti, E. and S. Zamagni, *An Outline of the History of Economic Thought*, Oxford, 1993

Seligman, B.B., 'Philosophic Perspectives in Economic Thought' in Samuels, W.J. (ed.), *The Methodology of Economic Thought*, New Brunswick, 1980, pp. 245–268

Shackle, G.L.S., *The Years of High Theory. Invention and Tradition in Economic Thought 1926–1939*, Cambridge, 1967

Shaw, K.K., *Keynesian Economics: The Permanent Revolution*, Aldershot, 1988

Shepherd, Ch.M., 'Newtonianism in Scottish Universities in the Seventeenth Century', in Campbell, R.H. and A.S. Skinner (eds.), *The Origins and Nature of the Scottish Enlightenment*, Edinburgh, 1982

Silverman, H.J. (ed.), 'Gadamer and Hermeneutics', *Continental Philosophy IV*, New York, 1991

Sinderen, A. van, 'Aanbodeconomie acht jaar later: de theorie en de praktijk van reaganomics', *Rotterdamse Monetaire Studies*, 1989

Sinderen, J. van, 'Over pre-economen, beleidseconomen en wetenschappers', *Research Memorandum 9300*, Research Centre for Economic Policy, Rotterdam, 1993

Sinderen, J. van and A. van Ravestein, 'Meer markt en minder overheid. De visies van nieuwklassieken en aanbodeconomen', *Economisch Statistische Berichten*, vol. 72, 1987, pp. 68–73

Skidelsky, R. (ed.), *The End of The Keynesian Era*, London, 1977

Skinner, A.S., 'Economics and History', *Scottish Journal of Political Economy*, vol. 12, 1965, pp. 1–22

Skinner, A.S., 'Natural History in the Age of Adam Smith', *Political Studies*, vol. 15, 1967, pp. 32–48

Skinner, A.S. (ed.), *The Wealth of Nations*, Harmondsworth, 1970/1981

Skinner, A.S., 'Adam Smith: Philosophy and Science', *Scottish Journal of Political Economy*, vol. 19, 1972, pp. 307–319

Skinner, A.S., *Adam Smith and the Role of the State*, Glasgow, 1974

Skinner, A.S., 'Adam Smith: Science and the Role of the Imagination' in Todd, W.B. (ed.), *Hume and the Enlightenment: Essays presented to Ernest Mossner*, Austin, 1974, pp. 164–188

Skinner, A.S., 'Adam Smith: An Aspect of Modern Economics', *Scottish Journal of Political Economy*, vol. 26, 1979, pp. 109–125

Skinner, A.S., see Wilson, T and A.S. Skinner

Skinner, A.S., see Campbell, R.H., Skinner, A.S. and W.B. Todd

Skinner, A.S., see Campbell, R.H. and A.S. Skinner

Skinner, A.S. and T. Wilson (eds.), *Essays on Adam Smith*, Oxford, 1975

Skinner, A.S., *A System of Social Science: Papers Relating to Adam Smith*, Oxford, 1979

Skinner, A.S., see Raphael, D.D. and A.S. Skinner

Skinner, A.S., 'A Scottish Contribution to Marxist Sociology?' in Bradley, I, and M. Howard (eds.), *Classical and Marxian Political Economy: Essays in honour of Ronald L. Meek*, New York, 1982, pp. 79–114

Skinner, A.S., 'Adam Smith' in Eatwell, J., Milgate, M. and P. Newman (eds.), *The Invisible Hand. The New Palgrave*, London, 1987/1989, pp. 1–42

Skinner, A.S., 'The Shaping of Political Economy in the Enlightenment' in Mizuta, H. and C. Sugiyama (eds.), *Adam Smith: International Perspectives*, London, 1993, pp. 113-139

Smith, A., see Works by Adam Smith (*The Glasgow Edition of the Works and Correspondence of Adam Smith*)

Smith, A., see Cannan, E.

Smithin, J., see Hamouda, O. and J. Smithin

Sobel, I., 'Adam Smith: What Kind of Institutionalist Was He?', *Journal of Economic Issues*, vol. 13, 1979, pp. 347–368

Sowell, T, *Classical Economics Reconsidered*, Princeton, 1974

Sowell, T., 'Adam Smith in Theory and Practice' in O'Driscoll, G. (ed.), *Adam Smith and Modern Political Economy. Bicentennial Essays on 'The Wealth of Nations'*, Ames Iowa, 1979, pp. 3–18

Stamm, V., *Ursprünge der Wirtschaftsgesellschaft*, Frankfurt am Main, 1982

Stark, W., *The Ideal Foundations of Economic Thought. Three Essays on the Philosophy of Economics*, London, 1944

Stark, W., *The Fundamental Forms of Social Thought*, New York, 1962

Stein, P.G., see Meek, R.L., D.D. Raphael and P.G. Stein

Stewart, D., 'Account of the Life and Writings of Adam Smith, L.L.D.' in Wightman, W.P.D., Bryce, J.C. and I.S. Ross (eds.), Essays on Philosophical Subjects, *The Glasgow Edition of the Works and Correspondence of Adam Smith*, part III, Oxford, 1980, pp. 269–351

Stigler, G.J., *Essays on the History of Economics*, Chicago, 1965

Stigler, G.J., 'Smith's Travels on the Ship of State', *History of Political Economy*, vol. 3, 1971, pp. 237–246

Stigler, G.J., 'Introduction' to Smith, A., *An Inquiry into the Nature and Causes of the Wealth of Nations*, Cannan Edition, New York, 1976

St John-Stevas, N. (ed.), *The Collected Works of Walter Bagehot*, London, 1968, parts 3 and 11

Stolper, W., see Recktenwald, H.C., Scherer, F. and W. Stolper

Stratum, R. van, see Berns, E. and R. van Stratum

Strauss, L., *Naturrecht und Geschichte*, Stutgart, 1956

Sugiyama, C. see Mizuta, H. and C. Sugiyama

Sweezy, A., 'The Keynesians and Government Policy, 1933–1939', *The American Economic Review*, vol. 62, May 1972, pp. 116–124

Taylor, Ch., *De malaise van de moderniteit*, Kampen, 1994

Teichgraeber III, R.F., *'Free Trade' and Moral Philosophy. Rethinking the Sources of Adam Smith's* Wealth of Nations, Durham, 1986

Teichgraeber III, R.F., '"Less Abused than I Had Reason to Expect": The Reception of The Wealth of Nations in Britain', *The Historical Journal*, vol. 30, 1987, pp. 337–366

Thoben, H., 'Mechanistic and Organistic Analogies in Economics Reconsidered', *Kyklos*, 1982 (35), pp. 292-305

Thompson, H.F., 'Adam Smith's Philosophy of Science', *The Quarterly Journal of Economics*, vol. 79, 1965, pp. 213–233

Thweatt, W.O. (ed.), *Classical Political Economy. A Survey of Recent Literature*, Boston, 1988

Tobin, J., 'Theoretical Issues in Macroeconomics' in Feiwel, G. (ed.), *Issues in Contemporary Macroeconomics and Distribution*, London, 1985

Todd, W.B. (ed.), 'General Introduction' to *An Inquiry into the Nature and Causes of the Wealth of Nations,* The Glasgow Editions of the Works and Correspondence of Adam Smith, Oxford, 1976, pp. 1–60

Tool, M.R., see Hodgson, G.M., Samuels, W.J. and M.R. Tool

Todd., W.B. (ed.), *Hume and the Enlightenment: Essays presented to Ernest Mossner*, Austin, 1974

Traa, P.C. van, *Geschiedenis van de economie*, Amsterdam, 1969

Trapp, M., *Adam Smith, politische Philosophie und politische Ökonomie*, Göttingen, 1987

Unger, J.A., 'The Resurgence of Adam Smithian Scholarship', *Polity*, vol. 12, 1980, 491–508

Vandewalle, G., '"New Keynesianism": een doctrine in wording', *Economisch Statistische Berichten*, vol. 74, 1989, pp. 152–156

Vandewalle, G., 'De Keynesiaanse leer: een speciaal geval in het neoklassieke bestel of een vertrekpunt voor een algemene vernieuwing in het economisch denken' in Nentjes, A. (ed.), *Keynesianisme vandaag. Jaarboek studiekring Post-Keynesiaanse economie 1987*, Alphen aan de Rijn, 1988

Vaughn, K.I., (Review in *Isis*, vol. 80, 1989, pp. 702–703 of Hutchison, T., *Before Adam Smith; the Emergence of Political Economy, 1662–1776*, Oxford, 1988)

Vercelli, V., *Methodological Foundations of Macroeconomics: Keynes & Lucas*, Cambridge, 1991,

Vermeulen, B.P., 'God, wil en rede in Hugo de Groots natuurrecht', *Wijsgerig Perspectief*, vol. 23, 1982, pp. 54–59

Vermeulen, B.P., see Eijffinger, A.C. and B.P. Vermeulen

Viner, J., 'Adam Smith and Laissez-Faire' in Clark, J.M. (ed.), *Adam Smith, 1776–1926*, Chicago, 1928/New York, 1966, pp. 116–155

Viner, J., 'Mr. Keynes on the Causes of Unemployment', *The Quarterly Journal of Economics*, vol. 50, 1936, pp. 147–167

Viner, J., 'Adam Smith and Laissez-Faire', *Journal of Political Economy*, vol. 35, 1927, pp. 198–232

Visser, H., 'Keynes en de neoklassieken: een herinterpretatie', *De Economist*, vol. 120, 1972, pp. 27–51

Vogt, W., 'Zur Kritik der herrschenden Wirtschaftstheorie' in Vogt, W. (ed.), *Seminar: Politische Ökonomie. Zur Kritik der herrschenden Nationalökonomie*, Frankfurt am Main, 1973, pp. 180–205 and pp. 306–322

Walker, D.A., *William Jaffé's Essays on Walras*, Cambridge, 1983

Walker, D.A., 'Is Walras' Theory of General Equilibrium a Normative Scheme?', *History of Political Economy*, vol. 16, 1984, pp. 445–469

Walker, D.A., 'Commentary' to Ménard, C., The Lausanne Tradition: Walras and Pareto, in Hennings, K. and W.J. Samuels (eds.), *Neoclassical Economic Theory, 1870–1930*, Boston, 1990, pp. 137–150

Walker, D.A., 'Walras' Theories of Tâtonnement', *Journal of Political Economy*, vol. 95, 1987, pp. 758–774

Walker, D.A., 'Another Look at Leon Walras's Theory of *Tâtonnement*', in

Walker, D.A., (Review in the *Journal of Economic Literature*, vol. 29, 1991, pp. 1742–1744 of West, E.G., *Adam Smith and Modern Economics: From Market Behaviour to Public Choice*, Aldershot, 1990)

Walker, D.A., 'Economics as Social Physics' *The Economic Journal*, vol. 101, 1991, pp. 615–631

Ward, B., *What's Wrong With Economics*, New York, 1972

Waszek, N., *Man's Social Nature. A Topic of the Scottish Enlightenment in its Historical Setting*, Frankfurt am Main, 1986

Weintraub, E.R., *Microfoundations. The Compatibility of Microeconomics and Macroeconomics*, Cambridge, 1979

Weintraub, S. (ed.), *Modern Economic Thought*, Philadelphia, 1977

Werhane, P.H., 'The Role of Self-Interest in Adam Smith's "Wealth of Nations"', *The Journal of Philosophy*, vol. 86, 1989, pp. 669–682

Werhane, P.H., *Adam Smith and His Legacy for Modern Capitalism*, New York, 1991

Werhane, P.H., (Review in *Ethics*, vol. 104, 1994, pp. 668 of Muller, J.Z., *Adam Smith in His Time and Ours: Designing the Decent Society*, New York, 1993)

West, E.G. (ed.), *The Theory of Moral Sentiments*, Indianapolis, 1969/1976

West, E.G., 'Scotland's Resurgent Economist: A Survey of the New Literature on Adam Smith', *Southern Economic Journal*, vol. 45, 1978, pp. 343–369

West, E.G., 'Developments in the Literature on Adam Smith: An Evaluative Survey' in Thweatt, W.O. (ed.), *Classical Political Economy. A Survey of Recent Literature*, Boston, 1988, pp. 13–44

West, E.G., *Adam Smith and Modern Economics. From Market Behaviour to Public Choice*, Aldershot, 1990

Wieacker, F. von, *Privatrechtsgeschichte der Neuzeit*, Göttingen, 1967

Wightman, W.P.D., Bryce, J.C. and I.S. Ross (eds.), *Adam Smith. Essays on Philosophical Subjects*, Oxford, 1980

Wightman, W.P.D., 'Introduction' to 'The History of Astronomy', 'The History of the Ancient Physics' and 'The History of the Ancient Logics and Metaphysics' in Wightman, W.P.D., Bryce, J.C. and I.S. Ross (eds.), *Adam Smith. Essays on Philosophical Subjects*, Oxford, 1980

Willis, K., 'The Role in Parliament of the Economic Ideas of Adam Smith 1776–1800', *History of Political Economy*, vol. 11, 1979, pp. 505–544

Wilson, T. and A.S. Skinner (eds.), *The Market and The State. Essays in Honour of Adam Smith*, Oxford, 1976

Winch, D., *Adam Smith's Politics. An Essay in Historiographic Revision*, Cambridge, 1978

Winch, D., *Economics and Policy. A Historical Study*, London, 1969

Winch, D., 'Science and the Legislator: Adam Smith and after', *The Economic Journal*, vol. 93, 1983, pp. 501–520

Winch, D., 'Commentary' to West, E.G., 'Developments in the Literature on Adam Smith: An Evaluative Survey' in Thweatt, W.O. (ed.), *Classical Political Economy. A Survey of Recent Literature*, Boston, 1988, pp. 45–52

Winch, D., 'Adam Smith: Scottish Moral Philosopher as Political Economist', *The Historical Journal*, vol. 35, 1992, pp. 91–113

Winch, D., 'Adam Smith: Scottish Moral Philosopher as Political Economist' in Mizuta, H. and C. Sugiyama (eds.), *Adam Smith: International Perspectives*, London, 1993

Wisman, J., 'Towards a Humanist Reconstruction of Economic Science', *Journal of Economic Issues*, vol. 13, 1979, pp. 19–48

Wisman, J., 'The Naturalistic Turn of Orthodox Economics: a Study in Methodological Misunderstanding', *Review of Social Economy*, vol. 36, 1978, pp. 263–284

Witteloostuyn, A. van, see Maks, J.A.H. and A. van Witteloostuyn

Wong, D., 'The Oversocialized Conception of Man in Modern Sociology', *American Sociological Review*, vol. 26, 1961, pp. 183–193

Wood, J.C. (ed.), *Adam Smith. Critical Assessments*, Beckenham, 1984, part I–IV

Worland, S.T., 'Mechanistic Analogy and Smith on Exchange', *Review of Social Economy*, vol. 34, 1976, pp. 245–257

Yeager, L, 'The Keynesian Diversion', *Western Economic Journal*, vol. 11, 1973, pp. 150–163

Young, B.C., 'Smith's View on Human Nature: A Problem in the Interpretation of "The Wealth of Nations" and "The Theory of Moral Sentiments"', *Review of Social Economy*, vol. 48, 1990, pp. 288–302

Young, B.C., (Review in the *Journal of Economic History*, vol. 51, 1991, pp. 765–766 of West, E.G., *Adam Smith and Modern Economics: From Market behaviour to Public Choice*, Hampshire, 1990)

Young, J.T., 'Natural Price and the Impartial Spectator: A New Perspective on Adam Smith as a Social Economist', *International Journal of Social Economics*, 1985, vol. 12, pp. 118–133

Young, J.T., 'The Impartial Spectator and Natural Jurisprudence: An Interpretation of Adam Smith's Theory of the Natural Price', *History of Political Economy*, vol. 18, 1986, pp. 365–382

Young, J.T., 'David Hume and Adam Smith on Value Premises in Economics', *History of Political Economy*, vol. 22, 1990, pp. 643–657

Young, J.T., *Economics as a Moral Science: The Political Economy of Adam Smith*, Cheltenham, 1997

Zamagni, S., see Screpanti, E. and S. Zamagni

Zijderveld, A.B., *De culturele factor. Een cultuursociologische wegwijzer*, The Hague, 1983

Zuidema, J., *School of stijl, een vraagstuk van indeling*, Afscheidscollege gegeven op 17 december 1986 aan de Erasmus Universiteit Rotterdam

Index of Names

Index of Subjects

Adam Smith Problem, Das 27, 28, 89, 168
Adam Smith renaissance v, ix, x, 1, 3,
  9-12, 15, 32, 167
- trends in recent Adam Smith research x,
  1, 7-10, 29, 31-32
admiration (*see also* knowledge) 24, 44,
  88, 90, 94, 118, 124-125, 158, 163
  (*see also* sympathy) 98-100, 104, 108,
  111
age of commerce (*see also* commerce,
  commercialization and liberalization of
  society, commercial society) v, xi, 103,
  106, 135
ages and periods of society 2, 23, 3, 39,
  63, 111
analogia proportionalitatis 171
analogia proportionis 171
atomism (atomistic) xi, 8-9, 14, 16, 21-22,
  35, 51-52, 55-58, 61, 63-65, 86, 91-92,
  119, 121, 133, 143-144, 147, 160, 167,
  171, 173
auctioneer 35, 91-93, 121, 141
auto-coordination 120, 146-147
benevolence 27, 47, 58-59, 78-80, 89, 94,
  95, 104, 105, 112, 143-144, 159, 167,
  175
bias (towards riches and power, in favour of
  the rich and the great) 89, 103-105
bonum commune x, 45, 103-105
categorical mistake 118
chain of intermediate, though invisible
  events 126
chrêmatistikê 45
collectivism (collectivistic) 21, 51, 89, 91,
  92
commerce v, xi, 37, 45-46, 53, 71, 81, 82,
  91, 102, 103, 106, 113, 131-132, 135-
  136, 145, 155, 177
commercialization and liberalization of
  society x-xi, 40, 44-46, 48-49, 55, 91,
  164, 172

commercial society x, xi, 2, 22, 37, 44, 48,
  64, 65, 82-83, 87, 89, 91, 105-106, 131,
  135, 144, 150, 160, 163, 170, 172, 173
corruption (of moral sentiments) 83, 103-
  106
cost of production theory of value 50, 52,
  139
crisis of/in modern economics vi, x, 21,
  157
decontextualization 18, 19
deism (deistic) 49-50, 87, 89, 114, 119,
  122-124, 126, 129, 131, 149-150
deus ex machina 142
dialogue (dialogic, dialogical) ix, x, xi, 1-2,
  13, 15, 17, 19, 22-23, 83-84, 87, 92-97,
  103-104, 117-118, 139, 157, 159, 167,
  172, 173
dichotomies in Smith's work xi, 22, 61,
  87, 159, 167-168, 170
- in modern economic thought 20, 159,
  167-168
distantiation 19
distinction of ranks 98, 99, 103
division of labour 25, 26, 36, 82, 134, 139,
  140, 144, 155
doctrine
- Schumpeter's use of 121
- Smith's understanding and use of (*see
  also* knowledge and system) 88, 94, 99,
  116, 131-132
dualism (dualistic) 157, 161, 172
economics (modern)
- a discourse about giving sense and
  meaning to economic phenomena in a
  commercial society x-xi, 44, 46, 49, 66,
  91, 103, 144, 160, 164, 170, 172-173
- mechanics of self-interest xi, 22, 47, 82,
  158, 171, 174
- a change from oppositional to relational
  interpretation of dual concepts xi, 20,
  21, 23, 157-158, 161, 167